Not I

ALSO BY JOACHIM FEST

Inside Hitler's Bunker: The Last Days of the
Third Reich (2005)

Speer: The Final Verdict (2002)

Plotting Hitler's Death:
The German Resistance to Hitler (1996)

Hitler (1974)

The Face of the Third Reich:
Portraits of the Nazi Leadership (1970)

The author with his father in early 1941

Not I

.

Memoirs of a German Childhood

JOACHIM FEST

Translated from the German by Martin Chalmers
Edited by Herbert A. Arnold

OTHER PRESS
NEW YORK

Production Editor: Yvonne E. Cárdenas
Text Designer: Jennifer Daddio / Bookmark Design & Media, Inc.
This book was set in 12 pt. Horley Old Style
by Alpha Design & Composition of Pittsfield, NH.

3 5 7 9 10 8 6 4

Library of Congress Cataloging-in-Publication Data
Fest, Joachim C., 1926-2006.
[Ich nicht. English]
Not I : memoirs of a German childhood / by Joachim Fest ;
Translated from the German by Martin Chalmers ; edited by
Herbert A. Arnold.
pages cm
"Originally published in Germany by Rowohlt Verlag GmbH in 2006."
Includes bibliographical references and index.
ISBN 978-1-59051-610-2 (trade pbk.) —ISBN 978-1-59051-611-9 (ebook)
1. Fest, Joachim C., 1926-2006—Childhood and youth.
2. Anti-Nazi movement—Germany—World War II—
Biography.   3. Historians—Germany—Biography.
4. National socialism.   5. Germany—National socialism—
Biography.   I. Chalmers, Martin, translator.   II. Title.
DD86.7.F47A313 2013
907.2'02—dc23
[B]
2013018230

For my parents

Contents

Introduction

BY HERBERT A. ARNOLD

This is a quite unusual memoir in several respects, yet it is a memoir all the same. Ever since St. Augustine's *Confessions*, the genre has been defined as an ex post facto ordering of selective parts of a person's past, to explain how he or she became who they are at the moment of retrospective. Achievements of adulthood tend to dominate, while childhood and youth are often underreported. Not here. Fest insists in his subtitle and in his book on describing in considerable detail his early years, between his birth in 1926 and the early postwar years; he leaves out altogether the adult achievements for which he is actually known, and ends with a brief postscript about his reaction to the unification of Germany in 1989–90.

All footnotes throughout this work are by Herbert Arnold, unless indicated otherwise.

Moreover, instead of focusing on his own life, he chooses to devote an extraordinary amount of attention to his father, of whom he presents an astonishing portrait. The other emphasis is on the times as experienced by an intelligent but naive youngster and his education, both formal and informal. And they are unusual times, indeed. Born into the Weimar Republic and its social and political turmoil, Fest has just begun school when the Nazis come to power in 1933. They and his family's firm and costly refusal to cooperate with the new regime will shape the narrative until near the end of the war, when young Joachim is drafted, survives the battle at Remagen, and is captured by American troops. He returns to Berlin, the city with which he identifies most strongly, and begins his work as a journalist and, eventually, historian of recent German history.

What makes this book so remarkable, however, and may well explain its extraordinary success in Germany, where it became a best seller with staying power, are the portraits of his family, of fellow Germans, and of the times. A major part of that success lies in the complexity, the contradictions, and the conflicts endured by the characters in this memoir. No simple black-and-white picture, good and evil, right and wrong conflicts—although they are there, of course—but the conflicted and sometimes self-contradictory nature of the protagonists makes for compelling reading. Here are real and not always likable people trying to live a life guided by principles which are in direct and consciously maintained conflict with the prevailing political and social environment. And here is the record of their battles, their survival, and the cost of refusing to collaborate with a state and a regime they recognized as evil earlier than most.

Focusing on the father, as the author does, demonstrates these contradictions most tellingly—and is a clever narrative stroke by the author, who clearly knows about his own internal contradictions, which he only touches upon on occasion. Johannes Fest is a bundle of just such contradictions. An upright conservative Catholic head of a primary school in predominantly Protestant Prussia, he is active in the Zentrum, the political arm of Catholicism in the Weimar Republic. He is also an active member of the Reichsbanner, a conservative paramilitary organization set up to combat the corresponding groupings of both Communists and Nazis, with whom they engage in bloody street fights.

Such associations normally clearly identify a right-wing conservative, middle-class radical, tailor-made for a career in the NSDAP, the National Socialist Workers Party, and the new order. Instead, and quite startlingly, he is a staunch supporter of Weimar democracy and intrepid opponent of the Nazis. He continues in this opposition, much to the consternation of his wife and to the detriment of the family, even after it costs him his job and social position and after the authorities try to tempt him to reverse his stance. Indeed, he revels in his outsider status, as does his son. That is the reason for the title, supposedly based on the Gospel of Matthew, and for the motto of the family: Us against the world. Again a contradiction, since this echoes *Viel Feind, viel Ehr* (Many enemies equals great honor), a popular saying of German right-wing conservatives and militarists. Yet here it means the inner emigration of the family unit, the mutual support, and the rejection of the dominant spirit of the times.

The father's life also demonstrates how ineffective even the most determined opponents of Nazism were in practice—and how conflicted. Every time Hitler achieved one of his early coups—the annexation of Austria, the defeat of France—Johannes Fest was torn. He had wanted the union with Austria for the Weimar Republic—but not for Hitler and not as annexation; he reveled in the defeat of France as a justified revenge for her intransigence and spitefulness toward Weimar—but not as a victory for Hitler.

The German patriot and the antifascist were in constant conflict with each other, a situation that would become even more serious as the war progressed and the first inklings of the Holocaust became evident. Here Fest—both the father and the son—depart most clearly from many other Germans who have argued ignorance after the war. The Fests insist that information was available, even if not easily corroborated, and that the nature of the regime and its deeds were clearly visible to all who wanted to see. They would therefore also not accept what they saw as the paroxysms of guilt after the war—and thus, once again, found themselves at odds with their society and their countrymen. It is this outsider status Fest sees as the distinctive characteristic of his family, a tradition honed under Nazism but proudly maintained throughout: they are mavericks, outsiders, not unlike the characters of Thomas Mann's narratives, which Joachim admires and his father condemns because of Mann's earlier "nonpolitical views."

There is another major influence on Joachim Fest's youth: the introduction to German and European culture, especially its music and literature, which are made available by both his home and his schools, but even more so by friends and mentors, who provide him with an academy of learning and questioning outside the confines of formal education. Whether it is an aunt who takes him to his first opera, a neighboring clergyman who loves Beethoven's *Fidelio* at least as much as disputing theological conundrums, or his older brother Wolfgang, who always seems a step ahead in his reading— young Joachim is a sponge and a classic example of the German *Bildungsbürger*, the broadly educated bourgeois who has gone to a Gymnasium.[1] They constitute a quite unselfconscious elite with an ethos derived from German idealist philosophy and popularized by the great German writers and thinkers of the past century and a half. This ethos is also shared by most of the Fests' many Jewish friends who populate this memoir. For many of them it became lethal because it kept them from leaving Germany in time to escape the Holocaust. Many of them argued that "their" Germany could never succumb to the rule of something as crude as Nazism and ignored the warnings of their friends like the Fests.

Few of them are still alive, therefore, during the postwar years, when Joachim makes his career in radio and

---

1 A Gymnasium in Germany is a secondary school that prepares students for university or graduate studies; its final exams, the *Abitur* (a secondary-school certificate), are a prerequisite for admission at all German universities.

television journalism and as a historian of the Third Reich. That adult portion of the author's life is totally missing, but it must be taken into account when one assesses the success of this memoir in Germany, because it is this public Joachim Fest—the conservative critic of the predominant cultural left in the Federal Republic of Germany—whose origins are here revealed. After two years as a prisoner of war and privileged by the known antifascist past of his family, he—as he recounts in these pages—more or less accidentally wound up researching and making public the Nazi past through his early work at Radio im Amerikanischen Sektor (RIAS, Radio in the American Sector of Berlin). His dream had been to become a *Privatgelehrter* (an independent scholar), working on obscure aspects of the Italian Renaissance, preferably supported by a beautiful and rich wife, while residing in some palazzo. Instead he was asked to work up portraits of some of the Nazi bigwigs for a radio series as a part of the American effort in reeducating the Germans after the war. These radio portraits led to books on Hitler, Albert Speer, the German resistance, and the end of Hitler, among others.

After rising through the ranks in radio and on German television to become editor in chief of Norddeutscher Rundfunk (NDR), the North German Broadcasting Network, Fest became responsible for the major political magazine *Panorama*, from which he resigned for political reasons. He then proceeded to write and publish his biography of Hitler (1973), the first by a German author, and aided Albert Speer, Hitler's protégé and armaments minister, in the publishing of his autobiography, before being invited to become coeditor of Germany's most prominent conservative newspaper, the *Frankfurter Allgemeine Zeitung (FAZ)*, whose cultural section he edited from 1973 through 1993. From that public platform he participated in the so-called *Historikerstreit*, a dispute initially among German historians about the nature of the Holocaust. At stake was the claim of the singularity or uniqueness of the Holocaust when compared to other mass atrocities of modern times, such as the Khmer Rouge's mass killings in Cambodia. The predominant view of the mainly left-leaning German historians, most of whom were social history adherents, was challenged by Ernst Nolte, Fest, and others. Jürgen Habermas, Eberhard Jäckel, and many others responded and a lengthy battle ensued, in which many non-German historians became embroiled as well, because of the historical and moral sensitivity of the issues involved. The current memoir allows the reader to see where Fest's skeptical and pessimistic challenge comes from: a dim view of human nature in general, pride in being an outsider to prevailing majority opinion, and a skeptical rejection of historical generalizations—all of which permeate the pages of his memoir. These are lessons, he insists, instilled by his father, the Nazis, the war, and postwar experiences upon which he has based his *Lebensregeln* (principles for life), as he likes to call them.

This memoir is unusual not just by focusing more on the father than the author, by leaving out major parts of the story, and by emphasizing contradictions rather

than linear narrative. It also takes certain liberties with
the conventions commonly observed. It is customary to
report only what is verifiable while indicating what is
conjecture, since few memoirists, if any, can recall exact
words or too much vivid detail. But Fest has decided
to include direct speech, especially of family members,
aided—he says—by notes taken in the past and consulted for this purpose. He thus imparts a distinctly
fictional, highly literary tone to his narrative, which ren-
ders it both lively and rather unreliable. But he delights
in language, especially the patois of Berlin which he likes
to reproduce in the puns and cheap wordplays popular
among schoolboys—all by way of creating an atmosphere
which, however fictional, is very convincing and familiar
to anyone who lived in Germany through those years.
The reader must decide how much of this comes across
in translation, which is not just one of language but also
of cultural ambience. One example may suffice: he talks
of cigarettes as the most valuable "currency" after the
war—immediately recognizable to contemporaries—
because the official currency was worthless and so was
the "official" economy. Everything was available only
through a universal black market with direct exchange of
goods or services. His descriptions of the general black-
out on the German side of Lake Constance contrasting with the blazing lights of neutral Switzerland on the
other not only refer to the obvious realities of the air war
but are also intended to contrast the darkness holding
Germany in thrall as opposed to the bright lights of freedom outside. Echoes of famous and well-known sayings

and precepts abound in the German text, ranging from allusions to Ranke's admonition to the historian to show things as they had actually occurred to Goethe's dictum that man (in the abstract) ought be noble, helpful, and good. In short, there is a quite self-conscious attempt at a literary shaping of the personal and historical subject matter, which is as much a part of who Fest is, given his education and background, as it is a recognition by a skeptical, practicing historian that there are distinct limits to the objectivity of the writer and the accessibility of all historical subject matter.

Amazingly, Fest manages to present himself—a wisecracking youngster who likes to have the last word—and his family, from choleric father to long-suffering mother, in vivid detail, embedding all of them in their frailty and humanity in terrible times, trying to keep their values and principles intact, even if it meant becoming and remaining isolated, outsiders, mavericks.

Preface

One usually begins to write memoirs when one realizes that the greater part of one's life has been lived, and what one intended to do has been achieved more or less well. Instinctively, one looks back at the ground covered: one is startled at how much has sunk into obscurity or has disappeared into the past as dead time. One would like to capture what is more important or save it for memory, even as it is fading into oblivion.

At the same time one comes face-to-face with the effort required in calling up the past. What was it my father said when my mother reproached him for his pessimistic moods, when she tried to coax him into a degree of flexibility toward those in power? What was the name of the German teacher at Leibniz Gymnasium, who, in front of my classmates, regretted that I was leaving his class? What were the remarks Dr. Meyer made as he accompanied me to the door on my last visit—were they somber or merely ironically resigned? Experiences, words, names: all lost or in the process of disappearing. Only some faces remain, to which, if one kept poking around long enough, a remark, an image, or a situation could be linked. Other information was provided by family tradition. But quite often the thread was simply broken. That also had something to do with the fact that when my family was expelled from our home in Karlshorst all keepsakes, notes, and letters were lost. Likewise the family photos. The pictures in this book were mostly given back to us after the war by friends who had asked for them at some point and were able to save their possessions through the upheavals of the times.

I would have been unable to record my earliest memories if in the early 1950s I had not had a radio commission to write an account of recent German history. Wherever possible I supplemented the published historical studies—which at that time were far from abundant—with conversations with older contemporaries like Johann Baptist Gradl, Heinrich Krone, and Ernst Niekisch.[1] Most frequently, however, and also at greatest length, I consulted my father, who, as a politically committed citizen, had experienced the struggles

---

1 J. B. Gradl (1904–88) and H. Krone (1895–1989) were both prominent members of the conservative, Catholic Zentrum party during the Weimar Republic and became founding members of the conservative Christian Democratic Union party in the Bonn republic. E. Niekisch (1889–1967) was an antifascist National Bolshevik imprisoned by the Nazis; he later taught in the German Democratic Republic. A tellingly odd collection of witnesses.

and suffering of the time as more than a mere observer. Naturally, these conversations soon extended to more personal matters and drew attention to the family's troubles, which I had lived through but hardly noticed.

On the whole I noted down my father's observations only as headings. That caused me some difficulties when I came to write this book, because if I could not reconstruct the context of a remark it inevitably remained sketchy and often had to be left out. Some of his opinions did not stand up in the face of the knowledge I had meanwhile acquired. In the initial draft, however, I reproduced rather than corrected them, because they seemed important as the opinions of someone present at the time; in part they reflect not today's historical view, but the perceptions, worries, and disappointed hopes of someone who lived through those times.

To make the book more readable I have also taken the liberty of reproducing some of my notes as direct speech. A historian could not possibly proceed in such a way, but it may be permitted the memoirist. Wherever possible these dialogues maintain the tone as well as the content of what was said. When individual remarks are placed in quotation marks they faithfully reproduce a comment, as far as memory allows.

Like all biographical notes, my observations make no claim to be indisputably valid. What I write about the friends of my parents, about teachers and superiors, remains my view alone. I present Hans Hausdorf and Father Wittenbrink, the Ganses, Kiefers, Donners, and others only as I remember them. That may not be accurate or even fair in every respect. Nevertheless, I was not prompted by any prejudice.

In several historical accounts I have dealt more analytically with the years covered in the following pages.[2] For that reason in the present book I could largely dispense with abstract reflections. They are left to the reader. At any rate I have not written a history of the Hitler years, but only how they were reflected in a family setting. That means actual living experiences, sometimes even the merely casual and occasionally the anecdotal, will predominate here, as they do in real life. When, as a teenager in the early 1940s, I described the grimaces of a friend of my parents who had a nervous disorder, my father admonished me, "Don't look too closely!" I responded that I neither could nor would close my eyes. Thanks to the generally nurturing environment in which I grew up that has never been difficult for me, nor was it used against me. It was actually a necessary prerequisite for writing this book. The temptation was much greater either to repress the grimaces of my youthful years or, even worse, to view them through a glorifying lens.

In writing this book I have accumulated many debts of gratitude. Here I would like to mention only Frau Ursel Hanschmann, Irmgard Sandmayr, my friend Christian Herrendoerfer, and my fellow prisoners of war Wolfgang

---

2 Fest is referring to the books which established him as one of Germany's foremost experts on the Nazi period. These books range from *The Face of the Third Reich* (1970) and *Hitler* (1974) to *Plotting Hitler's Death* (1996), *Speer: The Final Verdict* (2002), and *Inside Hitler's Bunker* (2005), to name some of the titles available in English translations.

Münkel and Klaus Jürgen Meise. The latter successfully escaped from the POW camp some time before
my failed attempt. I owe particular thanks to my editor
Barbara Hoffmeister for her numerous important comments. Finally, the many friends of my youth who helped
me with the order of events, dates, and names should be
acknowledged.

Joachim Fest
Kronberg, May 2006

Not I

ONE

·

How Everything
Came Together

The task I have set myself is called recollection. The majority of the occurrences and experiences of my life have as with everyone—faded from memory, because memory is ceaselessly engaged in casting out one thing and putting something else in its place or superimposing new insights. The process is unending. If I look back over the whole time, a flood of pictures presses forward, jumbled up and random. Whenever something happened, no idea was associated with it, and only years later was I able to discover the hidden watermark in the documents of life and perhaps interpret it.

But even then images intervene, especially when it comes to the early years: the house with the wild undergrowth at the sides (later, to our sorrow, removed thanks to our parents' sense of orderliness); catching crayfish in the River Havel; our much-loved nursemaid Franziska, who one day had to return to her home in the Lausitz; the trucks which raced down the streets with a bright flag, packed with bawling men in uniform; the excursions to Sanssouci or Lake Gransee, where our father told us a story about a Prussian queen, until we began to get bored with it. All unforgotten. And once we children had reached the age of ten, we were taken one Sunday in summer—when the band was playing and the aristocrats' two-wheeled carriages were standing in front of the emperor's pavilion—to the racetrack. Like the district of Karlshorst in Berlin, it had been developed by my grandfather on the out-of-the-way Treskow Estate, and had later gained the reputation of being the largest steeplechase course in the country. As if it were yesterday I see the parade of huge horses with the little jockeys in their colorful clothes, and the solemnly pacing gentlemen in their mouse-gray morning coats with bow ties at their throats and bulging starched fronts. The women, on the other hand, mostly stuck together and watched one another in the shadow of hats as big as wheels in the hope that some rival could be discovered and dismissed with a crushing remark.

It was a strange, genteel world that had brought my grandfather to Karlshorst. He had been born into the respected Aachen drapers' family of Straeter, whose branches were spread across the Lower Rhineland and which was so wealthy it could afford every two years to hire a train for a pilgrimage to Rome, where its members were received by the pope in a private audience. Circumstances had brought him into contact with the high nobility; in his twenties he was already travel marshal of the Duke of Sagan, and a little later he went to Donaueschingen as inspector of Prince Fürstenberg's estates. His early years were largely spent at aristocratic residences in France, and at Château Valençay (once the property of Prince Talleyrand) he had got to know my grandmother, who came from a Donaueschingen family and was a lady-in-waiting to the Fürstenbergs. It was a great love that like Philemon and Baucis's, lasted until old age, when the Second World War smashed everything.[1] For a long time French was mostly spoken in the family and the cooking—onion soup, duck pâté, and crème caramel—was also French. Most of the classics of the neighboring country were in my grandfather's library in awe-inspiring, leather-bound editions. I sometimes heard him declaiming Racine as he walked up and down in front of his desk, but his favorite authors were Balzac and Flaubert.

My grandfather had arrived in Berlin in 1890, at the time of a sensational murder case. The Heinzes, a married couple, had killed a night watchman. The Heinze case, which my grandfather and many others often compared to the murders of Jack the Ripper, had the side effect of drawing attention to the housing conditions of the poor. As a result two—and later three— groups of wealthy families joined together to establish

---

1 Philemon and Baucis are an aged couple in Greek mythology, a classical example of enduring marital loyalty and love, used by Goethe in *Faust* and thus familiar to any educated German.

philanthropic societies to build housing estates. The largest of these projects was initiated by the judge Dr. Otto Hentig, with Prince Karl Egon zu Fürstenberg in charge. Also involved were the Treskows, who had resided in nearby Friedrichsfelde (outside Berlin) since 1816, as well as August von Dönhoff, the Lehndorffs, and other respected families. The well-known architect Oscar Gregorovius also played a part, as did, somewhat later, the more famous Peter Behrens.

My grandfather had never accepted the Heinzes' excuse that the misery of the slums or the horrors of backyard housing in Wedding had driven them to it. So he tried to find out everything he could about Gotthilf Heinze, whom he often called "Gotthilf the Slasher." He even carried out detective work to discover masterminds, secret societies, and above all the depraved, red-haired beauty, who was mentioned in some sources, albeit dubious ones: the "angel of the gutter," as he once described her to me, years later. It was never clear to me, as a boy, whether she had been a prostitute victim or an accomplice of the murderer. My grandfather believed she was an accomplice, and growled, "Typical! He involves his wife in the murder. His lover stays in the background and is there for pleasure."

In May 1895 the district administrator signed the permit to build on the 150-acre Karlshorst Estate and immediately a kind of competition got under way for the best plots of land. The philanthropic society of Prince zu Fürstenberg proved more than a match for its competitors and appointed my twenty-seven-year-old grandfather as manager. His task, working with Oscar Gregorovius and the local authorities, was to establish a suburb on the land acquired, to lay down the street plan, to parcel up the plots, and to sell them at reasonable prices. At each stage of expansion a new quarter was added: there were streets named after the nobility, those with Rhineland names, the legend quarter, the Wagner quarter, and so on, step by step.

My grandfather mastered his task with great skill, but soon recognized that beyond the comfortable living quarters which still dominated Karlshorst when I was growing up, the place needed certain centers of attraction. So a hospital and a Protestant and a Catholic church were added, and a little park with a small lake that was laid out on previously marshy terrain soon began attracting strollers from a wide area. With prudent planning, the Treskow racecourse was expanded into a center of social life. In later years—in fact, just after my grandfather's time—a military school also came to Karlshorst. In the end the "little place of troubles," as he liked to call it, or the "barren sandy heath," as it was once described in an official document, which on his arrival had consisted of eight houses or rather farms with fewer than a hundred residents, had more than thirty thousand inhabitants.

In the years when I was consciously aware of him, my grandfather was a withdrawn, imperious, austere man, who, during crowded family gatherings, could silence a room with a single dry remark. On the street he was usually to be seen wearing a frock coat and a bowler and carrying a stick. Even then he had an old-fashioned aura, which he played up to with stubborn determination. Unlike my three younger siblings, who kept out of his way as much as possible, my elder brother Wolfgang and I enjoyed talking to him, no matter how monosyllabic he often was, because he was an attentive listener, who always knew how to ask questions that led somewhere. One of my sisters later complained that his face was all-too-glum and "the corners of his mouth always drooped so dreadfully." But even his silences, so Wolfgang and I found, carried weight. His handkerchief was always sprinkled with a couple of drops of eau de cologne. Passersby greeted him respectfully and doffed their hats with a low gesture that reached almost to the knee and often made us laugh. Older people still remembered that Karlshorst was, in part, his creation.

The woman at his side, my grandmother, was graceful and devoted, and was able to talk to each of her grandchildren in a different way, appropriate to their age. Her life had not always been easy and although the many troubles had left their mark on her face, she displayed no sign of unhappiness; instead, she was cheerful and practical. She was happy when she could make herself useful—that feeling made up for all the burdens, I often heard her say. They had five daughters and—to their everlasting sorrow—no son. Two of the daughters had entered a religious order: one worked on a mission station in Africa; the other (given the beautiful name of Sister Alcantara) was assigned by her superiors to a convent in Merano. She was tall and bore herself with the poise of an abbess but seemed oddly fragile. She had what she called "chest

trouble" and contracted in the "chilly convent vaults,"
as my mother sometimes complained, a lung infection,
from which she died before she was even thirty.

In 1917, during the First World War, the youngest
daughter fell ill with diphtheria at the age of fourteen,
resulting in complete physical paralysis. My grandparents spent a fortune on distinguished medical special-
ists and even consulted quacks without ever gaining
any relief for her. All day long my aunt Agnes lay on the
chaise longue in the dining room and, as she could not
move her head, every time someone entered she looked
sideways at the door with wide-open eyes, in which there
was a reflection of the futile effort of life. In the evening
my grandfather had to carry her into her bedroom, casting aside, as I once observed, the pride of an elderly gentleman. If one alluded to her suffering, she would merely
respond: "Please! I can manage!"

Dorothea, whom we called Aunt Dolly, was the elegant daughter. She was slim and striking in appearance
and, like my mother, had been educated at a boarding
school for young ladies in Silesia. Her wardrobe revealed
a fondness for bold patterns, which sailed close to the limits of good taste. She usually turned up wearing the very
latest hat, a fox fur over her shoulders, its silvered claws
glinting in the sun, and discreet gold jewelry around her
neck. She was well-spoken and frequently admonished us
for talking in a Berlin accent. My father thought that she
had acquired an affinity for the big wide world at boarding school in the small town of Liebenthal, whereas my
mother left there with poetry and good sense.

Emma Straeter, Joachim Fest's grandmother,
during her years at Valençay

Indeed, my mother, whose name was Elisabeth, but
who was called Tetta by the family, was considered the
strict one of the sisters. In contrast to her manner, however, which was self-confident and not without a touch of

pride, she had a charming side and an attractive warmth in company. The complexity of her character was also evident in her liking for "gentle music," to which her poetic tastes corresponded. She liked Eichendorff and Mörike, above all, but also Heinrich Heine, except that when she recited his poems she would leave out the last two lines.[2] "He doesn't stand by his feelings," she would say. "He's ashamed of them. When you are older and have the aptitude"—she said, turning to my brother and me—"you must write new endings to Heine's poems. Then I will at last be able to love him completely."

There was something to my father's otherwise quite unfair judgment on Dolly. She wanted to make an entrance. The moment her noisy children were out of the house, my mother sat down at the piano and improvised a little before playing her favorite pieces: Beethoven's "Für Elise," some Mozart variation or other, and many Czerny études. Finally, she would sing in a pleasant voice a few songs by Schubert and Schumann, and best of all some pieces by Carl Loewe, such as the one about "Herr Heinrich am Vogelherd" (Sir Heinrich at the fowling floor) or "Die Uhr" (The clock). "Why do you do that?" asked Aunt Dolly, puzzled. "Who benefits from it? Why don't you organize house concerts with guests?" But Tetta, my mother, would not be won over to anything like that.

---

2 These are major German poets of the nineteenth century to whom Fest will refer repeatedly: Joseph von Eichendorff (1788–1857) and Eduard Mörike (1804–75) are regarded as prime exemplars of German Romanticism, while Heinrich Heine (1797–1856) is often seen as the more critical and caustic.

Thanks to some family connections, my mother had been invited to balls at the Imperial Stables on a number of occasions and, even at an advanced age, she would talk enthusiastically about the cavaliers in tails and colored sashes who had paid court to her. She also talked of chests covered with military decorations and how a young man might let a monocle drop, significantly and revealingly, from the eye at a coarse joke or in feigned surprise. And then there were the lieutenants, who (as she said, losing herself in her memories) "were indeed dashing—I know how much foolish pink from a girl's face you can still see in that remark." She no longer remembered whether the attendants who stood around attentively everywhere, intercepting searching looks, wore *escarpins* with buckles. "But the servants had a matchless way of looking expressionless when one of the cavaliers helped me out of my coat. Beautiful, brilliant, and superficial, like some baroque music," she said—then, in her turn, without expression, "but gone, gone!" Yet she didn't mourn those days; because who would mourn a fairy tale once it was over?

For Aunt Dolly, on the other hand, who so relished talk of "higher things," which she loved for their inimitability, theater and especially music only became significant and affecting in a social context. She came to life in the hum of the gradually filling stalls or to the sound of the instruments tuning up, but she also enjoyed strolling in the lobbies and probably above all seeing the soigné gentlemen who, with a slight inclination, threw her reserved or occasionally brazen glances. She sometimes mentioned these to the accompaniment of girlish giggles, although she was by then almost thirty. It was then that I began to suspect that between men and women there were mysterious understandings that one would have to find out about later.

Everyone wondered why Aunt Dolly, who was everywhere courted by a certain type of experienced gentleman—the kind who (as my mother liked to say) had "unfortunately been around a bit"—never found a husband. Only much later was the answer discovered: she had for years been enslaved to a great love, which had robbed her of all sense: a married naval officer from Kiel. Around him she constructed an endless theater of dissemblance. Only my parents knew something of it, and after dropping a few hints they made us promise never to breathe a word. Once, when Aunt Dolly took me to the Gloria Palast at Karlshorst Station, where we saw a romantic film with a tragic ending, she began sniffling surreptitiously into her handkerchief, and then wept quietly to herself through the whole screening, sighing ever more deeply. At the exit, with a strained smile on her still-tearful face, she asked me to leave her alone and find my way home without her.

A couple of days later she turned up at Hentigstrasse at an unusual time and chatted away awkwardly. On my arrival she pulled me into the drawing room and apologized for her "faux pas." When I said there was nothing to apologize for, she retorted that at her age, too, one had to maintain one's composure and, even more important, have manners. "My weeping was discourteous."

Proud Aunt Dolly! I thought. To me, a fourteen-year-old, her every word seemed to betray how much she envied my mother. At the end of 1919 my mother had joined the Bleichröder banking house as an assistant and was going to the city center every day. There she got to know people, gained experience, and even climbed a rung up the career ladder. Aunt Dolly, on the other hand, had set limits to her ambitions early on and become a librarian because she had succumbed to the courtship of that damned naval officer, whose future she hoped to share. Tetta, by contrast, was not at all histrionic; reserved by nature, she did not need to make a splash emotionally or socially. She was not a diva, I once heard her say to one of my father's friends, who had reproached her for not showing her feelings sufficiently, and, for a while, the remark became a favorite saying in the family: "Mama isn't a diva!" Less than two years after starting at the bank she had got to know my father and (as she liked to say) "taken a girlish fancy to him," then "fallen a little in love with him," subsequently "really fallen in love with him," and married him soon after. All "quite unsurprising," all quite "normal," Aunt Dolly would sometimes say, and perhaps even a little boring, but promising so much more happiness than her own life.

On my father's side the family circumstances were considerably more remote and complex. As far back as the facts can be traced (that is, to the seventeenth century) his ancestors came from the small market town of Liebenau (Lubrza in Polish) in the Neumark of the province of Brandenburg. The parish registers, begun again in 1654 after the devastation of the Thirty Years' War, first mention their names in the 1670s. Most of them had made a living as craftsmen or tradespeople, and in one branch of the family also as brewery owners. Over the generations many of them had held office as "able councillors," church-wardens, or "village mayors." The first names common in the family also point to higher pretensions. In each generation there was a Rosina; many of the female ancestors were called Cäcilia or Justina; and my grandfather bore the first names (Latinized in the Baroque style) Robertus Tiburtius. He was an exuberant man full of the joys of life, who, it was once said, "set every dance floor in a state of excitement." Newly married and driven by the ambition (typical of the time) to settle new land, he had moved to the province of Posen, today called Poznan, and acquired a large farm there. Less than a year after his arrival, although only in his mid-twenties, he had become mayor and was respected by both Germans and Poles. His wife, however, did not get along with Polish conditions, and so, in 1895, the family, by now with seven children in tow, moved back to Liebenau. There my grandfather bought a flour mill close to the village.

He died in the early 1930s, before we got to know him well at all, and so any memories of him remain a tangled mixture of what one was told and what one remembers. Whenever we caught sight of him, he was walking like a shadow through the rooms, leaning silently and ghost-like on his walking stick, commenting in passing on our squabbling with a "Well, well!" He could only be induced to speak at length if my father asked him to recite

word for word one of the tales collected by the Brothers
Grimm, which he had learned as a child, or, on Sunday
evening, to say the lesson from the morning Mass. Then
he briefly shut his eyes before beginning: "And Jesus,
when he came out, saw many people, and was moved
with compassion toward them . . ." When we arrived in
Liebenau for the funeral he was laid out in the yard of his
house, a very old, unfamiliar, and seemingly fragile man,
who in death had shriveled up.

The coffin had been opened again for the last blessing, and in a final dutiful gesture my grandmother, bent
low and leaning on a stick, busied herself with some
overhanging corners and ends of cloth. Of the dead
man—who sank, his mouth slightly open, between
the lace-trimmed shrouds—we children saw only the
upper bony section of the face. After the solemn throat-
clearing of those present, which always precedes such
rituals, the priest spoke the funeral prayers and sprinkled the mourners with holy water, while disinterested
farmers' lads closed the coffin and carried it through
the yard gate and out into the road to the waiting horse-
drawn carriage. Almost fifty years later my younger
brother Winfried remembered that it was not so much
his quietly weeping grandmother or the psalm-singing
relatives gathered in a semicircle around the coffin and
the mountains of flowers that captured his attention
but a fly which rushed back and forth over the waxen
face of the dead man and several times disappeared into
the dark cavity of the mouth. For me, too, the sight was
something I never forgot.

My grandfather had been a down-to-earth man, tested by life. He was much respected (as I was later told) by his peers, and at council meetings the final word was often expected and indeed came from him. My father loved to tell a story from his youth that illustrated my grandfather's no-nonsense sense of reality. Five or six of what would in the end be eleven children had been sitting around the kitchen table with my grandfather, when one of the brothers asked what each of them would do if a huge sum of money were to fall into their laps, whether through God, the power of the angels, or by chance. "The jackpot!" he exclaimed. "It's being given to us! It'll be raining money! Remember my words!" Right away, twelve-year-old Franz revealed to the speechless company what he would do with the money. He would go into town and in Kurt Linke's inn, surrounded by beautiful women, order the best wines and liqueurs; the elder brother August confessed he would buy the most expensive dress for merry Maria Zietsch from the next village, and then hopefully dare speak to her for the first time; Cäcilie thought she would buy a dressmaker's shop with modern machines and employ at least five seamstresses. And so on, one after the other, until the slight Roni, who always looked a little starved, spoke up. "And I," he explained, swallowing frequently, "will buy myself Schlackwurst sausages with all the money—seventy or even a hundred—for as long as the money lasts. All day long, for a month—no, for a whole year—I will stuff myself with Schlackwurst. One after the other."

That was like a watchword. Everyone jumped up and agreed enthusiastically: Schlackwurst—yes! That's great! Schlaraffenland[3] forever! they yelled. Until my grandfather, who had said nothing throughout, went over to the tiled stove, took his stick, which was hanging from the side, and silenced the hubbub with a mighty blow on the table. Taking no notice of the daughters present, he shouted at the boisterous gang: "You damned rascals must eat bread with your sausage! You don't eat sausage without bread!"

My father drew the meaning of this story from his own experience. One could have dreams, build castles in the air—it was all allowed! But one had to keep one's feet on the ground! As a gifted schoolboy of fifteen he had wanted to study "something to do with religion or mathematics." After that he had for a long time been uncertain as to whether he should follow his love of nature and become a fisherman or a forester. When, finally, at his father's urging, he decided on the profession of teacher, the somewhat older son of our neighbor said it was a real shame that a lad with his practical talents should choose a typical "idler's job." Because of his ability my father was exempted from the first two classes when he started secondary school and later, on taking his school-leaving certificate, from the oral examinations. After several teaching posts he suffered a moderately serious wound at the beginning of the First World War, in France,

---

3 Schlaraffenland is the German equivalent of the Land of Cockaigne, an imaginary place of ease and luxury.—Trans.

returned to teaching, and immediately found himself back in Berlin. Politically committed from an early age, by 1919 he had established several local branches of the Catholic Zentrum party in southern districts of the capital and had occupied leading positions in the party, as he did later in the Reichsbanner, the paramilitary organization composed of members of the Zentrum party, the Social Democratic Party, and the trade unions set up to defend the Weimar Republic.[4]

He was a tall man with strong features; the "telegenic face" (as Wolfgang and I called it) which he displays in most pictures reveals only sternness and determination, without giving any clue to the cheerful character and even happiness that comes when a person is in harmony with himself. One of his friends once said that my father was a rare combination of energy, self-confidence, and mirth. His sharp wit could even turn into high spirits. Friends of my own youth whom I asked for the impression they had of him when they looked back, often said that as children there was hardly another adult whom they so enjoyed being with, because he was able to tell such crazy stories and sing such silly songs. Almost all spoke in these or similar terms of his ability to entertain and his enjoyment of practical jokes. Admittedly, he

4 The Zentrum party, established in 1870 and dissolved in 1933, was the political, conservative representation of German Catholicism in an essentially Prussian and therefore Protestant-dominated German Reich; it opposed the Nazis ideologically. After the Second World War the surviving members of the Zentrum founded and dominated the conservative Christian Democratic Union, including Protestants as well as Catholics. The first chancellor of the Federal Republic of Germany, Konrad Adenauer, was the candidate of the CDU.

sometimes suffered from a short temper; that may have
been because his good humor did not come from an inner
balance alone, but also had something to do with the certainty of being able to deal with all the trials of fate.

It should also be said that my father did not have the
least touch of social snobbery and could chat as easily to
the girl behind the counter at the baker's as discuss serious affairs of state with a senior civil servant. He was as
relaxed with a university teacher as with the children at
our birthdays. He enjoyed singing and he had countless
songs in his head from "Prinz Eugen" to the forgotten "Ich
hab mich ergeben . . ." (I have devoted myself . . .), which
survives only as a melody in Brahms's Academic Festival
Overture. To end a round of songs he liked to perform
boulevard or music-hall chansons, which, as I remember,
sometimes included the unforgettable assertion that "my
parrot don't eat hard-boiled eggs" or posed the question
"What, for heaven's sake, was Mayer doing in the Hima-
layas?" or, then again, praised a girlfriend called Titaisin,
whose lover boldly claimed (for the sake of the rhyme if
nothing else) that in his cake of life she was nothing less
than the raisin. He liked to laugh and could entertain a
company at table all evening with witty anecdotes or—if it
was required—more down-to-earth ones.

His origin, life, and strong convictions conferred on
my father four qualities, none of which seemed to go with
the others and each of which developed an impatience
with the other three. He was a republican, a Prussian,
a Catholic, and a *Bildungsbürger*. In his case, however,
all contradictions were held together by strength of

personality and each one of these strands contributed to his intransigence in the face of the Nazi regime. The inadequacies of the foundation of the Weimar Republic were perfectly clear to him, but he remained a committed republican. The problems of the moment must never place the principle in doubt, we heard him say repeatedly; and each one of us, his children, was a witness later on to his outrage when, after the end of the Hitler dictatorship, it was often argued that in 1932–33 there had been a choice only between the Nazi Party and the Communists, and that in Hitler people had chosen the lesser of two evils. Would it not have been more intelligent and, above all, more responsible to choose the republic, he objected, whether in the shape of the Social Democrats, the Zentrum, or the Liberals? In reality, all those who said later that there had been no alternative to Hitler had at the time lacked judgment and loyalty to the state, to say nothing of determination. My father had always been a militant republican; he wanted to resist the storm troopers of the Nazi SA (Brownshirts) not only with words, but with his fists. Consequently, following the election gains of the Nazi Party on September 14, 1930, he discussed with his friend Hubertus zu Löwenstein[5] the formation of a republican youth movement,

---

5 Hubertus Prince of Löwenstein-Wertheim-Freudenberg (1906–84), historian, journalist, and prolific author of books and articles on German and ancient history, was an early and outspoken antifascist who had to flee Nazi Germany. In England and the United States he became an active anti-Nazi spokesman. He returned to Germany and German politics after 1946; he was active in both the FDP (Free German Party) and the CDU (Christian Democratic Union) and attempted to help bridge the gap between the Catholic and Greek Orthodox churches.

which led shortly afterward to the establishment of the Vortrupp Schwarz-Rot-Gold.[6]

At the same time he was a dyed-in-the-wool Prussian, even if he didn't make an issue of it. The numerous "Old Prussians" who were to be found, in the old provinces of the Prussian crown at least, were overwhelmingly royalist and did not approve of the republic. "But I'm no unthinking Prussian," my father mocked, "and not sentimental enough to mourn the 'fugitive' Wilhelm the Second." His idea of what was Prussian, he said occasionally, was fairly out of step with the times. In addition to the familiar catalogue of duties, it included the voluntary self-limitation of demands, the avoidance of self-pity, and the ability to cope with life with a "pinch" of irony. "Just don't forget irony!" he frequently admonished us. "It's the entry ticket to humanity. Outwardly one displays a seriousness the situation demands, but inwardly one snaps one's fingers at the frustrations."

Certainly, he was critical enough to realize that Prussia and its much-praised ethos stood for nothing but itself—that it had no idea to give the world. Often he amused himself at the various efforts to lend Prussia a "soul" or even a "mission." As civilizing powers he accepted only ancient Greece and Rome. What had Spain, England, or France given the world, he once asked at table, apart from the swagger stick, five o'clock tea, Inca

6 Advance Guard Black-Red-Gold: black, red, and gold being the colors of the republican German flag, as opposed to the black, red, and white of the imperial and Nazi flags.—Trans.

gold, and a few fine phrases? Ultimately, each of these world powers had been about exploitation with a little added humane decoration. He preferred the unadorned will to survive, which embodies Prussia's idea of state. Like all the others, it had robbed, but at least it had not lied about it afterward. "A curtsey for Prussia," he concluded on occasion and with a smile; on the whole, Prussia didn't cut such a bad figure in the world.

Years later, when I asked him once again about his taste for irony, he responded that irony made almost everything in life more bearable, including the basically "chilly state air" of Prussia. A scene (unforgotten by us children) occurred on the annual trip to our relatives in the Neumark. As the train passed a small village almost swallowed up by the horizon, my father called us to the compartment window. "What you see over there," he observed, "is the silhouette of Kunersdorf, where Frederick the Great suffered the most terrible defeat of the whole Seven Years' War.[7] The Prussians," he continued, "among whom in this respect I do not count myself, always maintain that after every Kunersdorf there follows a Leuthen with triumph, fanfares, and the chorus 'Now Thank We All Our God!' That sounds elevating and fills the unthinking Prussian heart with pride. Unfortunately," added my father after a well-considered pause, "this fine story isn't true. Because the Battle of Leuthen took place in 1757, while Freder-

7 Frederick II, king of Prussia (1712–86), called the Great, is an icon of Prussian conservatives and advocates of German national greatness in the early twentieth century. In the Seven Years' War, which he started, he fought all major European powers and established the kingdom of Prussia as a key player among them.

ick did not meet with the defeat of Kunersdorf (whose disastrous consequences were only avoided by a change of rulers in Russia) until two years later. But," he concluded, "there has to be a little bit of cheating, if the Prussians are going to add another miracle of the House of Brandenburg to the first."

If Prussia and republicanism were not easily reconciled, then the contradiction was further sharpened by my father's strict Catholicism. He was a pious man, who accounted to the "Lord God" (as he usually put it in this context) for each of his private or political decisions. Not least because of his numerous offices, he maintained close relations with the senior diocesan figures and frequently met the papal nuncio Cardinal Pacelli.[8] He gave credit to Heinrich Brüning, the Zentrum party chancellor from 1930 to 1932, for pursuing, in principle and politically, the reconciliation of Prussianism and Catholicism; if he had succeeded, my father said, in retrospect, much would have turned out differently.[9] He was a friend of Bernhard Lichtenberg, the dean of St. Hedwig's Cathedral in Berlin.[10] In earlier years the latter had lived in Karlshorst as a curate; in 1941 he was sentenced for protesting against Nazi euthanasia and for publicly pray-

---

8 Eugenio Pacelli (1876–1958), later Pope Pius XII, was the Vatican's diplomatic representative in Munich and Berlin from 1917 through the 1930s, when he gained the most coveted prize in Vatican diplomacy, a concordat with the German Reich. He later knew of but did nothing to mitigate the persecution and extermination of Europe's Jews by the Nazis.

9 Heinrich Brüning (1885–1970) was the last democratic chancellor of the Weimar Republic; he died in exile in Vermont.

10 Bernhard Lichtenberg (1875–1943).

ing for the Jews, and he died in 1943 while being transported to Dachau concentration camp, in circumstances
that remain unclear. My father lost his usual calm when
advocating Catholic interests; at times it even seemed as
if he had been gripped by the siege mentality of diaspora
Catholicism. Although he tolerated almost all human
weaknesses, tellingly, he never got over the disgraceful
part which the leading figures of his party—Franz von
Papen and Prelate Ludwig Kaas—allowed themselves to
be talked into playing, out of ambition and opportunism,
during the course of the Nazi seizure of power.[11]

And finally, he was an avowed *Bildungsbürger*; the
pages that follow will provide some evidence of that.[12]
While at that time the term was not as discredited as it is
now, it already suggested old-fashioned values. After the
Nazi years the educated middle classes (*Bildungsbürgertum*) were seen as one of the principal social forces responsible for the rise of Hitler; when one looks more closely,
however, this accusation merely reflects the resentment of
spoiled children intent on being morally superior to their

11 Franz von Papen (1879–1969) was a monarchist member of the Zentrum whose
political machinations in 1932–33 significantly aided Hitler's rise to the chancel-
lorship and power in Germany. Ludwig Kaas (1881–1952) was the head of the
Zentrum party from 1928 through 1933 and a major contributor to the Vatican's
concordat with Germany, Hitler's first diplomatic success.

12 A *Bildungsbürger* is a member of that part of the German upper-middle class
which comes from and aspires to middle- and upper-range positions in German society's politically and economically dominant classes; she or he is highly educated
and will typically hold an *Abitur* certificate and a university or graduate degree or its
equivalent. She or he will also be widely read and traveled and show both knowledge
and appreciation of European high culture and be conversant in several languages,
including classical Greek and/or Latin. This class dominates German politics and
society to this day and represents only a small portion of the total population. It is
educated to be and thinks of itself as an elite.

parents, and on defaming all *Bildung* (humanist education) as pointless effort. Social science has, meanwhile, discovered that fewer than 1 percent of the population could be said to have belonged to the *Bildungsbürgertum*. Yet in the last halfway-free elections of March 5, 1933, Hitler's party received the votes of well over 40 percent of the electorate.

My father loved books. His pride was the chronological Goethe edition from the Propyläen publishing house, which he had bought with his first salary earnings, as well as a smaller edition of ten or twelve volumes with commentaries. Next to them in the bookcases, which covered three walls of his far from spacious study, stood works from Lessing to Heine, Shakespeare, of course, and much else up to Fontane, whom he admired.[13] "He's one of the family," he liked to say, when conversation turned to Fontane, and, pointing to the easy chair on the balcony, he would add, "He has a seat there every now and then." In the scholarly section there were two or three shelves of theological literature. My father was interested in arguments about the proof of God's existence and the stimulus Luther had given to the development of the German language; in the next bookcase was Prussian history, especially the period of the reformers during and after the Napoleonic Wars, also works on the Christian image of man and the spread of the faith to the remotest regions of the earth.

---

13 Theodor Fontane (1819–98) is the quintessential Prussian novelist of the nineteenth century. His novels provide a critical image of Prussian society's dominant classes; their realism is tempered by Fontaine's famous reticent irony and obvious affection for the people and landscape of the Mark Brandenburg.

The bookshelves stretching up to the ceiling clearly reflected my father's interests. Only above the desk was there a gap, in which—next to some family photographs and the silhouette of Goethe raising his finger in front of the young Fritz von Stein—hung an engraving after Raphael's *School of Athens*, with Pythagoras and Socrates, Plato and Aristotle, one pointing at heaven, the other at earth, as our father (to our amusement) explained to almost every visitor, and at the right-hand edge of the picture Raphael had portrayed himself, as was repeated to us at least as regularly. Standing in front of the portrait of the Catholic scholar and reformer Görres on the opposite wall (above which there was a bronze bust of Dante on a pedestal), my father was in the habit of assuring listeners that all of his life he had wanted to be like Görres: rebellious in his early years, moving things forward in the middle of life, and from the age of forty preserving what was good.[14] But the times have to lend a hand. In his they too often got in the way.

My father often talked about the period after the First World War, in which he had been wounded early on and spent time in hospital. He had no problem adjusting to circumstances then. He had been full of hope and, in his view, despite the painful defeat, there had been a strong attachment to the republic. He attributed this to three

---

14 Johann Joseph von Görres (1776–1848), a politically active writer and early adherent of the ideas of the French Revolution. He suffered political persecution throughout his life and eventually became an activist Catholic who advocated a liberal constitution and a federalist Germany—precisely the odd mixture of revolutionary and conservative Fest favors.

main causes, which, with the laconic brevity characteristic
of his new hometown, Berlin, he summed up as: the war
was over, the kaiser was gone, and the nonsense of the soldiers' councils was at an end. Furthermore, a constitution
had been debated and all of this combined had produced a
widespread sense of a new beginning, which took hold of
and united the middle classes and the workers.

"But even before the constitution was adopted, the
heavens darkened," he said. The first blow came with
the Versailles peace treaty, but it was not its draconian
exactions that weighed most heavily. It was the "humilia-
tions" imposed on the German delegation that produced
greater outrage, from the servants' entrance by which its
members had to enter the building in which the negotiations were held to the wounded men with serious facial
injuries, who, in an act of calculated offense, were posted
at the entrance to the conference room. These and similar
theatrical flourishes, he said, were intended to legitimate
Article 231 of the Versailles Treaty, which was formulated with the "unpleasant arrogance of the poor winner": the assertion that Germany bore sole responsibility
for the war. In truth, the victorious powers only proved
thereby that "they didn't measure up to their victory." It
was soon being said that the republic had returned from
Versailles "wearing a fool's cap," and the phrase was
repeated with contempt and bitterness.

My father talked a great deal about these setbacks.
The weaknesses already became evident, he said, in
summer 1919. Furthermore, the republic had not been
inaugurated with any great act of foundation that stayed

in the memory, but instead (as a growing number soon thought) with a shameful defeat which was the result of treachery. Many allowed themselves to be persuaded all too readily that they were the good-natured victims of deceit and vindictiveness. In the early days of the new state, my father related, as he was going to the local branches night after night, he had repeatedly pointed out in countering the agitation of the right that the emergent republic had been dealt two stabs in the back: first by the "Hindenburg swindle"[15] and second by the victorious powers, France in particular, for whom he made no allowances. As a result Hitler was allowed to present himself as the advocate of so-called German honor.

"There was one other great moment," he continued, when talk came around to the subject. That had been when the Kapp Putsch was launched in March 1920, and the young republic had even been granted a victory.[16] The coup d'état of the old "mustaches" had been thwarted not only by the workers' general strike but also by the more or less united resistance of the broad majority. There the republic had its long-awaited founding act after all, as my father had declared repeatedly in his speeches, and the listeners had sometimes even risen to their feet and

---

15 Fest senior was presumably referring to the wartime financial policy of the Reich, which in the expectation of victory increased the money supply, so initiating the inflation which reached a climax in 1923, or possibly to the myth of the undefeated German army, summed up in the phrase "the stab in the back."—Trans.

16 Wolfgang Kapp (1858–1922), conservative Prussian politician and administrator, attempted an armed takeover of power (March 13–17, 1920) which failed because of a general strike by the trade unions and a lack of support from both the bureaucracy and the army.

applauded. But the republic had not known what to do with this gift. Nevertheless, he and his friends had celebrated the victory in the assembly rooms and larger pubs of Neukölln, Kreuzberg, and Charlottenburg. At last, so they had all believed, their cause was safe. The republic appeared to have stood the test.

It was around then that he thought for the first time— after a life which had for so long been filled with meetings and endless evening appointments—that he could devote himself to his private advancement. At the end of 1921 he moved from the lower-class district of Neukölln to Karlshorst and bought an apartment house in Hentigstrasse, in which, already with an eye to a future family, he occupied a whole floor. At that time he felt he had made a success of the first part of his life. Professionally as well as politically everyone predicted a promising future for him. In addition, he had made the acquaintance of an attractive, well-brought-up young woman from a comfortable background and for the first time thought of marriage.

He approached everything with great seriousness. After he had satisfied himself about this young woman, her family, and its circumstances, he began one day to acquire, without the least stammer, a fluency in French conversation and for a while preferred popular literature in that language with extended passages of dialogue. In this way, my father later jokingly maintained, he had prepared himself for the traditional suspicions of future parents-in-law. Because it did not seem impossible to him that the strict Straeters might embarrass him by suddenly, as if unintentionally, switching to French and only after talking for some time apologize for the small discourtesy. He had not wanted to expose himself to that, he added with a laugh.

And, laughing, he also said that until that point his education had been all too greatly focused on the weighty themes; he therefore began to drape "garlands" on the "grand scaffolding," as he called it, adding the handsome accessories which, even if only socially, were part of an education. Then he made the rounds of all the specialist shops in order to achieve sureness of taste, because he came from the country and (as one said in the big city of Berlin) from "modest circumstances." He had already discovered fine-looking furniture and very pleasing craft work in the homes of friends and of political party acquaintances and formed an idea of how he wanted to live. When he believed himself reasonably well prepared he also went to the antique shops in the Hansaviertel district to form judgments with respect to furnishings, paintings, carpets, and whatever else belonged to setting up a home and corresponded to his financial possibilities. He even bought some pieces, mainly in old Berlin style. Meanwhile, from time to time, he sent a token of his intentions to the young miss in Riastrasse.

These were the eloquent love letters that my mother kept in a casket together with other mementos and buried in the garden in 1945 a few days before the Russians marched in. The evacuation order issued at short notice by the Russians prevented the little box from being recovered; to the lifelong sorrow of my mother it remained lost. There are even supposed to have been some love poems in it.

One day my father unexpectedly announced himself at the Straeters'. To his surprise the drawing room furniture was light in color. Decorated with flower vases and bright porcelain figures of courting couples, harlequins, and shepherdesses, the grace of the decor hardly seemed to match the stern image of my maternal grandfather. Certainly this visit (so my father thought) was full of possibilities for embarrassment; nevertheless, it passed more easily than feared. The future parents-in-law possessed French courtesy, and since they had worked out why the young man was calling on them, they first of all offered him a light liqueur and helped him in every possible way to cope with the situation. When, suddenly and without warning, he became formal and attempted to rise from his chair, they asked him to remain seated. The guest nevertheless responded that he was better able to say what he wanted to say standing, whereas for the sake of their well-being it would be better if they remained seated. After that the mood became more relaxed, so that my father was able to shed any stiffness and ask, without further ceremony, for the hand of their daughter Elisabeth.

A few weeks later the date of the wedding was set for the middle of 1923. When my father looked back he was able to feel a degree of satisfaction. He had been more successful than he could ever have expected; hints had been made recently that he had prospects of an appointment in the Prussian Ministry of Culture, Education, and Religious Affairs. And then things would continue. What could possibly get in the way?

TWO

•

The World Falls Apart

Karlshorst was a self-contained suburb on the eastern side of the capital, overwhelmingly inhabited by the middling middle class. Its origins as a planned community were still obvious from its orderly street plan, and one of my parents' friends, who liked to exaggerate, maintained that the architect's office had taken the place of the whims of princes.[1] It was part of the distinctiveness of Berlin that the Prussian rulers had built it arbitrarily but determinedly in the face of the waste of the Mark Brandenburg. Consequently, at its edges the city had not only a charming village quality, but attractively melancholy surroundings, interspersed with waterways and

---

1 Karlshorst was a planned community laid out by architects using grids with geometric patterns, an unusual origin for a European settlement.

marshes. On some weekdays one could travel by public transport to Gransee Lake or to Nauen without meeting anyone other than a dozen market women. There were the showpiece boulevards like Unter den Linden and not far away the village streets of Potsdam and Köpenick.

In my memory Berlin is still an open, green city, unlike London or imperial, stony Paris. It has to be said that aside from the most beautiful surrounding countryside it had scant charm, but it had an attractive modesty. On the other hand it was alert and intelligent with a quick wit. It compensated for its lack of elegance with urbane irony. Keeping up with the times was always more important here than formality. Berlin was not a town one took to one's heart, but one very quickly felt at home in it. And Karlshorst was a kind of small town variant of the great metropolis.

The house in Hentigstrasse, which my father had bought years before, was not in one of the villa quarters of the place, but in the middle of an area of tenement blocks. The residents were skilled workers, civil servants, technicians, and a few widows. At the sides and the rear of each house there was some green space, usually with an herb garden under a couple of fruit trees. Nearly always there was a toolshed next to the carpet rail. Distinctive features of our garden were a horizontal gym bar under the chestnut trees and a small, stepped swimming pool, in which we bathed in summer and in winter skipped down the iced-over steps in our hobnailed shoes.

Above all we loved the overgrown corners and edges of the plot of land. We crept around under the fruit bushes,

a cardboard tomahawk or a knife in our mouths, as noble
Sioux Indians against the Comanches, and played other
such war games. With my elder brother Wolfgang and
one friend or another we stuck together against all the
neighbors' children. We sent Hansi Streblow to the fat
baker's wife with six pfennigs to buy "puke cakes," as
we called her baked dough corners; we stretched a string
across the house doorway opposite, where the eternally
sour teacher, Müllenberg, was a tenant, and he promptly
stumbled over it; or we climbed over the fence to the garden of the parsonage next door and placed a worn, sweat-
stained bra from who knows where on the garden path.
Hidden in the bushes, stifling our laughter, we watched
old Father Surma discover the item as he was saying the
breviary and, after a brief hesitation pick it up, shaking
his head, then finally, though not before looking around
anxiously, hide it under his soutane. I was then five years
old and just beginning to develop a sense, if only a vague
one, of the impropriety of our idea.

We were five children, all born at intervals of two
years: Wolfgang, born in 1924, was our authority figure.
My younger brother Winfried, who was at once bright,
witty, and inward-looking, was followed by the affec-
tionate Hannih, loved by all, and then Christa, who was
often lively to the point of folly.

Wolfgang, like most elder brothers, was my undisputed model, and on his behalf I often got into fights with
other boys because of some unjustified slander or other.
He was brave, quick-witted, and casual to a degree that
sometimes appeared almost arrogant. At school, he not

In the garden at Hentigstrasse on my
first day of school in April 1933

only had the better marks but the more inventive excuses. I also heard him praised by the mothers of friends for qualities the meaning of which I did not understand. "Clever rascal," can "express himself very well," and "knows how to behave himself" I understood very well, but "has charm" or "knows how to flatter the mothers of his friends" were rather mysterious. Unlike me, he was never reproached for having a "cheeky mouth."

Wolfgang won my complete admiration in spring 1932. It was then that the DoX—a flying boat as big as a steamer with twelve propellers and able to accommodate more than 160 passengers on three levels—returned from New York after an Atlantic crossing and set down on the Müggelsee Lake, only a couple of stations from Karlshorst on the S-Bahn. Some weeks before, Wolfgang had asked my parents to take him to Friedrichshagen to see the plane land. His plea was repeatedly turned down. So on the afternoon of May 24 he set off unnoticed with just twenty pfennigs.

When he didn't appear for the evening meal at six o'clock my parents began to feel anxious. After checking in vain with neighbors they started making telephone calls and at eight my father informed the police, while my mother said silent but fervent prayers. Shortly after nine she left the house, extremely worried, to search the neighborhood, only to meet Wolfgang coming toward her in Dorotheenstrasse with outstretched arms, full of the joys of life. Immediately he began telling her what he had seen at the Müggelsee and how already, on the way there, at Karlshorst Station, he had met a married couple and had chatted with them "like an adult," and had got a good place at the lake and then watched as the DoX landed with a splash. The couple had even bought him two ice cream wafers and paid for the return ticket, so that he still had money left over. In the end they had come with him as far as Birkholz's milk shop.

My mother was tearful and relieved, but at the same time very upset; after she had brought Wolfgang to my father, who was looking very stern, they both gave him a serious talking-to. Wolfgang once again started on about his great day with the couple, the flying boat, and ice cream wafers, but my mother hardly let him get a word out. Finally, in the heat of the moment, she even threatened to lock him in the coal cellar should anything similar happen again. "That doesn't bother me at all," responded the seven-year-old with admirable calm, "because behind the partition are the water and light switches. I can easily get at them and turn them all off." My mother later admitted that she had been speechless at the impudence of this statement, but also a little proud. Increasingly proud, even. I, however, who had followed the scene through the half-open door, was only proud.

That happened in 1932. There's a dramatic image from about the same time which always appears when I shake the kaleidoscope of my childhood days. It dates from the months when the civil war in the declining Weimar Republic had also spread to the Berlin suburbs. One evening, after nightfall, footsteps thundered up the stairs and there was an impatient banging on the door of the apartment. When I jumped out of bed and opened up, my father was standing there, his jacket unbuttoned. He had a broad gauze dressing around his head, held in place by an adhesive; a sticky black patch the size of a fist was visible on the bandage. He had two companions with him, who bedded him down carefully on the settee and said something like, "Look after yourself, lad!" And while I was still astonished at the chummy tone that they dared to use with my father, the latter muttered his thanks, got up astonishingly quickly and disappeared—without paying any attention to me—into one of the rooms at the back. Surprisingly, my mother had been quite unaware of the course of events. Now, after the removal of the dressing and a brief moment of shocked silence, I heard her exclamation—"Heaven have mercy!"—then she ran to the telephone to call the doctor. Later we heard that a group of (Communist) Red Front Fighters had forced their way into a Social Democratic Party meeting at which Albert Grzesinski, the Berlin chief of police, was speaking. They had attacked the Reichsbanner stewards with clubs and broken up the gathering.

In the months that followed there was a constant coming and going in our house. Unfamiliar faces turned up and disappeared again without any greeting. Voices could be heard coming from my father's smoky study, fluctuating between fighting spirit, worry, and resignation. What it was all about was quite mysterious to Wolfgang and me, who were, of course, most interested in the fights. There was talk of street battles at Nollendorfplatz and in the district of Wedding, of bloody confrontations in places I had never heard of, like Altona and Leipzig, and each of these stories provided us with tales for when we went to bed, about revolt, car crashes, missing children, and, finally, because such stories have to become ever more gruesome, about heads bashed or even cut off. However little we understood of what we overheard, we nevertheless felt the atmosphere of embittered passion that was not only spreading on the streets but also surrounded every visitor to the apartment.

At this point I have to insert a comment which may be of help in understanding the pages that follow. In these passages there is often talk of the meek fall of the Weimar Republic. They refer only to the fragmentary memories of a six-to-eight-year-old who has preserved some inevitably sketchy images, which have only later become coherent. Events presented themselves to me in the form of stories current in every family, with almost everything dominated by politics. And yet the background events have to be sketched at least in outline, because in the course of the years they came more and more to dominate our lives.

The same applies to my father. On his picture, too, are superimposed the family stories which were passed on in the course of many evenings around the dinner table under the ceiling lamp with its silk cloth and tasseled shade. Tall, with short, parted hair, he cast a large shadow which to us children conveyed as much fear as it did security. He saw life as a series of tasks which one had to perform without making a fuss, with firm convictions and with as much good humor as possible. Precisely because of this he possessed an authority which was never challenged, still less doubted. In the family, fragments of this elevated image increasingly asserted themselves, in the face of all childish and later all adolescent resistance.

The character of my mother—with her then still rather mild eyes, frequently wide open in surprise—was no doubt different from the figure I remember. In those years, despite the five children she had borne, she conformed, evidently to a much greater degree than I recall, to the type of the daughter from an upper-class background: in love with beautiful feelings, with a big family as her goal and a solid basis in life, at the same time full of the certainty of having a claim to happiness. "I had everything," she said later, "and sometimes I even thought more than was due to me." But then her dreams and expectations had suddenly crumbled and without anyone having predicted it she displayed a firmness that could even turn into toughness. In retrospect, it appears to me that in the countless trials and tribulations of childhood each of us could find with her, more than with my father, understanding and support.

If I venture to make a few marginal remarks on political conditions and the way they affected the family, it should be said that the calamities of the late 1920s and early 1930s, especially the inexorable rise of Hitler, had stretched nerves to the breaking point. At the same time, as always in periods of crisis, the most bizarre prophets appeared: doctors of occult recipes for saving the world, sectarian preachers and those who promised the Garden of Eden and with unctuous, crazy eyes explained that mankind was doomed to destruction. The only hope was if the message they proclaimed found followers and a leader who would resolutely follow the path set by fate and issue new instructions to the world. They were well versed in the most eccentric texts of past ages, obscure prophecies, which strangely enough often corresponded to their follies. Soon my father began to collect literature on the subject.

What was disquieting about these bizarre predictions was that they imperceptibly cut the ground from under the republic. Given its manifest powerlessness both at home and abroad, the new state appeared to a growing number of Germans as a synonym for disgrace, dishonor, and political powerlessness. Increasingly, people surrendered to the idea that poetic, Romantic Germany, at home with profundity of thought and spirituality, had committed an act of metaphysical self-betrayal with the declaration of the republic. German culture had been worth far more than the shallow Western civilization it had been given in return.

In addition, as the crisis intensified, the need for diversion and cheap amusement appeared ever more unrestrained. "Soup kitchen at the front and around the back the Charleston and bobbed hair, La Jana[2] and hopping about on the dance floor," as my father mocked. The traditional values which until then had given people's lives support and orientation began to crumble in

---

2 La Jana was a "scandalous" dancer and film star, whose real name was Henriette Margarethe Hiebel.—Trans.

front of their eyes. There were many who contributed to this destruction, encouraged by the catchphrases of the time, which all pointed to crash and ruin: Twilight of Man, Storms of Steel, Apocalypse, Decline of the West.[3] "The process of decay," said one of my father's friends, the Zentrum party MP Richard Schönborn, "announces itself first of all in the world of ideas." A country and a society that employed such phrases as fashionable terms could not long survive.

Looking back at the major events of those years, a contemporary (as my father later remarked) might believe that he was not resisting a political movement at all, but rather the "Spirit of the Age." Today he knew, my father once said, long after the war, that one has already lost the battle the moment one accepts such a notion. His only compensation was the knowledge that he had been on the right side.

With Papen's Prussian coup of July 20, 1932, the Republic of Weimar had been destroyed, my father often said;[4] he and his political friends—the Riesebrodts, Mielitz, the Fechners—had all been in agreement on that. When a department head in the Prussian Ministry of the Interior, who likewise belonged to the Reichsbanner, begged for understanding that they would find

---

3 *Twilight of Man* (*Menschheitsdämmerung*) is the title of a famous anthology of Expressionist poetry, published in 1919; *Storm of Steel* (*Stahlgewitter*) is Ernst Jünger's 1920 memoir of the Western Front in the First World War; *Decline of the West* (1917) is a pessimistic work of historical speculation by Oswald Spengler.—Trans.

4 On that date, the German chancellor Franz von Papen removed the democratically elected government of Prussia from office.—Trans.

it difficult to act unconstitutionally, my father had for a moment lost his self-control, and as he left retorted: "Ever since the republic came into existence I wished it would have enemies as short-sighted and timid as we are. Then it would have survived. Now everyone knows that this state does not have the will to assert itself against its declared enemies." Many had responded that he should wait and see, that defeatism was no help, either. But he had not been defeatist; he had merely opened his eyes.

So the weeks passed in the timeless openness of childhood. We spent the summer largely in the garden, the winter with sleds and nailed boots in nearby Wuhlheide or then again in the neighboring sandhills and, ignoring my mother's worries, shot straight down ever steeper slopes. The skating rink was just behind the station. It was there that we attempted our first shaky steps wearing skates, fell, got up only to slip again, at last took three and then ten steps, before finally managing whole sequences of steps until we were counted among the "speed terrors." Outside, in the meadows at the edge of Karlshorst, we at first aimlessly kicked a ball around; then six or eight friends came together to form a team, which first played against another street and soon after that against another part of the district, with branches stuck into the ground serving as goalposts. On Hentigstrasse, refereed by "Motte" Böhm, we carried out bitterly fought games of dodgeball up and down the street. And anyone who complained about a ball thrown too hard or, like Helmut Sternekieker, cried because of the pain, was barred from one to three games.

Our garden was at the back of the house. It was about thirty yards long and overshadowed by trees. One reached it by crossing the small fenced-in yard and then going down a path lined with flower beds. In the middle was the big garden table and a little distance away to the right was a lower one for table tennis. About five yards to the left one came upon the horizontal bar, and beyond that was the tumbledown toolshed which my father knocked down in 1935 and with our help replaced with a simple little garden house made of planks. Right in front of it was the pool with its steps and a little fountain. Once, in executing a daring leap over several steps, I slipped and knocked an almost penny-sized hole in my left cheek on the pipe of the fountain and lost a tooth. The rest of the plot was divided into beds for flowers and herbs, carefully separated by large stones.

In retrospect the garden and what grew in it takes on giant proportions. The roses bloomed all summer long, the bushes bore fat berries, and the three or four trees in the middle of that modest magnificence were likewise weighed down with fruit. One autumn day at any rate—I was probably seven—my father said each one of us had his duties, and I was no exception. Wolfgang had to look after the rosebushes and keep the soil damp and loose, and from now on I was responsible for the just-harvested strawberry beds. "Could've told me before," I am supposed to have said; for this year all the strawberries were gone. All polished off! My father, however, had replied that success always starts somewhere.

I only remember January 30, 1933, because of stories later told in the family, but the days and weeks of shock that could be felt in our house ate deep into my consciousness.[5] As I later found out, on receiving news of Hitler's appointment as chancellor of the Reich, my father had immediately left his school office in Lichtenberg and gone to a meeting in the city center. He had not come home until about midnight and had talked with my mother until the early hours of the morning. He entertained none of the delusions to which so many politically informed minds fell victim at the time: that Hitler would become more reasonable, be moderated by success, or that, charlatan as he was, he would be a failure.

Engraved on my mind forever, on the other hand, amidst so much that has faded, is February 28, 1933. That day my father came down to the garden, where Wolfgang and I were playing table tennis, at about midday. "We're going into town now," he said. The order sounded at once stern and conspiratorial, and on the way to the station we tried to find out what this unusual excursion was about. At first my father remained tight-lipped, and only once we had sat down in the empty "cattle truck" (a third-class carriage on the S-Bahn) did he mention that we were going to see a burnt-out ruin. Had the fire already been extinguished? we asked. Had the fire brigade arrived? Would there be dead bodies? My father said nothing. Instead, when some other passengers got on at Ostkreuz Station,

---

5 On that day Adolf Hitler became chancellor of the German Reich, which sparked massive public demonstrations of joy throughout Germany.

he indicated that we should keep our voices down. And (so we later felt) during that journey he frequently talked about things we did not understand.

To our disappointment we didn't then go to the burnt-out Reichstag, whose importance my father meanwhile attempted to explain to us on the platform at Bellevue Station. He later related that while I had looked at him attentively as he spoke, it was obvious that I hadn't understood a thing. But that had, in fact, not been important to him. He had wanted above all to make us aware of the "gravity of the hour."

Instead of getting off the train and walking over to the building, from whose ruins a few pale trails of smoke were still rising, we traveled several times back and forth on the railway viaduct between Friedrichstrasse and Bellevue, and I probably paid more attention to my father's serious face than to the cityscape flitting past the train window. Repeatedly, I heard him utter the mysterious word "war," although I was unable to make sense of what he was saying. Years later, when I asked him if he had meant the Second World War, he denied it with a smile: no, he hadn't been as far-sighted as that. He had meant, rather, civil war. The Reichstag fire, he thought at the time, obviously signaled a settling of accounts with the now defenseless enemies of yesterday. And yet he had hoped that the fire would, at the last moment, still trigger the uprising, which he and others in the Reichsbanner leadership had constantly argued for, to no avail.

Indeed, those in power—now in possession of every power available to the state—began a new kind of civil

war that same February 28. My father, too, found himself in trouble. One month after the Reichstag fire there
were more and more signs that the regime suspected him
of "subversive activities." He was twice summoned to the
local education authority, and then later to the ministry,
and questioned on his attitude toward the Government.
He had not moderated a single word, he assured us on
his return. He saw no reason to alter his judgment on the
whole "rabble." My mother, who had put her hands in
front of her face during his report, rose at the end and
said with an unusual tone of reproach in her voice: "You
know that I have always supported you in what you
believe to be right. I always will. But have you thought
of the children and what your obstinacy could mean for
them?" When my father remained silent, she left the
room without a word.

The decision came a few days later. On April 20,
1933, my father was summoned to Lichtenberg Town
Hall (Karlshorst is part of the borough of Lichtenberg)
and informed by Volz, the state commissar responsible
for the exercise of the business of the borough mayor, that
he was suspended from public service, effective immediately.[6] When my father asked what he was accused of,
the official responded in a sergeant-majorish manner:
"You will be informed of that in due course!" But he was
a civil servant, objected my father, to which Volz replied,
"You can tell our Führer that. He'll be very impressed."
And then, in a derisive voice: "Look on the suspension as

---

6 April 20 was Hitler's birthday, hardly a coincidence.

a present! You'll be making the Führer happy! Because
today, as I'm sure you know, is the Führer's birthday."
According to my father's account, he had then responded
that he had no part in it and Volz retorted, provocatively,
"You can go now. I even urge you to do so! *Heil Hitler!*"

As he was on his way to the exit, all at once the building he knew so well seemed unfamiliar. It was the same
with the staff, some of whom he had known for years;
suddenly, one after the other, their eyes were avoiding
his. At his school, to which he went immediately, it was
no different, even in his office; everything from the cup-
boards to the stationery already seemed to have been
replaced. The first person he bumped into was his colleague Markwitz, who had clearly already been informed.
"Fest, old man!" he said, after my father had spoken a
few explanatory words. "Did it have to be like this?" And
when my father replied, "Yes, it had to be!," Markwitz
objected: "No, don't tell me that! It's something I learned
early: there's no 'must' when it comes to stupidity!"

On April 22, a good two weeks after the passage of
the Law for the Restoration of a Professional Civil Service, my father was summoned again. Remaining seated
and without offering my father a chair, the temporary
mayor, reading from a prepared text, formally notified
him that he was relieved of his duties as headmaster of
the Twentieth Elementary School and was suspended
until further notice. Given as grounds for the suspension were his senior positions in the Zentrum party and
in the Reichsbanner, as well as his "public speeches disparaging the Führer" and other high-ranking National

Socialists, and in particular the "martyr of the movement" Horst Wessel. Under the circumstances there
was no longer any guarantee that he would "at all times
support without reservation the national state," as the
law put it. "Is the authority aware that this is a breach
of the law?" asked my father, but Volz retorted that he
couldn't discuss legal matters with every man who came
in off the street. "Because from now on you are not much
more than that, Herr Fest, and no longer any colleague
of mine!" As he spoke these curt words, he continued
leafing through my father's file and one of the pages fell
to the floor—no doubt intentionally, thought my father.
Volz clearly expected my father to pick it up. My father,
however, remained motionless, as he later reported; not
for one moment did he consider going down on his knees
in front of the mayor.

Volz then continued in a noticeably sharper tone.
As well as being summarily suspended, my father was
required within two days to formally transfer charge
of the school to his successor, Markwitz. He would be
informed in writing of the details. With a gesture that
was part dismissal, part shooing away to the door, the
provisional mayor added that for the time being my father
was not allowed to take up any employment. Everything
proceeded as if according to a plan, said my father, when
he came to talk about what had happened.

To us children the effect of the event was at first hardly
noticeable, although (as I am supposed to have remarked
to Wolfgang later on) it made a boy's nightmare come
true: one's father is a teacher and is at home the whole

day long! At any rate the change, the mere presence of my father, gave the beautiful irregularity of my childhood a center and (as I thought) an annoyingly firm structure. Unusually, he even joined my mother a little later when with satchel, slate, and dangling sponge I set off for my first day at school, and it was he who handed me, after we had said goodbye, the colorful, shiny school cone.[7] After that he began to ask, as time passed, questions that he had never asked before: about homework, friends, pastimes. Also about my impudently answering back some neighbor, which I had long forgotten about, and once about a broken window pane.

At the end of April our nursemaid Franziska left. After our mother, she was the dearest person to us. To prevent her from leaving, my younger brother Winfried had even made her an offer of marriage; Hannih, our eldest sister, had declared herself willing to be a bridesmaid, and Fräulein Scheib, who helped out at the priest's office, had promised to make the little side chapel of the church available. A few days later the cleaning lady also stopped coming. From the beginning, anticipating a large family, my father had also taken the two neighboring flats, so that we occupied the whole second story. Now, one after the other, the two adjoining apartments were given up. Workmen came and walled up the connecting doorways. From now on there was no longer a playroom or the children's hall with the four rooms off

---

7 The author is shown with this cone in the photograph on p. 34; traditionally it is filled with candies meant to "sweeten" the start of school and its discipline.

it. Instead, we three boys all slept together in one of the
larger remaining rooms, in which, apart from the three
beds, there were two bookcases and, facing the balcony
window, a desk as well. Our two sisters were allocated
the room which had previously belonged to Franziska.

The new room shared by the boys had one advantage. It was next to the drawing room, in which guests
were received and where our parents sat together in the
evening. If we pressed our ears to the wall we could hear
every word. Much talk about politics, of course. But what
preoccupied us more was that little Lena with the unpronounceable Polish name, who lived on the estate behind
the racetrack, hadn't come home for three nights now. Yet
she was only fourteen, as my mother said, and was considered to be the prettiest and cheekiest thing. "Exactly!"
interjected my father drily, but my mother had already
moved on to the always forward Rudi Hardegen, who
had recently shown off with the "impossible" assertion
that "womenfolk" should be given a good hiding once a
day, then all marriages would be happy ones. A little later
we heard that Herr Patzek, who lived a couple of houses
along and already had six children, had almost apologized to our father because his wife was pregnant for the
seventh time; he could hardly conceal the fact that he was
already fifty, he said. At that age it was improper to show
off one's lust, not least for the sake of the reputation of
his dear Magda. We were in early puberty at the time
and we slapped ourselves so hard on the shoulders at this
story that I fell against the wall and we heard our mother
say, "What was that?" In an instant we buried ourselves

Der Bürgermeister.   Berlin-Lichtenberg, den 18. April 1933,
      Schv.II.

                    Herrn

                        Rektor   Johannes F e s t ,

Mit Zust.-Urk.!   20.   Volksschule.
                            ================================

                    Als Staatskommissar zur Wahrnehmung der
            Geschäfte des Bezirksbürgermeisters des Verwaltungs-
            bezirks Lichtenberg, zu dem ich durch den Herrn
            Oberpräsidenten der Provinz Brandenburg und von
            Berlin bestellt worden bin, beurlaube ich Sie vorbe-
            haltlich der Zustimmung des Herrn Oberpräsidenten ab
            sofort bis auf weiteres.
                    Mit der kommissarischen Leitung der Schule ist
            Herr Lehrer   M a r k w i t z   beauftragt.
                    Ich ersuche Sie, sich am Donnerstag, dem
            20.4.33 um 12 Uhr in dem Amtszimmer der Schule ein-
            zufinden und dem kommissarischen Schulleiter die Amts-
            geschäfte zu übergeben.

                        Staatskommissar zur Wahrnehmung der
                        Geschäfte des Bezirksbürgermeisters.

Johannes Fest's suspension notice of April 18, 1933,
signed by the Acting Borough Mayor Volz, who had been
installed by the Nazis. The letter appoints Markwitz
as provisional headmaster and continues: I request you
to present yourself in the school office at midday
on April 20, 1933, and hand over all official
business to the provisional headmaster.

in our pillows and, as she looked in at the door, Wolfgang even managed a couple of sighing snores as if fast asleep.

Gossip like that gripped and amused us far more than all household worries, all politics and disputes between neighbors. At some point during the summer the letter came which turned my father's suspension into dismissal, because no change of attitude could be discerned in him. The date for his removal from the civil service was given (as the law required) as October 1, 1933. He was allowed, in accordance with unexplained decisions by the local authority, a pension of less than two hundred Reichsmarks, plus child allowances. It was a plunge into *Povertät*,[8] as they used to say in Berlin, and although my mother was often worried about it, she did everything she could to make sure we were affected as little as possible. There was to be no talk of lack of money. As soon as anyone infringed that rule she called out his name across the table as a reprimand. From time to time, she even tried to see our new circumstances in a positive light. "The situation has one advantage," she would remark to us. "You can never be spoiled!"

But of course our meals became more modest. There were no toys anymore and Wolfgang did not get his remote-controlled Mercedes Silver Arrow model racing car or I the football, which (as I've never forgotten) cost three Reichsmarks, seventy-five pfennigs. The model railway already lacked gates, bridges, and points, so to

---

8 Pseudo-French, used in Berlin slang, showing the influence of the important Huguenot presence and tradition in Berlin.

make any progress at all we built hills out of papier-mâché
on which we placed home-made houses, churches, and
towers. At Christmas, instead of the model racing car,
Wolfgang got a jacket, I a leather-looking pair of trousers, and both of us some long brown socks, which we
thought "girlish" and which, on leaving the house, we
rolled down to knee length even before we reached the
street. When he saw my disappointment, my father said,
consolingly, "Things will get better! Sometime!" My
mother said nothing in response to her children's worries, which were brought to her again and again, and at
most she pursed her lips. In bed one evening Wolfgang
said that her eyes were red from crying; he knew about
things like that.

Gradually, however, the continuation of the familiar
blurred any sense of a break. In the afternoons, as soon
as the weather allowed, the family still gathered around
the garden table, friends often came from nearby as well
as farther away, the Lensches, the Schönborns, as well
as Hans Hausdorf with his pies and his puns, the Kör-
ners and others. Sometimes also the fat son of Frau Dölle
showed himself at the ground-floor window simulating
gymnastic exercises, while from the first floor Frau Bik-
king, who was more than seventy, could be heard singing
in a tremulous, old woman's voice her favorite song: "A
soldier stands on Volga's bank . . ."[9] or "Give the marble
a beating heart . . . ," and again and again after three
or four numbers the modulated wail: "It was long, long

---

[9] A then quite recent song from Franz Lehar's *The Tsarevich.*—Trans.

ago." She had lived alone with an old cat for years and accused us of only liking animals as "Sunday grub, preferably with red cabbage and a thick gravy." When she complained of the noise we made, she pretended to twist something in her hands and a creaking sound came from her throat to represent a neck being wrung. And, as they had done before, the SA (Brownshirt) units came marching down Marksburgstrasse singing their battle songs: "When the golden evening sun" or "The brittle bones tremble," interrupting each song to shout up at the windows, "Germany awake!"

For a while one saw uniformed patrols everywhere, although there was neither unrest nor brawls in public halls. Instead, the more or less declared opponents of the regime were abducted and sometimes beaten to death. Many of those arrested without justification were taken to informal concentration camps, usually set up by the SA in out-of-the-way cellars. Among the images of those months is a drunken man who, close to Karlshorst Station, stopped in front of my parents and me and, raising both arms, shouted in a hoarse voice, *"Heil Hitler!"* Curiously, I often recollect distant cries for help, yet I do not know what gave rise to them and where they came from. It may be that they were an echo of the fear, which for all our ignorance of what was going on outside had also taken hold of us and made the air strangely thick.

There were good reasons to be afraid: the men in belted leather coats who came from time to time and with a *Heil Hitler!* entered the apartment without waiting to be invited were more than enough to create a threatening

atmosphere.[10] Without another word they shut themselves in the study with my father, while my mother
stood in front of the coat recess, her face rigid. At table,
friends were mentioned who had suddenly disappeared;
others disappeared from conversation, because they were
no longer friends. Among the close connections that
remained there was a circle of ten or twelve Reichsbanner people, as well as Hubertus zu Löwenstein, whose
influence on postwar politics later attracted some attention. During one evening meal he telephoned in a state of
great agitation and asked for my father's advice: the SA
were causing a commotion outside the door of his apartment. "Can you hear the noise?" he said, and then he
asked how he should respond. Perhaps he should open
up, after all? "No!" shouted my father, so loudly that
around the table we fell into a terrified silence. "Under
no circumstances! Don't let them in! Leave by the fire
escape! Only by the fire escape, if the house has one!"
Löwenstein didn't open up and he escaped the bloodhounds; soon afterward he fled Berlin and later made his
way by hazardous routes to the United States.

At first, the countless violations of the law by our
new rulers still caused a degree of disquiet. But among
the incomprehensible features of those months, my
father later recalled, was the fact that soon life went on
as if such state crimes were the most natural thing in
the world. Although I did not grasp much of what was

---

10 Fest is describing the appearance of the Gestapo or Secret State Police (*Geheime
Staatspolizei*) and its typical mode of operation.

happening around us, he never answered my questions. I didn't understand anything about it yet, he said. In two or three years he would explain it to me. Wolfgang, to whom I turned after that, responded with a secretive air that it was about politics. The family story goes that I (then seven years old) replied, "But I'm political, too!"

As I later found out, many of the agitated conversations really were about the state's illegal actions, and how people paid so little attention to them. To my parents' satisfaction there was only one Hitler supporter in our building, Herr Schimmelpfennig, although his wife once told my father ("in confidence") not to take her husband too seriously. This business with the Nazis is just "silly stuff," she said, adding with a laugh that years ago—to her lifelong regret—she had foolishly taken seriously his proposal of marriage.

Even tenants who disapproved of the regime made mollifying remarks. "What do you want, then?" asked Herr Deecke from the ground floor, who was the father of that cute little Traute. "You're exaggerating!" Everybody could see that things were improving by the day. Frau Dölle talked the same way; she liked to play the concierge and missed no opportunity to go into raptures about her paunchy son, who was always ready with an obscenity, in word or deed. Herr Patzek, with the deep, open voice, spoke of the mere "fairground tricks" of the Nazis, which were very far from being a threat to the Western world; with such scare stories one was only playing into the hands of the "Hitler gang." Herr Leopold, who worked in some ministry or other and was known for his earthy cynicism, thought that, apart from the usual teething troubles, the whole Nazi dictatorship amounted to a limitation of freedom of thought. And that "doesn't even hurt the left side of my ass," as he put it. Because one just had to listen to the nonsense the famous "man in the street" talked; one should really be grateful to the new rulers for putting an end to all that "political blathering." My father usually replied to such objections (as he later told us) by saying it wasn't about the unemployed at all. And still less about freedom of thought. In reality, everyone was simply searching for an excuse to look away from the crimes all around.

Soon a growing indifference began to spread even among declared opponents of Hitler. To a not inconsiderable degree it could be put down to the deliberately euphemistic vocabulary of the regime. My father was "let go," as it was called; others were "provisionally" retired; arrests were called "preventive custody"—how bad could that be? At the end of 1933 my father went for a walk with his Social Democrat friend Max Fechner in the pine woods near Erkner. For reasons of safety he liked to go there to discuss politics. "So we allow ourselves to be ruled by louts for a while," said Fechner, they wouldn't last long. My father listed everything that contradicted this view and pointed out the "disgrace" of their seizure of power. The republican associations had millions of members, but had not even managed a general strike. Instead, within a few days of a mere government decree, they had dissolved into thin air without resistance and followed the Nazi flags at the big Labor Day parades.

Now everyone was constantly thinking of new justifications for having gone along with it.

There had then been a lengthy argument, said my father, reporting on the walk in the woods. Fechner had pointed out that the Nazis' smartness had scuppered all of their plans: he and his friends had always expected a coup d'état; all of their plans for action had taken that as their starting point. But there had been no coup, and Hitler coming to power halfway legally had completely thrown them. The executive committee of Fechner's party had been unable to deal with the fact that the law was against them. Consequently, it had forbidden every form of resistance. My father had replied, as Max Fechner confirmed after the war on a visit to my parents, that he understood: as proper Germans, upholding the law was more important to them than justice.

Karlshorst, as it had meanwhile developed, was a small town in which everyone knew everyone, as well as their predilections, bad habits, quirks, and vanities. And also their affairs, minor marriage crises, or children's school reports. Since spring 1933 everyone knew, too, whom he could trust and with whom caution was necessary. A civil servant from Number 12 suddenly shaved his head and started going around in his National Socialist Motor Corps uniform, even when he wasn't on driving duty; the uncle of the newlyweds in the corner house was a big shot in the party and drove up every second Sunday wearing his golden brown uniform; Harry Kehl, with whom we played football in the street, had risen to section leader in the Deutsches Jungvolk (the junior version of the Hitler

Youth), and in order to convince everyone of his new importance he wore the red-and-white cord of his rank even on
his sailor suit. Once I heard him loudly reciting the Hitler
Youth "camp prayer" to the house walls: *Du Volk aus der
Tiefe / Du Volk in der Nacht / vergiss nicht das Feuer /
bleib' auf der Wacht!*"[11] and a little later a somewhat older
girl from the street parallel to our own sent my brother
packing at the door of her apartment, saying that no one
was allowed to enter unless they had read *Mein Kampf.*

But most of those around us were "decent people" (as
the saying goes). There were hardly any denunciations at
this time. At any rate we never felt ourselves excluded,
and our clothes, which were soon patched a dozen times
over, allowed us to roam around the poorer quarters,
while we were already at home in the more middle-class
ones. The friends I made at school also came from "reliable" families: Gerd Schülke, Clemens Körner, and
Ursel Hanschmann from the floor below, whose father
was employed in the university administration. The
families had become friendly after Herr Hanschmann
had several times refused to join the party at the cost of
discrimination at work. The relationship became so close
that the Hanschmanns were given the key to the apartment when our parents visited friends in the evening,
and they gained a lot of respect in our eyes, because they
never said a word about all the noisy fun and games we
children got up to on such evenings.

---

11 Roughly (and without the rhyme): You, nation from the depths / You, nation in
the night / don't forget the fire / stay on your guard!—Trans.

All of that continued in the happy present time of childhood, and reinforced the impression of familiarity. We continued to play dodgeball on tree-lined Hentig-strasse; collected cigarette cards of art works, film beau-ties, and football players; competed as to who could do the most knee circles on the horizontal bar in the garden; or made fun of Fat Dölle. When the milk cart rattled through the streets, we begged the driver for a piece of ice or, if need be, knocked it off the big pole when he wasn't watching. "You're stealing!" Fat Dölle would then accuse us. "You're taking things that aren't yours!" Once I am supposed to have asked him where all the fat on his stomach came from, and said that maybe his mother stuck it on.

In the evening, when we had gone to bed, our father told us stories about his schooldays and youth in the Neumark; how he had gone hunting rabbits with ferrets, or in winter had broken through the ice of Packlitzsee Lake while angling for carp. Later, he read to us from Schwab's *Heroic Legends*. I also remember the tales of the Grimms and of Hauff. "The Seven Swans," "Dwarf Long-Nose," "The Severed Hand," and "The Cold Heart," and how they filled our imagination and even our dreams with knights and princesses, witches and dwarves.[12] Next came the stories of Hector and Achilles and the adventures of Odysseus, whose traces, my father said, were still visible in Sicily today: for example, he had

---

12 "The Seven Swans" appears in a collection by Ludwig Bechstein. "Dwarf Long-Nose," "The Severed Hand," and "The Cold Heart" are among Hauff's tales.—Trans.

seen the boulder which the blinded Polyphemus hurled after Odysseus and his companions lying in the water near Syracuse.[13]

Early on the reading and the "told stories" (as we called them) became a firm feature of every evening, though they became progressively more sophisticated. When we were one or two years older my father read us pieces by Johann Peter Hebel, then a children's edition of Swift's *Gulliver's Travels*; later also writings by Ernst von Wildenbruch or Christian Morgenstern. And so on through the years to Heinrich von Kleist's novellas or to Ricarda Huch, whose stories, insofar as I got to know them, were mostly set during the Italian Renaissance and were read so often possibly because Italy was the country my father particularly liked, and so, imperceptibly, we did, too. Yet Huch's most impressive story had the title "The Last Summer" and was set in prerevolutionary Russia in 1906. Even today it still takes my breath away, when I think of the end of the story: how the typewriter literally flies into the air in the middle of a word, bringing both the scene and the tale to an abrupt end.[14]

---

13 This mix of Germanic heroic tales, fairy tales, both ancient and modern, and classical literary masterpieces is typical for the exposure to literature of the *Bildungsbürger*, at least through the first half of the twentieth century.

14 Johann Peter Hebel (1760–1826) is the author of popular, humorous poems and stories of everyday life, some in his native Alemanian dialect. Ernst von Wildenbruch (1845–1909), the grandson of a Prussian prince, wrote patriotic and historical novels, poems, and songs, often on Prussian themes. Christian Morgenstern (1871–1914) is best known for his scurrilous nonsense poems with both a humorous and a melancholy tinge. His more serious poetry and his translations of Scandinavian literature are less known.

Heinrich von Kleist (1777–1811) was a Prussian officer and remains a major German dramatist whose plays, short prose narratives, and essays, while related to

Naturally, we had countless questions about what
was being read to us, but before my father gave us any
answers he turned off the little reading lamp, and it is
these explanatory sessions in the twilight or darkness
which over the years, more than anything else, meant
home to me. After that the evening prayer was said, following which no more talking was allowed. From the
street came only the suburban silence: echoing steps that
drew closer, combined with a couple of voices as they
passed, and then were drowned out by the goodbye shouts
of some customers at the corner pub. Soon I discovered
that Wolfgang was continuing to read with a flashlight
under the blanket. He was always one step ahead. When
I was reading Mörike's *Mozart's Journey to Prague*, he
was already on to Wassermann's *The Maurizius Case*; a
few years later, when I told him about Stefan Zweig, he
merely smiled and said one had to read Nietzsche.[15]

Despite so many things continuing unaffected by
current events, it was sometimes possible to discern
signs of the strain being placed on society. From the end
of 1934, a few months after the so-called Röhm Putsch,
following which Hitler raised himself to unchallenged
leader, the powers-that-be visibly intervened in everyday

---

all the major intellectual currents of his time, are largely sui generis. His drama *Prinz
Friedrich von Homburg* poses central moral questions in the context of Prussia's military legacy and history, as does his most complex novella, *Michael Kohlhaas*, for the
time of Luther and the Protestant Reformation.

Ricarda Huch (1864–1947) is the author of neoromantic and historical novels
and novellas who renounced her membership in the Prussian Academy of the Arts
in 1933 to protest its takeover by the Nazis.

15 Jakob Wassermann (1873–1934) specialized in novels with a sensationalist content; *Der Fall Maurizius* (*The Maurizius Case*) became a film.

life.[16] Already six months earlier, one or two petitions by my father for reemployment had been turned down. Then he had brought home from conversations with friends the information that the subject of "racial science" had been introduced in schools, and that air-raid drills in anticipation of war had begun. He also came back from his monthly meetings with news of the imminent ban on Neudeutschland (New Germany), the Catholic strand of the youth movement. Soon there were no more hikes on which, as part of a group, we watched the fire burn down in some clearing as night fell; without much fuss, the Hitler Youth took over the songs of the old youth organizations as if they had always belonged to it.

In the summer of 1934 my father was once again summoned to Lichtenberg Town Hall. A counter clerk told him—in a voice loud enough to be heard by the half dozen other people waiting—that the ban on employment imposed on him was comprehensive. It had come to the knowledge of the authorities that he was giving private lessons. He was therefore informed (and in relating this episode my father imitated the official's deliberate pauses) "as—a—final—warning—that—he—was—also—forbidden—to—give private—tuition."

In the course of the autumn, my grandfather, then seventy years of age, went back to work. He had been a

16 "Röhm Putsch" was the Nazi designation for three days of murder by the SS (Schutzstaffel) at the end of June 1934, during which the entire leadership of the SA (Sturmabteilung or Brownshirts), including its head and Hitler's close friend Ernst Röhm, was eliminated; the SS also used this opportunity to kill numerous political opponents within the Nazi movement and outside.

Berlin Lichtenberg

✗ Reg.-Bez. Berlin

Personal-Karte für Lehrer.

Name und Vornamen: *Fest, Johannes*
(Rufnamen unterstreichen)

Geboren am (Tag, Monat, Jahr) 6. 2. 89. Religionsbekenntnis *kath.*
in Ostrowo, Kr. Samter

Gegenwärtige Dienststellung[1]) *Rektor*

Anstellungsverhältnis[2]) *endgültig*

Im Volksschuldienst endgültig angestellt am *1. 3. 1914*

Erste Lehrerprüfung abgelegt wann? *24. 2. 1910* wo? *Paradies*

Zweite Lehrerprüfung abgelegt wann? *8. 1. 1914* wo? *Lindenheim*
Kr. Czarnikau

Sonstige Lehramtsprüfungen abgelegt (welche? wann? wo?)

Mittelschullehrerprüfung, 22. 10. 22 in Berlin
1. Eintritt in d. Schuldienst 1. 4. 10
1. " in d. Berlin " 1. 10. 16

An welcher Schule gegenwärtig angestellt oder beschäftigt?[3])

Schulort und Kreis		Genaue Bezeichnung der Schule[4])	Seit wann an dieser Schule beschäftigt?
Ort	Kreis		
Bln.-Lichtenberg		20. kath. Schule	1. 12. 29
20.4.33 beurlaubt	1.10.33 entlassen	54. L.L.G. (66)	

Unterschrift des Ausfüllenden:

Johannes Fest.

Anmerkungen siehe Rückseite.

*Personnel file card for Johannes Fest, with entries on his
suspension and later dismissal in April and October 1933*

wealthy man for most of his life until the war loans took half of his fortune and the currency devaluations of the postwar years eliminated the rest. He no doubt had a pension, but his own needs and, above all, his desire to help my parents in the difficult position they now found themselves, caused him to become active again. Although as managing director of a private company he had had no professional training, the Köpenicker Bank, simply on the basis of the respect he enjoyed, offered him the opportunity, after a short period of training, to work for them. And so, only a few months later, as manager of the Karlshorst branch of the bank, he went to work every day as an employee, which was something he had never done before.

One momentous, never forgotten experience of the year that was drawing to a close remains to be mentioned. I no longer know what I expected after its announcement; at any rate I could hardly wait—given all the mysterious hints, of which I tried to make sense— for Aunt Dolly to take me to the opera for the first time. Weeks beforehand she asked to speak to me and demanded a clean collar and polished shoes for "our great evening." Apart from that she emphasized that I must read the libretto, and two weeks before the performance quizzed me about scenes and arias. I am grateful to her to this day that she chose for me (I was not yet nine years old) Mozart's *The Magic Flute* as my entry to the magical world of music. For all my reading efforts and Aunt Dolly's additional explanations I didn't understand a word of the meaning of the thing, of Sarastro's order of priests, the Queen of the Night, or the

Trial of Fire and Water, and only Papageno made sense to me, even though no one could tell me why Papagena appeared as an old witch for so long and only toward the end of the piece, when Papageno played his magic music, as an enchanting maiden. But the music has stayed with me all my life. "And once again: no Berlin accent!" Aunt Dolly admonished me as we entered the theater; theaters were "hallowed halls" and she hoped I knew where the term "hallowed halls" came from. In fact, if I remember rightly, it was merely the foyer of the Rose Theatre.[17]

But overall, the performance was an overwhelming experience. I am even supposed to have asked whether we couldn't see the opera again the next day. Aunt Dolly merely laughed. But when she realized what a success her invitation had been, we saw Lortzing's *Zar und Zimmermann* only five weeks later, then *Il Seraglio* in a local hall, and later *Der Wildschütz*, also by Lortzing.[18] After many other performances we finally applauded, shortly before my departure from Berlin, *The Marriage of Figaro*, as well as (so my aunt said) its textual precursor and musical continuation *The Barber of Seville*. These early opera visits with an "aunt intent on higher things" awakened my taste for all music and gave it a solid foundation.

In early 1936, from our place by the wall, Wolfgang and I eavesdropped on a rare argument between our parents. There had been a strangely irritable atmosphere all

---

17 "Holy halls" is a quotation from *The Magic Flute.*—Trans.

18 Albert Lortzing (1801–51) composed and wrote the libretti for popular, often humorous operas.

day. My mother evidently started it, reminding my father in a few short sentences what she had put up with, politically and personally, in the last three years. She said she wasn't complaining, but she had never dreamt of such a future. From morning to night she was standing in front of pots, pans, and washboards, and when the day was over she had to attend to the torn clothes of the children, patched five times over. And then, after what seemed like a hesitant pause, she asked whether my father did not, after all, want to reconsider joining the party. The gentlemen from the education authority had called twice in the course of the year to persuade him to give way; at the last visit they had even held out the prospect of rapid promotion. In any case, she couldn't cope any more . . . And to mark the end of her plea, after a long pause she added a simple "Please!"

My father replied a little too wordily (as I sometimes thought in the years to come), but at the same time revealed how uneasy he had been about the question for a long time. He said something about the readjustments that she, like many others, had been forced to make. He spoke about habit, which after often difficult beginnings provides a certain degree of stability. He spoke about conscience and trust in God. Also that he himself, as well as my brothers and I, could gradually relieve her of some of the work in the household, and so on. But my mother insisted on an answer, suggesting that joining the party would not change anything: "After all, we remain who we are!" It did not take long for my father to retort: "Precisely not! It would change everything!"

My mother evidently hesitated for a moment. Then she responded that she knew that joining the party would be to lie "to those in charge," but then let it be a lie! A thousand lies even, if necessary! She had no qualms in that respect. Of course, such a decision amounted to hypocrisy. But she was ready for that. Untruth had always been the weapon of the little people against the powerful; she had nothing else in mind. The life she was leading was so terribly disappointing! Now it seemed to be my father's turn to be surprised. At any rate he simply said, "We are not little people. Not when it comes to such questions!"

Head next to head we pressed our ears to the wall in order not to miss a word. But we did not find out what happened in the longer intervals, amidst the clearing of throats, the adding of fuel to the tiled stove, and, if we really did hear it properly, occasional sobs. My mother said something about the reproaches of many friends, according to whom my father was too inflexible and only thought of his principles. My father, however, replied that he could not go along with the Nazis, not even a little bit. That, exactly that, was how it stood. Even if their expectations of life had been disappointed as a result. It happened to almost everyone that their dreams ended up on the rubbish heap. Once again there was a pause, before my mother replied, "My dreams aren't in danger. I'm not talking about them! They were shattered long ago! Don't fool yourself!" Both of them knew that nothing would change in their lifetimes. They would never get rid of Hitler again. And at the very end, after another of those long delays which were impossible to interpret: "It is just so hard to make that clear to oneself every day."

Years later, after the war, when I asked her about this argument, my mother remembered it immediately. She had considered every word for some time and had to gather up all of her courage to speak, since she knew what the answer would be and that my father would be in the right; it had taken her a while to get over it. The ten years of their marriage before that had been untroubled. Then from one day to the next everything had turned "dark." She had only been in her early thirties. The argument I was talking about had been the beginning of a second phase in her being-in-the-world. After her eternally beloved young days with boarding school, piano and Eichendorff poems, and the early years of marriage, she had been forced to learn that life showed no consideration; more or less from one day to the next everything had been turned upside down.[19] For her girlish mind it had been a catastrophe. Sometimes she had thought the rupture would destroy her life. "But we saw it through," she said after a pause, which I did not interrupt, "even if to this day I don't know how we managed it."

On that February day Wolfgang and I became aware for the first time of a serious difference of opinion between our parents. It was a cold winter evening; there was snow on the balcony in front of our room and layers of ice had

---

19 The references from boarding school through early marriage are all intended to show how protected from real life the upbringing of a young "lady" like Fest's mother was; they also set up the contrast to what she would endure later on.

formed at the edges of the window panes. Only when the conversation ebbed away and we climbed down from the desk did we notice how frozen stiff we were. Wolfgang took me into his bed so that we would warm up and said, finally, "I hope it turns out well!" I responded that it had turned out well. What did he mean?

Once I was in my own bed again, our parents came into the bedroom to check that everything was all right. They whispered something I couldn't make out. When they had gone I said to Wolfgang that now he could see that I had been right. He replied in a questioning tone, which to me at the time seemed exaggerated, "Perhaps."

·

THREE

Even If All Others Do . . .

One afternoon at the end of 1936, as Wolfgang and I were trying out new slides and leaps on our garden skating rink, my father told us to come to his study. The unusual tone he adopted as he did so made me ask, cheekily, "What's the matter? Is there a problem again?" With visible reluctance, my father asked us to sit down at the smoking table. First of all he talked about the little summerhouse which had just been completed. He had decided to partition off the front part as living space— a sort of "den" with a desk, books, and drinks—and to keep a number of animals at the back. But, he interrupted himself midsentence—that was not why he had called us.

He wanted to talk to us about a subject, he began, that had been giving him a headache for some months now. He had been prompted by one or two differences of opinion with our mother, who was terribly worried and was hardly able to sleep anymore. No doubt it was also harder for her than for anyone else in the family, and, furthermore, she took everything more seriously than he did. Of course, he knew that with the Nazis taking power, her life—for the time being, at any rate—had come to a stop. Perhaps his trust in God was greater, or perhaps he was only more foolhardy, although to reproach him with being so, as Aunt Dolly did in her haughty moods, was quite wrong. He knew what his responsibilities were. But he also had principles, which he wasn't going to let anyone call into question. Least of all the "band of criminals" in power.

He repeated the words "band of criminals," and if we had been a little older we would no doubt have noticed how torn he was. He had discussed what he was about to say with my mother and they had with some effort reached an agreement. From now on there would be a double evening meal: an early one for the three younger children and another one as soon as the little ones were in bed. We belonged to the later sitting. The reason for this division was very simple; he had to have a place in the world where he could talk openly and get his disgust off his chest. Otherwise life would be worth nothing. At least not for him. With the little ones he would have to keep himself in check, as he had done for two years now whenever entering a shop, in front of the lowliest counter clerk, and—by force of law—every time he picked up his children from school. He was incapable of doing that, he said, and concluded with the words, more or less, "A state that turns everything into a lie shall not cross our threshold as well. I shall not submit to the reigning mendacity, at least within the family circle." That, of course, sounded a little grand, he said. As it was, he only wanted to keep the enforced hypocrisy at bay.

He took a deep breath, as if he had got rid of a burden, and walked back and forth between the window and the smoking table a few times. In doing this, he began again, he was turning us into adults, so to speak. With that came a duty to be extremely cautious. Tight lips were the symbol of this state: "Always remember that!" Nothing political that we discussed was for others to hear. Anyone with whom we exchanged a few words could be a Nazi, a traitor, or simply thoughtless. In a dictatorship, distrust was not only a commandment, it was almost a virtue.

And it was just as important, he continued, never to suffer from the isolation which inevitably accompanied opposition to the opinion on the street. He would give us a Latin maxim for that, which we should never forget; it would be best to write it down, then brand it on our memory and throw away the note. The maxim had often helped him, at any rate, and even saved him from making some wrong decisions, because he had rarely made a mistake when he had followed his own judgment alone. He put a piece of paper in front of each of us and dictated: "*Etiam si omnes—ego non!* It's from the Gospel According to St. Matthew," he explained, "the scene on the

Mount of Olives."[1] He laughed when he saw what was
on my piece of paper. If I remember rightly, I had written
something like *Essi omniss, ergono.* My father stroked my
head and said, consolingly, "Don't worry! There's time
enough for you to learn it!" My brother, who was already
at Gymnasium, had written the sentence correctly.

That, more or less, was how the hour in the study
passed. I have, understandably enough, reproduced only
the gist of my father's words, no matter how often I
later thought of them. After we returned to our room,
Wolfgang repeated, with all the superiority of an older
brother, that we were adults now. He hoped I knew what
that meant. I nodded solemnly, although I didn't have a
clue. Then he added that all of us together now formed
a group of conspirators. He proudly pushed against my
chest: "Us against the world!" I nodded once again,
without having the faintest idea what it might mean to
be against the world. I simply felt myself to be favored
in some indefinable way by my father, with whom in the
recent past I had increasingly got into arguments because
of some piece of cheek or other. The way he sometimes
acknowledged me from then on with a passing nod, I also
interpreted as approval. That evening, after the parental "Good night," my mother came into our room once
more, sat down for a few minutes on Wolfgang's bed, and

---

1 This line, which gives Fest the title of his memoir, may be translated as "Even if
all others do—I do not!" The King James translation of this verse (Matthew 26:33)
reads rather differently: "Peter answered and said unto him: Though all men shall
be offended because of thee, yet will I never be offended." German Bible translations don't really correspond, either.—Trans.

later on mine. "I only say cheerful things—or prefer to say nothing," she had once declared as a Liebenthal rule of life. She stuck to that now. But she looked depressed.

It was an adventure, as I often, in the weeks that followed, happily persuaded myself before falling asleep. Who had the opportunity of entering upon such an enterprise with his father? I was determined not to disappoint him. Possibly my happiness also had to do with the fact that the dominant childhood feeling of being defenseless against one's parents returned now and then; but there wasn't only powerlessness; on the whole, I was imbued with a sense of privilege. And trust in others— that, too, was one of the lessons of that afternoon—was not a present that one doled out casually, but a rare remuneration, which had to be earned.

Only when I was older did I understand the horror of the situation, in which constant watchfulness was required as a kind of law for parents as for children, mistrust was a rule of survival, and isolation a necessity— where the mere clumsiness of a child could lead literally to death and ruin. Fifteen years later, when I asked my father about the dark side of his afternoon talk, his expression again immediately revealed just how worried he had been then. He recovered himself and replied that at the time he had been very conscious of the risk to which he exposed himself and his family. Perhaps he had gone too far. But he had hoped to God it would turn out well. And, indeed, the gamble had paid off. At any rate, neither we nor Winfried, who had been allowed to join the second sitting of the evening meal later on, had ever caused him any embarrassment. And, just as he had wished, none of us had ever forgotten the maxim which, he remembered, he had bequeathed us. Indeed, the fine Latin maxim "Even if all others do—I do not!" belonged to every truly free life.

Otherwise, everything remained as before. The petty quarrels between us children, the great reconciliations. In spring the lilac bushes bloomed, and when it rained the white and violet flowers bowed almost to the ground. Soon after the berries, the plum tree in front of the Deeckes' window bore juicy black fruit, and once every three months my mother dressed up and went in her dark blue dress with the pale collar and the pearl necklace, which my father had given her on their wedding, to the Liebenthal Club, "dress informal," where, as we joked, she heard the latest "market gossip" of the upper ranks, about the worries of bringing up children, about daughters' romances that had come to nothing, and once even, amidst whispered agitation, about a premarital pregnancy.

In the early summer of 1936 my father and I had erected a pigeon loft on the roof of our little summer-house. When we were finished, he said that in appreciation he was freeing me from the strawberry fields and instead entrusting me with a bigger, more instructive responsibility, of caring for the pigeons: feeding, watering, keeping the loft clean. Typically, he handed me a pale blue booklet with the title *Everything about the Pigeon for Beginners and the More Advanced*, and within a few days I was able to distinguish the different kinds: the vain pouters with their mechanical nodding; the tumblers, who during vertical flight abruptly let themselves drop and, as if at a word of command, came to a standstill; the puffed-up fantail pigeons; and the carrier pigeons, which I soon took to friends and, bearing tiny messages, sent back to Hentigstrasse, address "Kitchen Window." Then there were the evenings, when the greedy scrapping of the sparrows had come to an end and the talking in our room had stopped, while from outside, from the bottom of the garden only the sleepy sounds of the chickens could be heard, and farther away the clacking of the passing S-Bahn trains. Gradually, the day faded into darkness, only occasionally was there a shout or, when we were already drowsy, the bell of a cyclist.

The pleasant regularity of the days ended in autumn 1936. That was the point at which more and more neighbors and acquaintances began to go along with the rulers, not only formally but with increasing conviction. At any rate, that was the case in Karlshorst, where the big defection to the Nazis did not begin until then. At second dinner my father said this turn of events could probably be explained by the many benefits which the regime offered to people. Herr Patzek reported, delightedly, that for the first time he could hear Willi Domgraf-Fassbender and Elly Ney for an affordable price, and see *Faust* in the theater, and, of course, Ibsen's Nora, or an opera production conducted by Arthur Rother.[2] When it was said

---

2 Willi Domgraf-Fassbender was a famous and popular baritone, Elly Ney a pianist. Ney was a notably enthusiastic Nazi. Arthur Rother was likewise a keen Nazi; his career continued without a break after 1945.—Trans.

that Hitler's rise was the history of how he was underes-
timated, my father would add that one should rather talk
of Hitler's history of "popular appeasement." This had
then evolved into the dramatically staged history of his
acclamation.

Hitler was not only acclaimed in Germany, but (and
this was possibly much more disastrous) also abroad. How
all those bowing and scraping delegations of French war
veterans, of journalists and sports officials, who virtually laid Europe at the dictator's feet, had made my father
despair. Not to mention the trade unionists who had
commented so appreciatively on Hitler's social policies.
A further impetus had been provided by the Olympic
Games in 1936, staged as a festival of reconciliation. And
one had to add all the pseudo-romantic embellishments
of the modern world, which in its National Socialist guise
was no longer defined by jazz bands, box architecture,
and Cubism, but by folklore, braided hair, and the art of
the Old Masters. Anyone who wasn't impressed by all
of that had persuaded himself he was going along with it
"to prevent anything worse." In truth, none of those who
talked like that had prevented anything worse; instead
they enhanced the regime's prestige and provided it with
expertise, and so actually promoted the worst.

The gains that the regime was making were also evident in everyday life. The previously friendly sales assistant in the grocer's fell silent now as soon as my father
came through the door; acquaintances of many years disappeared into doorways or quickly crossed the road when
he approached. At second dinner they were henceforth

called "the other-side-of-the-street walkers." Herr Henschel, whose garden adjoined ours, now appeared on his balcony wearing the black uniform of the SS instead of the brown one of the SA. His fists on the solid fat of his hips, he would shout over in a commanding voice, scolding the "girl brats" for making such a row; when the elder of my two sisters organized a Chinese lantern procession on her birthday, he called the police to come and put an end to the "mischief." He was not only disturbed by the "fidgeting" with naked flames, but by the risk of fire. Others again informed the *Blockwart* (block warden) when we put itching powder under their children's shirts or perhaps had talked them into handing over their gobstopper candies so that we could fire them at sparrows or streetlights with our catapults.[3] Herr Fest—said nice Frau Köhler, who lived a couple of houses down, to my mother—was the father of "little criminals"; she didn't mean any offense by it. But she would report the recent theft to "higher authorities," even if it had only been a matter of a couple of fallen apples. Anyhow, said Frau Köhler, the party had immediately seen the sort of person it was dealing with, and had rightly shown my father the door.

Malicious talk of this kind was new and it showed that something alien had entered the quiet world of the suburb, in which there had been, at most, personal or family differences. It was frightening to see how, after a

---

3 This was the lowest rank of National Socialist party officials above the regular rank and file, the most zealous of whom enforced petty Nazi requirements, such as the hoisting of flags and attendance at rallies, often to the annoyance of their neighbors.

The parental home in Karlshorst, Berlin,
with the eight-year-old author in the foreground

brief pause, the stable social structure of Karlshorst fell apart. Suddenly, enmities appeared which were given an ideological justification, but in reality gave free rein to nothing but envy, malice, and sheer spite.

My father observed these changes with dismay. When I later asked him what had affected him most, he said it had been the "empty space" which had opened up, raising a "wall of silence and looking the other way" around him. That had hit him harder than expected. Because there had been nothing unexpected about the misdeeds of those who suddenly wore a uniform and had power; he had foreseen that and had been more surprised that many behaved more decently than he would have thought. But in the end base instincts had come to the surface, as with Frau Köhler, who had been nice for so long. He would gladly have dispensed with the satisfaction of having been proved right in his skepticism about human beings. Once, in the course of an outburst of anger, he let slip that he felt "like puking" all the time. But all too few people puked with him.

He found a degree of compensation in his circle of acquaintances and friends, which drew visibly closer. Its eleven members met every four weeks in out-of-the-way taverns or pubs; each of them had belonged to the Reichsbanner. Paul Mielitz, the former mayor of the borough of Friedrichshain in Berlin, was one of the group, as were Max Fechner, who in the late 1940s—after the forced unification of the Communist and Social Democratic parties in the Soviet Zone—became minister of justice of the new German Democratic Republic; some school inspectors and headmasters, most of them unemployed; and Franz Künstler, a former MP and chairman of the Berlin SPD, who had spent the first twenty months of Nazi rule in Oranienburg concentration camp (later known as Sachsenhausen) and was then at liberty for several years.[4] He never, however, spoke about his experiences. He was not allowed to, he told those who asked; he had signed an undertaking to remain silent, and their meetings already made him suspect. "We even cover up the concentration camps with our silence," complained my father. At the outbreak of war Künstler was conscripted to do forced labor; he was badly treated and died as a result. My father used to say that the funeral in autumn 1942, which almost two thousand people attended, had been the last mass demonstration against the Hitler dictatorship. Arthur Neidhardt, a senior officer of the Reichsbanner when it was dissolved, took part in the early meetings, occasionally also Heinrich Krone, later a Christian Democrat minister in West Germany, and a number of other friends of former days.

Every time, my father brought back stories of troubles from the meetings, of arrests or family tragedies, and some things he kept so secret that he didn't even relate

---

4 Max Fechner (1892–1973), SPD (Sozialdemokratische Partei Deutschlands) member, survived the Sachsenhausen concentration camp and joined the SED (Sozialistische Einheitspartei Deutschlands), but was demoted from his positions, imprisoned, and excluded from the party for supporting the striking workers in the uprising of 1953. He was rehabilitated in 1958.

Fest mentions Fechner and Franz Künstler (SPD) to show his father's connections to and openness for leftist ideas and persons, to counterbalance his father's otherwise mainly right-wing leanings.

them at second dinner. Consequently, Wolfgang and I soon started taking up our eavesdropping position after these gatherings. From time to time, so we heard, the circle was able to help some of the persecuted, providing documents or some money. Beyond that my father managed by circuitous ways to discover the latest figures for political prisoners. At the outbreak of war, they numbered, if I remember correctly, well over 200,000.[5] In the early months of the Hitler period the friends also exchanged information about the torture chambers of the SA, which were taken over by the SS in 1934. There was much discussion of how Himmler's men proceeded much more coldly and bureaucratically than the SA had done. The SS, we heard our father say several times, had invented "administrative death" in place of "bloody arbitrary killing," a phrase which made a considerable impression on us, although even Wolfgang couldn't say what it actually meant. Then again, my father talked about a renowned legal expert who called the constitutional state an invention of Jews and Communists.[6] The judgment on the contemptible role played by Papen was unanimous, because out of a craving for prestige he had gone down on his knees before the dictator dozens of times. He had repeatedly talked about taming Hitler. Riesebrodt now called him "the lion tamer who lies down on his stomach in front of the lion."

---

5 This is a much higher estimate than professional historians would currently give.—Trans.

6 Presumably a reference to the jurist and political theorist Carl Schmitt.—Trans.

Besides this it was mostly everyday matters that were discussed at second dinner. Perhaps, I later thought, my mother had after all managed to persuade my father to be more discreet. There was talk of an argument with Rudi Hardegen; of the measured, impressively dignified appearances of the new priest; and, unquestionably the most amusing point of discussion, of giving names to the newly hatched chickens. Wolfgang and I got endless pleasure from inventing mad, made-up names: a particularly vain young cockerel was called Chicken Coop Dandy; his shy brother Wallflower; a splashing young hen Dribbler; another (to my mother's dismay, because it constantly let itself be covered by every male in the coop) Old Faithful. Sometimes the two of us interposed dinner-table topics to avoid questions about the previous week's school essay or the apology to Frau Weyen because of the racket we had made recently. To conclude, my father delivered brief, witty sayings from a seemingly inexhaustible stock: *"tempi passati past,"* for example, or someone with modest intellectual gifts was "sure not to have invented the soup plate."

These were the times of the most cheerful harmony, which, however, could change abruptly. For a long time I was considered to be hard to control, and every couple of days my parents had to hear the complaints of friends or neighbors. My bad behavior was held against me for years. According to one story, when my father had problems with an antiquated camera, I, in a recalcitrant mood, had smashed the thing; according to another, as a six-year-old I had put a young rabbit high up in a bird box so

that it would see the world; and so on. My younger sister
Christa, who was three during my wild days, repeated
into old age how she had to cling to my father's trouser
leg to prevent him from punishing me. She could not,
however, save me from dozens of clips around the ear.
On the other hand, if any rebuke failed to come, I was
equally dissatisfied; only a thrashing or at least a scolding
set the world to rights again.

The most serious trouble ensued when I, as often
happened, insisted on having the last word even against
my parents. One time, at table, I muttered that Frau Vaupel, one of my parents' closest friends, was a "silly goat."
When my father angrily protested that he did not want
to hear anything like that from me even one more time,
I repeated without the slightest hesitation that Frau Vaupel was "a silly goat, a silly goat." When my father chided
me, pointing out that he had just forbidden this effron-
tery, I replied that he had said "one more time"; as I had
said it twice, I had merely obeyed his wishes. My father
changed the topic, shaking his head, but I saw that my
mother, who briefly left the room, suppressed a chuckle.

Sometimes my father also talked about political topics, or more precisely, ones that were almost historical,
for which the second dinner had really been set aside.
After an admonishing glance, he would tell us about
the difficult emergence of the republic or about its long
dying; of bitterly unjust judicial decisions; of the SA
torture chambers in Columbia Haus, a former military
prison, and many other places. Once, as I've never forgotten, I heard him describe Papen and Kaas as traitors

and the SPD leadership as a bunch of cowards. "When we set up our organization Black-Red-Gold,[7] our slogan was *Deutsche Republik, wir alle schwören: Letzten Tropfen Bluts soll dir gehören!* (German Republic, we all swear: our last drop of blood shall be yours!). But what did we do? We handed over our arms stores to the Nazis."

On another occasion he mentioned an argument with Dr. Goldschmidt, a lawyer he had known for years. In 1935, after the promulgation of the Nürnberg race laws, my father had begged him to leave the country as soon as possible. But Dr. Goldschmidt, who, as a German patriot, had always felt it his duty to drink only German red wine instead of the far superior French and to buy only German clothes, shoes, and groceries, had paid no heed. Germany, said Dr. Goldschmidt, was a state of law; it was in people's bones, so to speak. In the eighteenth century, under King Frederick William, his family had been received almost without prejudice, first near Teltow and then in Berlin, and his was now the sixth generation to live in Germany. Of course, there had been moments of hostility, but his ancestors had survived it all. One should not get into a panic.

There were constant discussions. But neither Dr. Goldschmidt nor other Jewish acquaintances like David Jallowitz and Dr. Meyer were convinced. Most of them I only saw on occasional visits. The dominant type had

---

7 The full title of the left-of-center paramilitary force supported by the SPD, the trade unions, and the Catholic Zentrum party, among others, was *Reichsbanner Schwarz-Rot-Gold* (Black-Red-Gold, after the colors of the republican flag).—Trans.

an ascetic face, was intellectual, and had that unexpected wit that my father loved so much. Remembering some of these Jewish friends, my father said to me after the war that in their self-discipline, their quiet civility and unsentimental brilliance, they had really been the last Prussians; in any case, he had more often encountered his idea of Prussianism among the long-established, often highly educated Berlin Jews than anywhere else.

They had, he once went on, only one failing, which became their undoing: being overwhelmingly governed by their heads, they had, in tolerant Prussia, lost their instinct for danger, which had preserved them through the ages. Like Dr. Goldschmidt, Jews came up with the most diverse reasons for remaining in Germany. Almost all of them protested that their families had always been "nationally minded"; they talked of family sacrifices or of decorations awarded during the First World War for service at Verdun and Chemin des Dames, at Ypres and on the Marne front.[8] They did not want—as many of them put it—to be infected by the general hysteria; and a businessman from the Spittelmarkt,[9] whom my father had known since Weimar days, assured him that one of his great-uncles had donated considerable sums to the Empress Auguste Viktoria for her "church quirk."[10] The

---

8 This invocation of the most notoriously deadly battles of World War One is often used to stress the bravery, patriotism, and sacrifices of German Jews in that war.

9 The Spittelmarkt was the center of Berlin's rag trade, in which Jews were very prominent.—Trans.

10 Empress Auguste Viktoria, wife of the last German emperor, was noted for her promotion of church buildings to overawe the godless Berliners.—Trans.

most paradoxical argument was the one my father heard from Harry Hirschberg, a legal secretary, who claimed that driving the Jewish inhabitants out of the country was precisely what the Nazis wanted, so the Jews should not be urged to flee. My father was involuntarily aiding and abetting criminals. And, Hirschberg added with an admonitory glance, anyone who knew anything at all about the law knew that, too, was punishable.

Hardly anyone, added my father, took his pleas seriously, and of those he knew a little better only the Rosenthals and the eldest son of Herr Lausen paid heed. He suspected, however, that Aby Lausen had emigrated to England less because of the warnings about the Nazis than because of an early love interest who had already gone there the year after the Nazis seized power. Another frequently put argument was—after the anti-Semitic campaigns of Stöcker, Fritsch, and others had come and gone—who was going to run away from mere hooligans? Wolfgang asked who was being talked about, and the conversation went from the *Handbook on the Jewish Question*[11] to the copious anti-Semitic pamphlet literature and the idea of the "national community."

My father persisted; he was without any social snobbery—his own background precluded that. The idea of the national community, which had had passionate

---

11 Adolf Stöcker (1835–1909) was a Protestant pastor and right-wing politician, central to whose program was anti-Semitism; for some years Stöcker was cathedral and court preacher in Berlin before being removed because of his extremism. Theodor Fritsch was an anti-Semitic journalist and pamphleteer, defender of the rights of small trade, active before and after the First World War; he compiled the *Handbook on the Jewish Question.*—Trans.

advocates on the left as on the right, had always seemed to him to be quite offensive. He would never want to have anything in common with the SS man Henschel, who lived opposite, or with the Communist leader Teddy Thälmann, never mind Franz von Papen.[12] On other occasions he talked about the war, love of the Fatherland, or what the words "the bosom of Abraham" meant. Wolfgang and I found such instruction no less exciting than football matches at the Oberschöneweide Sports Club, which we often went to and sometimes even continued talking about in bed—until one day it all became too much for my father. He suggested other conversations we might have: about the best book we had read; the difference between the Benedictine Order and the Jesuits; the origin of some popular Berlin sayings; the history of building on Schwanenwerder Island (in the River Havel in Berlin), and other more appropriate themes.

Twice every summer the family traveled "to the west" on a weekend, which usually meant to Potsdam, or Prussia's Arcadia, as my father always put it in a tone of voice which, regardless of his frown, I called his "devout Prussian irony." I had picked up the expression from Hans Hausdorf, a close friend of my parents. He loved everything about the idyllic royal town, from Frederick the Great's showy New Palace to the Dutch Quarter where we often stopped for lemonade. But his favorite

---

12 Ernst Thälmann (1886–1944), German Communist leader who ran for the presidency of the Weimar Republic against Hindenburg and Hitler. The Führer hated him intensely and had him sent to the Buchenwald concentration camp in 1933, where he was executed on August 28, 1944.

places were less obvious: Glienicke Palace, the Belvedere on the Pfingstberg—Pentecost Hill—or the Italian-style villas with their towers built by the architect Persius, which could be encountered everywhere in Potsdam.

And above all the Church of the Redeemer at Sacrow. As we approached the campanile on the winding paths along the river, inevitably the dark "rathole" would be mentioned, which one had to recognize as a reference to Theodor Fontane's *Travels*. My father thought the union of early Christian modesty and Prussian industriousness that was realized in the building was especially success-ful. Nowhere else, he said, expressed more vividly that the world of Prussia was not just a matter of riding crops, the cane, and regimentation. Instead it could also reveal itself as relaxed and even charming, once the somewhat rough "Prussianness" had received a suitable polish.

I have never forgotten the remark my father made later on, shortly before I left Berlin, that really the landscape of the Mark Brandenburg around Berlin displayed in every direction the same melancholy poverty. But around Pots-dam the art-loving Prussian rulers had placed, here and there, a church, a little temple, once even what looked like a mosque, and much more amidst marsh, sand, and pines. And wherever that had happened, what had been a mere "district" had been transformed as if by a magic hand into a "landscape." Arcadia, in short. To him it was (as he liked to explain in his schoolmaster's manner) a kind of proof that the always somewhat shabby Prussia, breathlessly stumbling through history, not only served the well-being of its subjects through conquest but also in humane ways. And on one of our last excursions "to the west," I heard him say of Sanssouci Palace, alluding to a quotation from Frederick the Great, that in the end Prussia's history, despite all the not unjustified objections, had indeed been a "rendezvous with glory."

He could never get enough of the light effects on the pink and bluish glazed bricks of Sacrow church. Occasionally, he would express his annoyance if we could not properly appreciate them, and found the frogs hopping into the water from the paths at our approach or the crayfish, which we sometimes brought up whole handfuls at a time, to be far more entertaining. From Sacrow one could look along the "passages of light," as my father put it, to the steam-engine house[13] and Babelsberg Castle, built by Schinkel, as they lay in the dusty sunbeam veils. They were touching attempts—already marked by an uncertainty of style—to conceal the cool ugliness of advancing modernity.

The other summer excursions I remember were to Neuruppin, the "Mark Brandenburg's town of genius," as my father ironically called it, because both the architect Schinkel and the writer Fontane were born in the "eternally wretched little place"; to Gransee Lake, associated with Queen Luise of Prussia; to Stechlin Lake, where we waited in vain for the geyser to erupt; to Rheinsberg with the Friendship Obelisk; and to Lehnin Abbey. Somewhere at the sandy edge of a wood, by ranks of slim pines drawn up as if on parade, the tablecloth was brought out

---

13 The "mosque" mentioned above.—Trans.

and the picnic basket opened. Usually, there were Kiel sprats from the market hall (a small wooden box cost one mark) or dried fruit (likewise packed in a wooden box and costing the same), which was praised as "good German Cameroon banana" from the former colony. These would be combined with thick slices of bread and afterward an apple. I found the mixture unspeakable and for years wondered how it tallied with my sensitive mother.

Once Dr. Knessel, who wanted to show off his new Horch to my parents, drove us out to Potsdam.[14] He had his pretty daughter Sophie, who was about two years older than me, with him. My mother's impression was that she was much too flirtatious: the girl was indignant that Wolfgang was allowed to sit on the separate passenger seat next to her father; we all knew that she had her eye on Wolfgang. On the long straight highway to Glienicke Bridge, while the adults were talking about the charm of the Marble Palace (Marmorpalais), she had, out of pure boredom, pulled faces. Then, just before we reached the Town Palace in Potsdam itself, she had, without warning, sat on my lap and pretended to kiss me; she merely laughed at the grown-ups' protests that she should stop immediately. On the drive back, when I summoned up my courage and, more or less in revenge, sat on her knee, she didn't fend me off, but instead embraced me and began to smooch in a way I took to be passionate. After some futile warnings Dr. Knessel stopped at the side of

---

14 A Horch is the ultimate prestige motor car of the period; Adolf Hitler was driven in one.

the road, tore open the door, and said sternly, "Sophie, I must ask you to behave!" But the girl was not so easily put down. "My misbehavior here," she retorted naively, "is the same as yours in your bedroom in the morning." Clearing his throat, Dr. Knessel took his place at the wheel again. "This isn't the end of the matter," he rebuked his daughter. My father, too, was clearly going to have a word with me.

The reproaches I was subject to at home were at first milder than I had expected. My father went over my recent "misdeeds" and accused me of coming to enjoy the role of the rowdy. Then earlier instances of bad behavior were brought up, such as my kidnapping of the Deeckes' tomcat in my school satchel; I had released it far beyond the racetrack to find out whether it knew its way home as well as our carrier pigeons. And ages before—with my friends Ecki and Hoppi Scholz—I had shouted at the windows a couple of cheeky verses we had made up. Were things going to go on like this? And now today, just to cap it all, I had sat on Sophie's lap . . . I interrupted him with all the fury of a bad conscience, because of the misdeeds which had been dealt with long ago: "Today, I had to do it! You can't let Sophie get away with what she does! I can't anyway! At some point you've got to show someone like Sophie that enough is enough!" When my speech of vindication was finished and when, after the subsequent exchange of words, my father was still looking bad-tempered, it was my mother, surprisingly enough, who sat down beside me on the settee. "You're right, my boy!" she said and then, turning to my father:

"Don't take everything so seriously. Children his age do sometimes squabble. Apart from which Sophie did start it. One doesn't just sit on a stranger's lap." In the family ever after that the incident was called "the lap-squabble story."

Our excursions to the west usually took place on Sunday, in order (as my mother put it) to avoid the snooping of Block Warden Fengler. She had the impression he particularly liked to call on her household, to see whether she had the monthly "Sunday hotpot" on the stove, an austerity measure already decreed shortly after the Nazi seizure of power. She hated him and his way of talking about how hard it was to track down all that suspicious behavior, especially as on each of these inspections he was also responsible for collecting two marks fifty for Winter Aid. Once when my mother summoned up her courage and observed during the "pot test" that his labors about which he complained so much were conducted with great zeal, he retorted that he performed every task with "unreserved commitment." She didn't say any more, but she had yet another reason to loathe "the little man with the big mouth," as she once called him with unusual sharpness. The fellow almost made her doubt God, so that at her next confession she had two sins to admit: hate and weakness of faith.

At the end of 1933, in order not to waste the unexpectedly empty time, my father began to brush up on his English and French, which he had learned while he was a student. He took classes at the Hartnack School on Nollendorfplatz, which (a great sensation at the time) made use of gramophone records for language teaching. Soon the languages he had learned years before were no longer enough for him; he took Italian and Russian courses. As a result he simultaneously expanded his circle of acquaintances to include several colorful, occasionally even bizarre characters. Of the French ones, I remember Roger Reveille, who was quick-witted and animated and seemed to have a command of almost every European language. Also among the new guests were three Russians, who had emigrated to Germany in the early 1920s, and Saverio Aprea, a counselor at the Italian embassy.

From now on the sounds of unfamiliar languages mingled in our apartment or in summer around the garden table. What I particularly remember about the Russians is the lost-sounding "humming song," which they struck up in their growling basses, usually at a late hour. From time to time they interrupted these solemn melodies with staccato sequences, but all this, to their sorrow, was performed only in low voices, in order not to annoy the neighbors, and in particular Herr Henschel, who repeatedly appeared on his balcony, a finger raised threateningly. Roger talked about Marcel Proust and then jumped to Clemenceau, the war, and his father, who in 1914 had been deployed close to the place where my father had been wounded.

We developed the closest attachment—affection almost—to Signor Aprea, who possessed the unique Italian combination of knowledge of human nature, charm, and the craftiness born of an experience of dictatorship. What made him irreplaceable, however, were the tickets to events which he acquired thanks to his diplomatic contacts and passed on to us. For Wolfgang and me he obtained entry to two days of the Olympic Games, so that we weren't just limited to "looking for Negroes" round about the Brandenburg Gate, but could watch Jesse Owens in his unforgettable long-jump duel with Luz Long. We were also able to go to several variety shows at the Admiralspalast, likewise to the six-day cycle races in the Sportpalast, where, as a token of the greatest expert knowledge, we learned to whistle Paul Lincke's hit song "Das ist die Berliner Luft, Luft, Luft" (That's the Berlin air, air, air), and finally, thanks to Saverio Aprea, we were able to attend free opera performances, as well as big shows like *Menschen, Tiere, Sensationen (People, Animals, Sensations)*.[15]

We had a factotum in the shape of old Katlewski, our "good household spirit." He was short in stature, had cropped gray hair and a fat, turned-up nose. His face was at once sorrowful and traversed by laughter lines. By profession he was a house painter, but now long retired. Once he showed me his apartment, which was several streets away, and I remember the bedroom with the vast marriage bed, above which hung a framed print, in which Jesus, his hand raised half in instruction, half in blessing, walked through a cornfield with his disciples, and on the wall opposite St. George, mounted on his horse, in the act of plunging his lance into a hissing dragon. Old Kat, as he was called, was

---

15 Paul Linke's "Berliner Luft" song is to Germans what Frank Sinatra's "New York, New York" is to Americans. And the big show *People, Animals, Sensations* was turned into a popular movie.

ready to help the family whenever any odd job needed to be done. "I think highly of yer dad for political reasons," he said, "because I'm an old Socialist"; but, he added, "I'm a gentleman, too, and so I admire yer mother as a lady." He repaired our bikes, and once even the seam of a friend's burst football, trimmed the lilac bushes, stood on the tall wooden ladder to pick fruit, and from obscure sources obtained bags of chicken feed. For a church festival he wove garlands of daisies for my sisters and altogether was always at hand when help was needed.

Katlewski also supplied us with the latest political jokes, regularly giving notice of them between tightly closed lips. As soon as he had made us sufficiently curious, he referred to the "huge trouble" he could get into for passing them on. But then, after about a quarter of an hour, Wolfgang and I had softened him up to the point where, there among the currant bushes or the pots of paints with which he happened to be busy, feigning annoyance, he gave way. "But not a word to a soul!" he began each of his jokes, thrusting a hoe or a brush dripping with paint in front of our noses. "Not to your brother and sisters, neither. Not even them." One of the few jokes I still remember was about the stupidity of the Nazis as demonstrated by the *Blockwart* who showed up for a review wearing one black and one brown shoe. "Man, Larsunke"—Katlewski caricatured the commanding official in his best version of the Berlin dialect— "I've told you again and again that you must pay attention to your shoes. One black, one brown—what are you thinking?" Larsunke saluted and replied: "Yes Sir, Herr Kreisleiter! I don't get it either. I have mulled it over and over but I don't get it. Even my wife doesn't know what to make of it because, you see, I have got another pair like that standing around at home."

I have forgotten most of Old Kat's jokes long ago, though I remember him quoting Shakespeare with reference to Göring, saying a man may smile and smile and yet be a villain. "I got that from the Workers' Educational Association," he said.

In summer 1937 it was time for me to go to secondary school, and since there was no classical Gymnasium in Karlshorst my parents decided to send me—as Wolfgang had been two years earlier—to the Canisius Kolleg, a Catholic school run by Jesuits, even though it was in Westend, on the other side of the city. Because of its excellent reputation it was inundated with applicants, and to limit the annual rush for places a difficult entrance exam had been introduced. Nevertheless, that same year the Education Ministry declared it had decided to close the school due to lack of demand. A few days after I discovered I had passed the test and been accepted for the school, another letter arrived to cancel the admission.

That was one disappointment. The other was that in that same year the school caps with colored ribbons were banned. Wolfgang's, as far as I remember, had white and shiny green ribbons. The braiding on the caps was graded according to year;[16] now they were abolished in

---

16 These German schoolboy's caps of various shapes, in the colors of the school, were normally the only item of uniform worn by Gymnasium students and identified them as such.—Trans.

the name of national unity. Some compensation was provided by the briefcase, which my grandfather gave me as
replacement for the ridiculous school satchel which I had
carried to elementary school.

So I found myself at the Leibniz Gymnasium, a huge
reddish-brick building on the Mariannenufer by the
River Spree, not far from the Silesian mainline station.
For generations the area had been a gateway for the mass
of immigrants from the east, like the Scheunenviertel
by Alexanderplatz not far away. The classroom smelled
of stale sweat, leather bags, and margarine sandwiches.
During breaks and after lessons we played football in the
schoolyard or practiced taking corner kicks, complicated
passes, and, individually, even the high art of the backheel.
We also enjoyed, three or four of us at a time, just keeping
the leather ball in the air with headers, and we often spent
whole afternoons on Hentigstrasse playing dodgeball
with Hansi Streblow, "Kutti," and Sternekieker. "Motte"
Böhm, a somewhat older girl, who always had an inherited
tram conductor's bag with a polished silver buckle around
her shoulder, invariably took the part of the referee.

It must have been around this time or a little later
that my father returned depressed from one of the
meetings with his friends. There were still nothing but
defeats, he said. Mielitz had reported—and Classe,
with his English contacts, had confirmed it—that Fleet
Street from *The Times* to Lord Rothermere's *Daily Mail*
showed undisguised sympathy for the Nazis. *The Saturday Review* front page had recently been taken up with
HEIL HITLER in large letters. All had agreed that next

to nothing could be expected from Britain. Acknowledge the benefits of dictatorship was the message coming from the island, only a halfway civilized form of tyranny held the prospect of moving things on.

He himself would never understand, continued my father, why everyone who opposed Hitler was inevitably, sooner or later, left out in the cold. There had been a long, sometimes heated discussion about that. Agreement was only reached when it was concluded that they had been hopelessly unprepared for the dictatorship. What had come out on top in Germany might occur in darkest Russia or the Balkans, but surely not in their law-abiding country. What had happened? That was the question raised on all sides, but no one had an answer. In this agitated atmosphere Krone had finally said that in critical situations leaving a question unresolved was the best means of sticking together. One just had to accept that there were no easy answers.

Long-established bonds were not always equal to the pressures of the situation. Kalli Vaupel, one of my father's close friends from his student days, had spent many years in the rural Uckermark not far from Berlin, and had failed to make the longed-for move to the capital. He was bald (to the degree that we called "polished"), had a wiry figure and an inexhaustible sense of humor, and even appreciated bad jokes. Later, he became less and less cheerful and began to drink. He couldn't see a way out of the dark hole he was in, he said, yet he had to get it behind him; he just didn't know how.

Perhaps, as some acquaintances suspected, the cause of Karl Vaupel's depression was really his conspicuously attractive, very sporty wife. At any rate she was the reason the two friends drifted apart, because she, in the jargon of the time, was an enthusiastic *Nazisse*. She was capable of maintaining in all seriousness that the Führer had been "sent by God" and that the Lord had great things in store for Germany. Again and again there were arguments because of her, so that at some point both sides preferred to meet only occasionally and let the decades-old friendship peter out.

Irmi Vaupel was active in a party organization and, after the outbreak of war, in a uniform-wearing one; it was even rumored that, driven by admiration and ambition, she had risen through the ranks of the guard unit of a women's concentration camp. After the war she was interned together with her husband. I have forgotten her further career. Kalli Vaupel got to know a very attractive American Jewish woman while he was being interrogated in a camp in Bavaria. She was employed in the U.S. camp administration and he fell in love with her. Since he was not accused of anything he was released after a few months, obtained a divorce, and married the American. Kalli was a weaker and more fickle personality than he had thought, said my father. The times were full of lives which took an absurd course, often dramatically and crazily so. Many were unable to resist the folly of the times. When, toward the end of the Hitler years, they regained their senses, it was too late.

One of my classmates, with whom I was friends and shared a number of interests, was Gerd Schülke, who lived in public housing close to the hospital. He had an alert, quiet character and lent me books that had made an impression on him. On a map of the world divided into squares we played Battleship; later we replayed historic sea battles from Salamis to Trafalgar and Jutland.[17] We threw dice for each movement of a fleet. He also invented the impending naval war in which the German Reich always put to sea against the British fleet. England was the enemy, he said, no other, because one needed to have a strong opponent if the victory was to be worth anything. Yet the course of battle was left to the throw of the dice. Reality, Gerd said, was not so very different.

Among the high points of the end of the year was the Christmas market around the royal palace. The memory of the majestic yet comfortable building designed by the architect Schlüter is for me always linked to the blissful fairground world of the days before Christmas, to colored lights, tinsel, and gingerbread. We admired the radiant Christmas tree, the merry-go-rounds and the Father Christmases bobbing up and down on them, and enjoyed the smell of baked apples and burnt almonds. And no visit was complete without explanations about the building of the palace or a look at the Schlüter courtyard. And, rising above it all, the somewhat squeaky

---

17 These are major historical maritime battles from the Greeks via the Napoleonic Wars to the First World War; to Germans it is the Battle of Skagerrak, not Jutland.

harmoniums playing Christmas carols. At the booths one could shoot metal arrows at stars, rubber candles, or Christmas balloons, and once by a stroke of luck I won five sticks of candy floss, which was so good for making my sisters' hair sticky. It was a world of magic, fairground, and pre-Christmas happiness, and every one of these excursions ended with a childhood tragedy: when our parents called out that it was time to go home. From the S-Bahn train we still saw the sky above the palace glowing red, before the image faded away in the twilight of the great city.

Sometimes one of our parents' friends also accompanied us. Once it was Felix Ernst with his sleeked-down hair who joined us, and whose little, mysterious smile never left him all evening. Not even on the ghost train, which Wolfgang and I had with a great effort persuaded him to go on, did it change. On another occasion we were joined by Hans Hausdorf, who, during the whole three hours in which we were pushed along between the booths and the candles, balanced a box of pastries for my mother on the tip of a finger. Sometimes the Goderskis also came with us, and once the Patzeks came, with (as we whispered to one another) the "whole flock of kids."[18] But there were always tears when we left.

In the early days of 1938 we received a call from Dr. Goldschmidt. By chance I picked up the phone. He asked

---

18 This is an allusion to a children's song in which all the birds return in spring: "Amsel, Drossel, Fink und Star, und die ganze Vogelschar" (Blackbird, thrushes, finch and starlings, and the whole flock of birds).

what the new school was like, what my favorite subjects were, and how I got on with the boys from the proletariat. Then he asked to speak to my father. There was something interesting he had to tell him. I stayed in the room and observed from the guest's chair as my father listened with an increasingly somber expression. Now and then he came out with a "So!" or a "Really!" and toward the end of the conversation made an unintelligible remark. When he had put down the receiver he remained silent at his desk for a while, and then said that in his incorrigible patriotism Dr. Goldschmidt had been trying to convince him that people were making a misjudgment in their eternal touchiness about the Nazis. Today he had gone to a government office on behalf of a client. The official he had had to deal with had been altogether accommodating, despite the "big" party badge in his buttonhole, and in clipped sentences had assented to everything Dr. Goldschmidt had requested, or at least hinted at one or another loophole. When Dr. Goldschmidt had thanked him, the official had replied with a smile, "But Herr Doctor! We're not monsters after all!"

"I ask you!" Dr. Goldschmidt had added. "There you have it: not monsters! Just a little bit barracks square in tone! Too loud for our civilian world!" Nevertheless, he preferred that to noncommittal talking around a thing; he had always said that distrust makes one blind. At this remark, said my father, he had been dumbfounded, so that he had merely been able to interject: "And trust even more so." After this remark Dr. Goldschmidt had said goodbye with a laugh and ironically urged my father to

turn over a new leaf. "One more thing that's incomprehensible," said my father, when he came to talk about the
incident at second dinner: someone who didn't notice
that he was down on the ground, "Even when you shout
it in his ears."

As usual, when my father was beside himself, my
mother's lips began to tremble and it was easy to imagine that she was about to exclaim, "Please, Hans. Not in
front of the children!" Instead, she only looked anxiously
from one to the other and remained silent. Hardly had we
swallowed our last mouthful when she began to clear the
table to prevent any further conversation.

•

FOUR

Don't Ever Become Sentimental!

It was an utterly politicized world in which we were growing up. Many conversations and almost all personal decisions were made with an eye to the prevailing situation. Certainly, I know contemporaries who also grew up in Berlin at this time who perceived things differently. Apart from the National Prayer, which in some schools was recited in chorus on National Socialist celebration days, the Hitler Youth uniform, and the youth movement songs like the one about the wild geese sweeping through the night with shrill cries, they were not affected by politics.[1]

---

1 The Hitler Youth had taken over both the organizations and the songs of the independent German youth movements of the years after the First World War. After the second war the German Boy Scouts would continue the tradition.

Nevertheless, the traditional rules of upbringing still applied, in our home perhaps even a little more than elsewhere. But they were never talked about, except in the form of the fixed formulas that we heard again and again, but whose cryptic meaning we did not understand until later: Don't pout!, Don't make such a fuss!, Children shouldn't talk without being spoken to! And at table one was not to mention money, scandals, or the food being served. The principles expressed in such rules were never expanded on. No words were lost on them. They were taken as self-explanatory and were considered as basic to proper behavior. Once, when my mother complained about my impudence, my father said, "Just let him be! Let him be cheeky! Here at least. We just have to teach him where the limits are. If he doesn't grasp it here, then outside he'll be shown the limit soon enough."

With all of that, our almost implicit upbringing was the very antithesis of the regime with its anticivic impulse, and today, after the passing of the years, I see it as a kind of story of civil development in uncivil times. Those in power knew nothing of civilized social intercourse, my father assured us, and consequently they were not ruling over a thousand-year Reich, but one that went back at least five thousand years, "deep into the primeval forest." In a paper on education he noted: "All theories of education derive from a chorus of many voices. It stretches from the Ten Commandments to the moral treatises of philosophy and the great works of literature, and to much else to which whole libraries bear witness. And all of it is directed at a really quite modest goal: to teach human beings a few self-evident truths."

Translated into everyday terms these self-evident truths amounted to setting store by "decency" and "good manners" and to showing "consideration." Apart from which one should not regard formality, as Hans Hausdorf, my parents' friend, with his love of paradox, once said, "as mere formality." And my mother liked to conclude her educational epistles with a sentence we had heard countless times since early childhood, whether one of us had cut his knee and my mother was attending to it with her bottle of iodine, or one of us complained about unfair marks or about a referee whom we thought had constantly blown his whistle to penalize our football club SC Karlshorst: "Just don't get sentimental!"—which for her meant don't moan, don't feel sorry for yourself, don't weep tears for what can't be helped. Once, when Christa, the wilder of my two sisters, had fallen and sought help from my mother with a bleeding knee, I heard my mother say, while soothingly stroking her, "Don't cry, my dear! Don't cry! Weeping is for the maid's room!" A certain amount of social pride was always involved in the ban on self-pity. But far more important than that was the feeling of being subject to a stricter code of conduct.

Much more often, however, there was the world of untroubled days, on which no homework had to be done, none of our duties—increasing in number as one grew older—had to be carried out, and there were no bottles of iodine to be seen far and wide. The summer holidays were the high point. When July came we regularly traveled to the Walken, my grandparents' isolated farm, a couple of miles from the village of Liebenau in the Neumark of Brandenburg. My uncle Berthold had taken it over when he married one of my father's elder sisters. He was a capable, hardworking man. Everyone feared his strictness; and his mustache, stiffly drawn out when he went to church, further increased the impression of a rough countryman's temperament. The farm was situated in a landscape of frugal dignity, and the gentle hills across which plow and harrow had to be drawn made cultivation that much more difficult. But my uncle had two sons and two daughters, who were as hardworking as he was and blessed with as practical an intelligence. They were between five and ten years older than us. As far as we were concerned they coped quite effortlessly with a difficult role somewhere between that of minder and playmate. We children were particularly taken by the cheerful Irene. She taught us to swim, accompanied us as we lay in wait for and tried to hunt wild rabbits (usually in vain), and instructed us how to catch field mice, which bit us if they could, on the freshly harvested fields. Authority can often make children flinch, but she exercised it without the least trace of intimidation. We all loved her.

The farmstead formed a square, with a domestic wing, two stable-and-stall wings, and a barn with a threshing floor. It had two gates, one opening onto the sandy road to Liebenau, the other onto a slightly sloping track, which led past a pine wood to nearby Lake Packlitz. The farm buildings with the large inner yard lay at the center of more than two hundred acres of scattered fields, which demanded at least ten months a year of exhausting work. When we were announced at holiday time, Uncle Berthold hitched up the horses and waited for us at Schwiebus Station twelve miles away. In his good suit, wearing a homburg hat and with an "anointed mustache," as we called it, he sat on the "throne" of the shiny Sunday carriage. With awkward courtesy he invited one of us children to sit up on the driver's seat beside him. If it was too hot my mother opened her little parasol, and we children poked fun at her and said she looked like a princess, who on some whim had ordered her liveried servants to climb down and make their way back to the castle on foot. She smiled then and hugged whichever of her children had the funniest idea as the story was spun out further and further. And sometimes, if the child was sitting farther away on the coach seat, she stroked his or her head.

The drive from Schwiebus seemed endless and often took two hours or more. When it was along deep, bumpy, sandy tracks, the flanks of the horses were stained by sweaty foam in the afternoon heat, and the buzzing horse-flies circled excitedly around them. Once at the farm-yard we used a couple of rags to kill the insects, which, exhausted by their bloodsucking, had mainly settled on the horses' necks and haunches. Meanwhile, Uncle Ber-thold changed into his working clothes and with a long peel, which our aunt handed him, drew eight to ten trays of still-steaming cakes out of the oven: crumble-topped *Bienenstich* and apple cake, whose scent spread to the farthest corners of the house.

As a tireless workingman, my uncle had only one blind spot: he could not imagine that beyond work and perhaps prayer there was any other meaningful activity in life. So it was usually already on the evening of our arrival that he allocated our tasks for the next day. "We rise at five!" he said. "That's normal here, even for city layabouts!" Over the years a running battle developed between him and us boys, when, always at nightfall, he issued his instructions for gleaning, haymaking, or stacking sheaves. Only my sisters, gentle Hannih and boisterous Christa, were spared. In the beginning we asked or pleaded for a couple of hours of swimming in the lake or for time to read. But my uncle simply growled something about "nonsense" and that was the end of it.

We, however, thought as obedient sons: No complaining! Just don't get sentimental! Every evening, after we had gone across to one of the tiny bedrooms from the kitchen with our candles, Wolfgang, with Winfried and me, elaborated cunning strategies that would enable us to slip away while passing through a wood and gather mushrooms or on a hilly field chase partridges. But soon the cleverest tricks we thought up came to nothing, because my uncle kept an all too suspicious eye on us. Sometimes we also hid fishing rods in a hazel bush and the next morning made our way to the nearby lock, where the fish liked to linger in the bubbling water. But neither the pail with barbels, tench, eels, and puny whitefish we brought back or the middling pike we now and then transported in a second pail were enough to pacify my uncle. We had not obeyed his instructions, he barked.

And our beloved uncle could do no more than shake his head when I once asked him whether in winter he did nothing more than carry out the necessary repairs. Good-naturedly he responded, "Why? Of course, there's nothing else!" At that I retorted that then he should understand that we had our winter in the summer; that's how it was in the city! The long holidays were our repair time, as it were. So he shouldn't be always forcing us to work. There was a long pause. Then my uncle tugged at the tips of his mustache and grumbled, his arms outstretched on the table, "That's going too far for me!"

My parents usually stayed only a few days, and later I asked myself whether it was only after their departure that we began to "run behind the barn." During his stay on the parental farm my father worked too, and showed that he still knew how to handle a scythe and a pitchfork, whereas my mother appeared rather lost in a world that was foreign to her. Our greatest love as children was the smithy, in which the horseshoes were made. As soon as the fire was kindled we were allowed to blow air into the embers until the charcoal in the middle of the forge began to glow deep red. Then the iron was placed in the fire until it too glowed, and then, blow by blow on the anvil, it was shaped to fit the horse's foot. Hammer raised, my uncle stood in front of the hearth and was surrounded by the smell of burnt hoof when he nailed the shoe to the patient animal. And once, in the course of the holiday, usually toward the end, a pig was slaughtered, a process we followed with a mixture of horror and fascination.

The three brothers in 1933 at the Berlin Zoo:
(left to right) Joachim, Winfried, and Wolfgang

Despite the constant running battle with my uncle, the Walken was the carefree, much loved playground of our early years. Packlitzsee, by which the farmstead was picturesquely situated as if placed there by the hand of an artist, was a modest stretch of water a couple of hundred yards long and broad. Since its surface lay a little below the woods around it, I remember it as a dark, smooth lake, rippling and glittering only at the edges. I shall never forget the gentle, bluish light above its surface, the scent of the pine woods behind us, and the fine white sand at the bathing place, which always got stuck between our toes. In addition, the sounds of the summer afternoon heat: the gurgling of the waves, the woodpecker hammering away somewhere, the splashing of the leaping fish and a little further on the cries of the diving birds, which at every call dipped head first into the water. It was as if time stood still. Only the myriad mosquitoes that feasted upon us disturbed the feeling of never-ending holidays.

The greenery of the beeches, birches, and weeping willows which lined the shore of the lake, and whose branches at points trailed in the water, was only broken on the opposite shore. This was particularly evident in the early evening sun. Then the glowing yellow facade of a baroque monastery with two towers stood out. It had been founded in the thirteenth century by Cistercians and later rebuilt in the Silesian Baroque style. With its bright magic it spread an atmosphere of silence and solemnity, which ever since I have associated with this style. The small village behind the monastery, hidden by the trees, bore the name which for each one of us has since that time represented the ideal interplay of natural and architectural beauty: it really was called Paradies— Paradise. It was, indeed, ours.

The other Eden, which began to open up for me at the age of eight or nine—as if at a secret "Open sesame!"— was the world of books. Like more or less everyone else, Heinrich Hoffmann's *Struwwelpeter* had been read to us before we started school, and we could recite by heart some of the morally intimidating verses. Later, to our insatiable pleasure, came Wilhelm Busch; I remember that his verse stories and pictures—*Pious Helene, Fipps the Monkey*, and above all *Max and Moritz*—were the first texts that I read before starting school, initially with the help of my finger. We knew nothing, of course, of Wilhelm Busch's Schopenhauerian pessimism, which sooner or later become obvious to every knowledgeable reader, yet some of his verses still make me happy today, and certain lines took on almost proverbial stature in our family. At every stage of my life, as soon as I set eyes on one of these parables, written and drawn with such a masterly, malicious wit and knowledge of human nature, I have involuntarily read on.[2]

That was, apart from my father's goodnight stories, the other literary pleasure of my early years. No Dr. Doolittle, no Germanic sagas, no *Uncle Tom's Cabin* could match the verses of Wilhelm Busch. Reading became more demanding, also more time-consuming, when, after dinner one evening, Wolfgang told me I now had to read "Kamai." He was, meanwhile, on the third volume, and Hansi Streblow claimed he had already read five. When I asked how many books there were by this "Kamai," and heard something about sixty or seventy titles, I was close to having nothing to do with him. But then I read *The Treasure of Silver Lake* and instantly became so addicted that within a year I went on to read *Winnetou* and about twenty other books, only once interrupted by one of Fenimore Cooper's Leatherstocking

<hr>

2 Heinrich Hoffmann (1809–94) was a medical doctor and author of satirical and children's books, including the universally popular and familiar *Struwwelpeter*, translated into most European languages.

  Wilhelm Busch (1832–1908) was a painter and writer whose satirical and humorous exposure of self-importance and pettiness, among other things, made his illustrated stories told in simple doggerel household items throughout the German-speaking world, especially *Max und Moritz* (1865).

volumes, which, however, despite the numerous explanatory drawings, I found boring, even silly.

The works of one other author interrupted my reading of the adventure stories of Karl May (as I now realized he was called).[3] Mark Twain's *Tom Sawyer* and *Huckleberry Finn* now became the other great literary experience of those years. For some time I considered the author of *Tom Sawyer* to be at least the equal of Goethe, who was admired everywhere as the world's greatest poet, whereas I maintained that the correct order was in fact: Wilhelm Busch in first place, far ahead of all the others, then Mark Twain, closely followed by Goethe.

Later—I must have been about thirteen or fourteen—I read *Moby-Dick*, the story of the white whale, which Wolfgang had recommended to me. I had to get away from my father's collection of bourgeois literary treasures, he said, and although I angrily disagreed, I soon began to read the heavy volume. There was much that I hardly understood, yet the tension of this mysterious book did not let me go. The drama of Ishmael and the grim, one-legged Captain Ahab with the dark scar on his face, as if struck there by lightning, and the harpoon baptized with the name of the Devil, restlessly traversing the oceans of the world, is something I have never forgotten. I realized for the first time that my father's taste was not everything, and that in addition to the legends

---

3 Almost unknown in the English-speaking world, the adventure stories of Karl May (1842–1912) have had an unbreakable hold on the imagination of adolescents in Central Europe since the late nineteenth century.—Trans.

and calendar tales whose endings were always certain, there was a strange and sinister world. Melville opened the gates wide.

At that time it offended me that, like my brother, given the circumstances, I got only ten pfennigs a week pocket money, and the only way of earning more was to learn poems by heart, because my father had offered a one-mark reward for every ten poems recited without a mistake. So I learned Goethe's "The Erl-King," Schiller's "The Pledge" and "The Cranes of Ibycus," and numerous other ballads; above all to please my mother, I gradually moved on to nature poetry and reflective verse, and finally to Rainer Maria Rilke and Stefan George.[4] When, returning to the classics again, I could recite "The waters rushed, the waters rose . . ." by Goethe,[5] my father recommended Gottfried Keller's ballad "Seemärchen" (A lake tale), which even today I think of as a continuation. It is at once brilliant and slides into the demonic, while Goethe's contemplative verses only have a suggestion of threat at the end. The penny-dreadful literature by John Kling or Tom Shark and the rest, which was so popular with friends and schoolmates, passed me by, oddly enough. One day I started a book with the title *The War of the Miami*. I got

---

4 Johann Wolfgang von Goethe (1749–1832) and Friedrich Schiller (1759–1805) represent the absolute pinnacle of German and European culture in the nineteenth century to educated Germans; together they constitute the German *Klassik* or classical period. They serve here as a counterpoint to the "other" reading of young Joachim, such as Gottfried Keller (1819–90), a Swiss prose writer who actually did work in the spirit of Goethe's large prose works, and to the popular literature cited immediately afterward.

5 From the poem "The Fisherman"; there's a famous setting by Schubert.—Trans.

bored, however, and then began a novel set in the empire of the Incas, *The Divine Sacrifice*, which was no better, so I went back to Karl May. But it was different with Hans Dominik, whose novels opened up vistas of a highly technological future, filled with shiny machinery.

At the beginning of 1938 I saw our neighbor Herr Hofmeister draw my father into the hallway and reproach him in a subdued voice for being too contrarian. He told him he should open his eyes at last! At the evening meal, when I asked my father why he put up with something like that, he conceded that basically Hofmeister was right. Things really were better than they had been. The seven or eight million unemployed had disappeared, as if by a conjuring trick. But the ten million or more Hofmeisters didn't want to see the means by which Hitler achieved his successes. They thought he had God on his side; anyone who had retained a bit of sense, however, saw that he was in league with the Devil.

Wolfgang asked if that was more than conjecture and whether there really were pacts with the Devil—and what was the theological explanation for it? We frequently came back to this topic, which had a strange fascination for us. Of course, my father soon brought the conversation around to the historical Dr. Faustus and attempts by the medieval alchemists to produce gold, jewels, or the philosopher's stone in their laboratories, then he regularly concluded with Goethe's great play, *Faust*.

These discussions came to an abrupt end in March of that year, when German troops crossed the border into Austria under billowing flags and crowds lined the streets,

cheering and throwing flowers. Sitting by the wireless we
heard the shouted *Heil!*s, the songs and the rattle of the
tanks, while the commentator talked about the craning
necks of the jubilant women, some of whom even fainted.

It was yet another blow for the opponents of the
regime, although my father, like Catholics in general,
and the overwhelming majority of Germans and Austri-
ans, thought in terms of a greater Germany, that is, of
Germany and Austria as one nation. For a long time he
sat with the family in front of the big Saba radio, lost in
thought, while in the background a Beethoven symphony
played. "Why does Hitler succeed in almost everything?" he pondered. Yet a feeling of satisfaction pre-
dominated, although once again he was indignant at the
former victorious powers. When the Weimar Republic
was obviously fighting for its survival, they had forbidden a mere customs union with Austria and threatened
war. But when faced with Hitler, the French forgot their
"revenge obsession," and the British bowed so low before
him that one could only hope it was another example of
their "familiar deviousness." The Weimar Republic, at
any rate, would probably have survived if it had been
granted a success like that of the Anschluss.[6]

Nevertheless, my father continued, the union brought
with it a hope that Germany would now become "more
Catholic." It was only a few days before he realized his

---

6 The Anschluss or union of Austria and Germany had been forbidden by the Allies in the peace treaty of Versailles, at the urging of France in particular; it proved
to be a major success as a propaganda slogan of the Nazi agitation against that treaty
and aided their rise at the polls.

error. Already at the meeting with his friends, which had been brought forward, he learned of the persecution of the Jews in Austria, heard dumbfounded that the admired Egon Friedell, whose *Cultural History of the Modern Age* was one of his favorite books, had jumped out of the window as he was about to be arrested, and that in what was now called the Ostmark there was an unprecedented rush to join the SS. "Why do these easy victories of Hitler's never stop?" he asked one evening after a pensive listing of events. And why, he asked on another occasion, was this mixture of arrogance and hankering for advantage breaking out in Germany, of all places? Why did the Nazi swindle not simply collapse in the face of the laughter of the educated? Or of the ordinary people, who usually have more "character"?

So there were ever more occasions for that conspiratorial feeling that bound us together; at least that's how my father interpreted the course of events. During the summer several members of my father's "secret society," as Wolfgang and I ironically called it, visited us: Riesebrodt, Classe, and Fechner. Hans Hausdorf also came regularly again, and brought us children "presents to suck" and, as always, a pastry for my mother. His center-parted hair was combed down flat and gleamed with pomade. We loved his puns and bad jokes. And, indeed, Hausdorf seemed to take nothing seriously. But once, later on, when we took him to task, his mood turned unexpectedly thoughtful. He said that human coexistence really only began with jokes; and the fact that the Nazis were unable to bear irony had made clear to him from the start that the world of

bourgeois civility was in trouble. He went on to say that
he, at least, had the impression the bonds were loosening.
Once, as Hausdorf was leaving, I heard my father complain that for the foreseeable future nothing was changed
for him by the regime's relaxation of pressure. He had
always kept a hospitable house, but that was no longer possible: at present his means allowed him at most to invite
friends to a modest supper once a month. In truth, not
even that. For that reason he had started to invite people
for afternoon tea; he could still afford that.

David Jallowitz (known as "Sally"), who dealt in
suitcases and used to call occasionally, now came more
frequently than before, and examined the pots in the
kitchen in front of my indignant mother. Once when she
grumbled about the heat, thirty degrees C. in the shade,
he gave her the "good advice" simply not to stand in the
shade, and Jallowitz laughed when she said the joke was
stupid and inappropriate.

Other visitors were Walther Rosenthal and his wife,
who, according to Wolfgang, was as "sensitive as a teen-
age girl," but always listened with a serious, melancholy
expression, and had intractable frizzy hair, which stood
up at the side.

Sonja Rosenthal hardly ever said a word, and so it
was especially surprising when she once contradicted her
husband, of all people, and his assertion that the world
had never before been so brutish and violent. He was
mistaken, she interrupted gently, absolutely mistaken.
Because there had never been a different world, different
people, and more peaceful conditions than today. Life

had always been quite unreasonable, extremely cruel—
and she had hardly finished before she fell back into her
alert silence, quietly examining the guests around her.

Among other friends who came regularly was August
Goderski, whom (despite his modest reserve) we called
"the man with the lip," because of a bulging growth at
his mouth. At the beginning he was usually accompanied by his grown-up son Walter. It was also Walter who
on December 6 appeared as St. Nicholas in our home.[7]
Year after year he repeated the Christ child's intermi-
nable personal admonitions to me, and declared that
after the boorish behavior of the past year a whole troop
of angels would be keeping a watchful eye on me. Naturally, I promised to say the required prayers of repentance
and to be exemplary henceforth, and accompanied St.
Nicholas to the door with folded hands and many pious
bows. But then I aroused general annoyance when, as
he was still on the half-landing, I called after him: "And
a Happy Christmas to you, Herr Goderski! And come
again soon! We're always pleased to see you!" I was eight
years old at the time. Hardly was the door shut when my
parents accused me of spoiling the St. Nicholas fun for
my sisters Hannih and Christa with my cheeky remarks.

In fact, Walter Goderski's visits were always a particular pleasure, because he was funny and a great joker. Even

---

7 December 6 is St. Nicholas's Day, celebrated in Germany with the appearance of
a figure, most often dressed as a bishop, accompanied by some coarse fellow with
a sack and cudgel; they would reward the good, usually with nuts, dried fruit, and
sweets, and punish the bad with taps with the cudgel and the threat of being put in
the sack and taken away.

today I still remember some of his "crazy" stories, as we called them; for instance, the one where a half-educated fellow rebukes his friend: "So you think yer 'telligent, Maxie? Let me tell you what you really are: Yer totally in-telligent!" Finally, also in my gallery of favorite guests was Dr. Meyer, who, whenever there was a pause in the conversation, talked about the books he was reading for the second, third, or fourth time. Among his preferred authors were Grimmelshausen, Lessing, Fontane, as well as, of course, Goethe, Heine, and—as he assured me with a smile, in answer to a question—"all the others, too."[8]

But then this apparently relaxed, increasingly close circle was struck by a virtual bolt from the blue. On November 9, 1938, the rulers of Germany organized what came to be known as Kristallnacht, and showed the world, as my father put it, after all the masquerades, their true face.[9] The next morning he went to the city center and afterward told us about the devastation: burnt-out synagogues and smashed shop windows, the broken glass everywhere on the pavements, the paper blown in the wind, and the scraps of cloth and other rubbish in

---

8 Johann Jakob Christoph von Grimmelshausen (1621–76) was Germany's greatest Baroque prose writer, best known for his exuberant novel *Simplicius Simplicissimus*. Gotthold Ephraim Lessing (1729–1781) was one of Germany's foremost theoreticians and practitioners of drama, a great Enlightenment humanist, best known for his parable of tolerance *Nathan the Wise*, which advocates the peaceful coexistence of Muslims, Christians, and Jews.

9 Kristallnacht, so called because of all the broken glass, was the first massive and overt Nazi attempt at hurting the Jews of Germany physically and publicly, following the previous legalistic and administrative systematic reduction of their civil and property rights. As an attempt at arousing the German public to a general pogrom it failed; its intimidating effects, however, were significant.

*In April 1938 Wolfgang photographed the family
with Aunt Dolly and Grandfather Straeter. In the foreground
(left to right): Hannih, Winfried, Joachim, and Christa*

the streets. After that he called a number of friends and advised them to get out as soon as possible. "Better today than tomorrow!" I heard him shout into the receiver once. But only the Rosenthals saw sense.

It was at this time that, without notice, the only Jewish pupil in our class stopped coming. He was quiet, almost introverted, and usually stood a little aside from the rest, but I sometimes asked myself whether he always appeared so unfriendly because he feared being rejected by his schoolmates. We were still puzzling over his departure, which had occurred without a word of farewell, when one day, as if by chance, he ran into me near the Silesian Station, and took the opportunity to take his leave personally, as he said. He had already done so with a few other classmates, who had behaved "decently"; the rest he either hadn't known or they were Hitler Youth leaders, most of whom had also been friendly to him, often "very friendly indeed," but he didn't see why he should say goodbye to them. As a Jew he would soon not be allowed to go to school anyway. Now his family had the chance to emigrate to England. They didn't want to miss the chance. "Pity!" he said, as we parted, and he was already three or four steps away. "This time it is forever, unfortunately."

Not long after the beginning of the new year, in March 1939, my father called Dr. Meyer to ask why he had not come to tea for such a long time. Dr. Meyer replied that since the death of his wife he hardly went out at all, and also November 9 had seen his worst premonitions come true. He would never have believed how much malice dwelt behind the doors of the apartments

around him. He had had to give up his practice. Now
and then he still attended the events put on by the Jewish
Kulturbund, but he even found shopping difficult, likewise going to the bank, to the postbox, or the post office.
Toward the end of the conversation they agreed on afternoon tea for the following week.

Dr. Meyer came to Karlshorst on an early spring day.
Since it was warm he suggested taking tea in the garden;
if one wore a coat it was comfortable outside. When he
arrived I was in the garden shed cleaning some tools; at
a signal from my father I brought the heavy stoneware
crockery from the sideboard over to the table, while my
mother made tea upstairs in the flat.

Dr. Meyer, who was in his mid- to late fifties, said that
his wife had died from "a lack of will to go on living." He
continued to reside in the old-fashioned, somewhat run-
down building, by now shabby with age, at Hallesches
Tor. My mother, who had accompanied my father there
to offer her condolences, told awful things about the state
of the apartment: dirty plates lying around; cups half
full of greasy tea; clothing thrown everywhere. The sole
room in which there had been any effort to impose order
was the library, only disturbed by two or three stacks
of framed pictures by German Expressionists.[10] When
she arrived, reported my mother, she had immediately

---

10 Many modern German artists, especially painters, were patronized by Germany's Jewish upper-middle class, which was an additional reason for Hitler and
National Socialist cultural officials to deride their work as non-Aryan and ban it
from museums and public sales. Nazi taste ran more toward the gigantic and heroic
representational in both painting and sculpture.

begun to rinse the dishes lying around and tidy up the
most obvious mess. But Dr. Meyer had said that she
shouldn't bother. He spent nearly the whole day in his
library, because the window looked out onto the courtyard, where he did not have to see or hear any people.

My father said of Dr. Meyer that he always walked
bent forward, as if the medical sounding of a patient's chest
determined his habitual posture. Also, if one looked more
carefully, one could discern a slight trembling. He spoke
with a somewhat hoarse voice and constantly cleared his
throat while reciting his favorite poems, perhaps out of
respect or because of a throat problem. My father assured
me that he had never had an inconsequential conversation with Dr. Meyer, and so that afternoon, once I had
finished work on the tools, my father called me over to the
garden table. "Listen," he said, "to what Dr. Meyer has to
say." The latter was just on the German *poetae minores*,
Geibel, Rückert, Gellert, and Bürger, as well as the "won-
derful Droste-Hülshoff." With the exception of Bürger,
none of these names as yet meant anything to me.[11] But
Dr. Meyer had changed the subject and later—to the

11 Emanuel Geibel (1815–84) is best known as the poet of German unity under
Prussia and for popular nature poems and songs. Friedrich Rückert (1788–1866) is
the author of many narrative poems on patriotic themes, but also of the *Kindertoten-
lieder* (Songs of dead children), set to music by Gustav Mahler, and his translations
introduced Persian and Arabic poetry to German readers. Christian Fürchtegott
Gellert (1715–69) was a transitional figure combining Enlightenment and early Romanticism in his fables, novellas, and plays. Gottfried August Bürger (1747–94) is
famous for some of the best-known ballads in the German language, especially his
"Lenore" and his version of the travels of the notorious Baron von Münchhausen,
teller of tall tales. Annette von Droste-Hülshoff (1797–1848) wrote primarily poems
but is best known for her novella *Die Judenbuche* (The Jew's beech); she was also a
close friend of the writer Levin Schücking.

accompaniment of more involuntary throat-clearing—made some disparaging remarks about immigrant Jews, who some years before had come to his area of the city; he didn't belong to them, he said. He had always felt himself to be German. He didn't even feel that culturally he was a Jew. His parents had already taken a few steps out of that world, only the Nazis had forced him back into "alien Jewishness." Then he returned to his poets of the second rank: Matthisson, Hölty, Stolberg.[12] Curious, I thought, the two men there in the spring light, wrapped in their thick coats, look as if they're sitting in a waiting room.

In the evening my father related that he had reproached Dr. Meyer for his snobbish attitude toward the Eastern European Jews around Silesian Station. Without hesitation, the latter had admitted that like all Jews he was arrogant. But that one was allowed to make fun of one's own relations. My father, however, should never dare say anything like it—at least not if he valued their friendship. Then I learned that my father had arranged that I should visit Dr. Meyer every Saturday after school. I had heard, hadn't I, how tiresome shopping and every postal errand was for him? Dr. Meyer had assured him that he had taken a liking to me and, since he was a highly educated man, the calls would surely do me no harm. Besides, it was the least one could do for people like him. After brief reflection my father continued: he

---

12 Friedrich von Matthisson (1761–1831); Ludwig Heinrich Christoph Hölty (1748–76), author of ballads and emotionally evocative poems; the Stolberg brothers, Counts Christian (1748–1821) and Friedrich Leopold (1750–1819), are best known as Goethe's travel companions; both dabbled in poetry and drama.

would ask the Rosenthals if it suited them for Wolfgang
to call on Saturdays. In fact, it was a few months before
the visits began, because Dr. Meyer unexpectedly raised
objections, and my father said he was evidently shy-
ing away from allowing an outsider to see how he lived.
However, in late summer 1939 I visited Dr. Meyer for the
first time and from then on almost every Saturday, while,
as far as I remember, Wolfgang walked the ten minutes
from his school in Neue Kantstrasse to the Rosenthals
about once every four weeks.

For me it was an instructive period, full of ever new
discoveries. I usually got to the old Berlin "musty house"
at about two in the afternoon. First, I went to the shops
in the neighborhood with Dr. Meyer's list. Unlike him,
he told me in the hallway, I didn't have to have a briefcase
in the hand that wasn't carrying the shopping bag. He
always held something in each hand in order to avoid the
Hitler salute, with which he, in particular, was repeatedly greeted, even if only with a forearm brought up
toward the shoulder. "I don't even salute with one hand
free," I responded, showing off somewhat, and added,
"my father doesn't even do it with two hands free."

The chaos in the apartment, which had so discon-
certed my mother, hardly bothered me. Naturally, it
didn't escape my notice that Dr. Meyer lived in grand
bourgeois surroundings, which had meanwhile become
impoverished and dilapidated. In the library the bookcases with their dark wood carving reached up to the
ceiling, and although the room was kept reasonably tidy,
Dr. Meyer apologized for the mess. He had always only

kept his study in order; everything else had been the
responsibility of his wife and, earlier on, of the servants.
At some point he began to talk about his last trip to
Provence, about meeting his sons, how happy they had
all been. But just under a year ago his wife had simply
stayed in bed one morning and, after having been urged
many times to get up, had explained she was not made
for these times and simply didn't want to go on anymore.
Finally, she had put her hands over her ears, mutely
shaking her head, and had not taken another bite of food.
As he related this Dr. Meyer walked restlessly back and
forth in the library. Then he stopped abruptly and said,
"On the eleventh day Hilde Meyer was dead."

I have sometimes asked myself whether it was the
memory of the holiday in Nice or the refusal to accept his
wife's death that caused Dr. Meyer to receive me almost
every time in a beige summer suit with a red neckerchief.
Recently, I remembered again how quickly he spoke.
My father said, no doubt rightly, that when he talked,
Dr. Meyer was driven by the thought that he didn't have
much time left. When I returned from the errands he
began to talk about his wife again, and three sons who
had emigrated some time before. Two were, meanwhile,
living in South Africa, where, in his opinion, they didn't
belong.

Life permitted itself many mistakes, he continued
after a pause for thought. Sometimes, however, people
threw it completely off course. He was really a failure.
His grandparents had been peddlers plying their trade
between Krakow and Lodz, before they had left their

NOT I

Berlin. Had his family history taken something like a
"normal" course, then he or one of his sisters would have
got at least to one of the better parts of Kreuzberg, his
sons then to Charlottenburg, and their children, in turn,
to a villa in Grunewald. Now two of them were living in
Johannesburg, one in Mexico. "Life is no longer sticking
to the rules," he concluded. "But why?" He said it in a
tone of voice that suggested there was no answer to the
question.

Wordlessly, he turned away and gloomily looked
across a number of shelves and names in the bookcase.
Then he asked me to read him poems from an anthology.
I told him about my father, who awarded one mark for
ten poems, and for the next occasion Dr. Meyer recommended one or two poems by Heine, Platen, and Rilke.[13]
Without thinking, Heine's "I bear no grudge" comes
to mind, and Rilke's "The Merry-go-round, Jardin du
Luxembourg." Once, when I was reciting, I noticed that
Dr. Meyer's eyes were wet. As if it were today I remember that I was reading the Goethe poem "Schlafe! was
willst du mehr?"[14] I thought perhaps he felt it to be the
fulfillment of a last wish of his beloved wife. Later we

---

13 August Count von Platen (1796–1835) was a master poet who preferred demanding forms like sonnets and ghasels; he also wrote popular ballads and political
songs. Rainer Maria Rilke (1875–1926) was one of the greatest poets of the twentieth century, whose complex and profound works span a wide variety of forms; the
poems cited here and later are an integral part of any educated German's cultural
vocabulary.

14 This is actually the last line of Goethe's poem "Nachtgesang" and the first line of
a poem by Hoffmann von Fallersleben written in 1840.

turned to prose: I read Fontane's *Schach von Wuthenow* and some Kleist stories. Dr. Meyer added literary or historical references, then I read some of Conrad Ferdinand Meyer's curiously cool stories; on another occasion, Droste-Hülshoff's *Die Judenbuche* (The Jew's beech) and Emil Strauss's *Freund Hein* (Friend death). Dr. Meyer was my school.[15]

Apart from that he gave me rules to follow in life, some of which I have never forgotten. It is less of a problem for the world if people are stupid than if they have prejudices, was one of his maxims; another: nothing is as expensive as a present one gets. Once he also warned me always to keep my distance. "One shouldn't embrace people," he explained, "because the person you embrace all too often has a knife up his sleeve." "At most one embraces a woman," and even she often has a knife under her nightdress. At this revelation I must have stared at him in disbelief, because after these words I heard him laugh for the first time: "Just a bad joke!"

Through visiting Dr. Meyer I got used to not going home immediately after school. In early summer 1939 I was almost fourteen. My father had suggested it was now time to take the Italian Renaissance more seriously, and even perhaps to make its study my career. Because if I were to devote myself to history, it would be a good idea not to get any nearer to the present than the

---

15 Conrad Ferdinand Meyer (1825–98) is famous for his tightly constructed, powerful prose and poetry, including oft-quoted ballads blending form, rhythm, and content in masterful fashion. Emil Strauss (1866–1960) was a minor prose writer, mainly known for the novel mentioned here.

fifteenth century, otherwise I would inevitably come too close to the period occupied by the Nazis. Around this time I discovered Alfred Hentzen's illustrated book on the Berlin Nationalgalerie on his bookshelves, so I had this additional material to fuel my interests. After classes I often went to the Museum Island in the city center.[16] The spacious yet intimate group of buildings, the majestic stairways, the halls and rows of columns captivated me in themselves. In terms of painting, however, I was most taken by the rooms of the Romantics, the Nazarenes, and other German painters who went to Rome for inspiration: Anselm Feuerbach, Hans von Marées, Böcklin, and everything else between late David and Manet. Of the Italian painters from Giotto to Reni, on the other hand, I admired above all their technical brilliance—the tangibly heavy brocade in the paintings of Titian or the beautiful flesh of the nakedly displayed bodies—while simultaneously asking myself why the dramatic turmoil of the times was so little reflected in these pictures. I often talked to my father about it. In the end, our conclusion was that the Italian Renaissance was historically infinitely more brilliant and somber than the idylls of Olevano or Barbizon, and much more attractive as a scholarly and literary subject. Nevertheless, beneath the fogs of Caspar David Friedrich or in the undergrowth and ponds of Monet there

16 This complex of several large museums, dedicated to major exhibits of ancient monuments and art as well as paintings through the ages, is located on an island and constitutes the heart of Berlin's immense collection of cultural treasures even today.

was more life to be discovered than in the paintings of Salvator Rosa or Guido Reni, where saints fought with dragons and other poisonous, hissing monsters. But my father said both were appealing: the intimations of art and the way it transcended reality.

With Gerd Donner or some other classmates I occasionally went a few stops farther on the S-Bahn to the Planetarium at Zoo Station. It was basically an ordinary cinema, except that before the newsreel and the main feature the starry sky of that day was shown on the domed roof and commented upon. My parents were somewhat naive in assuming that a movie theater offering such an instructive supporting program could hardly be showing any second-rate films; and so, undisturbed, I saw at the Planetarium the films of popular stars like Heinz Rühmann, Willy Fritsch and Zarah Leander, Heli Finkenzeller and Heinrich George—in short, everything that was being talked about at the time. My parents would have been a little surprised. Only the fact that—out of instinct and on Gerd Donner's advice—I avoided all propaganda films would have halfway set their minds at ease.

That summer Emil Lengyel announced that he would be coming to see us. He was a friend of my father's from his Weimar days and had meanwhile made a considerable reputation for himself in the United States as an academic and a political commentator. In early summer 1939 he had set out on an extended trip through the capitals of Western Europe to investigate the increasingly threatening political situation. In his letter he had written openly about Hitler's responsibility for the impending war and described the Nazi regime as a version of the Hungarian dictatorship—which he had fled after the First World War—but established with German thoroughness.[17]

My mother was dismayed. "I certainly don't care for any fiery czardas temperament in politics.[18] And on top of that an American utterly hostile to the Nazis in our house," she said at second supper to my father. "Think of your family! They'll use it against us. Why don't you just go to a bar?" My father stared angrily ahead and seemed to be thinking that he hadn't initiated the so-called second supper to have arguments with my mother in front of Wolfgang and me. Finally he replied, "Like you I am thinking of all of us here. But cowardice is not allowed either. You're forgetting that." My mother stood up and with her hands on the table retorted quite curtly, "You don't think about courage or cowardice. You only have your principles in your head." In all those years it was the only argument our parents had in front of us.

But my father didn't give way. Lengyel came to Hentigstrasse and we spent, not least at my mother's prompting, an amusing evening around the garden table with czardas steps and hand-clapping. When night fell, our guest produced five paper lanterns out of nowhere and we continued the fun for a while longer. Then the

---

17 The reference here is to the de facto dictatorship of Miklós Horthy de Nagy-bánya, the plenipotentiary ruler of Hungary from 1920 through 1944.

18 This reference to Hungary's national dance, the *csárdás*, invokes the popular stereotype among German speakers of the Hungarians' alleged fiery temperament, in love and argument.

insufferable Herr Henschel appeared on his balcony and requested quiet. "Ten o'clock!" he roared. At that Lengyel and my father withdrew to the study.

I was still calling on Dr. Meyer, and one day he got around to talking about Thomas Mann, "indisputably the greatest German writer," as he repeatedly emphasized. Until then I had no more than heard the name, but now, in his hoarse voice, Dr. Meyer talked about the writer's stature, the Nobel Prize, his elder brother Heinrich, and the great literary talents of his children. As he talked, he poured out so many names and titles that I soon had everything mixed up. Finally, he read me some passages from *Tonio Kröger* and said that the book was the briefest summing-up of Thomas Mann's lifelong problem. All his principal characters were outsiders and every one of his books was a variation on that theme. Once he had got going, he also quoted some phrases from *Royal Highness* and *Buddenbrooks*. He stood on a stepladder and brought down several volumes by the author. After leafing thoughtfully through them he handed me *Buddenbrooks* for the "next fortnight," and told me insistently neither to turn down the corners of pages nor to damage the book in any other way, never mind lose it. Because, under present conditions, Thomas Mann was no longer in favor and new copies were hard to come by.

I began to read the first pages on the S-Bahn, but said nothing about it at supper, because I knew my father's reservations about novels. When Aunt Dolly, who was a librarian, once brought Hermann Hesse's *Narcissus and Goldmund* for Wolfgang, my father thought her action incomprehensible, and said novels were mostly for housewives or maids with time on their hands.[19] After a long argument he read the first two or three pages of the book and gave it back to Wolfgang with an amused "Well, have fun, Miss Magda!"

With Thomas Mann it was different. After a few days, when I had just reached the description of Uncle Gotthold's death, my father discovered the book and asked where I had got it from. When I told him about Dr. Meyer's special liking for Thomas Mann, he was unimpressed: Dr. Meyer couldn't know that, but he wasn't having Thomas Mann in the house. He was certainly a significant author, but a politically irresponsible person. My father had lost all respect for Thomas Mann with *Reflections of an Unpolitical Man*. Precisely because it was so well written it had done more to alienate the middle classes from the republic than Hitler.[20] That sort of thing was impossible to forgive. He demanded that I send the book back to Dr. Meyer immediately; he himself would include a few lines of explanation.

When I came home from school the next day, the book had already been taken to the post office. My mother

---

19 Hermann Hesse (1877–1962), writer and pacifist, received the Nobel Prize in Literature in 1946 before his novels were discovered by British and American youth of the counterculture movement of the 1960s, especially his novel *Steppenwolf*.

20 Thomas Mann (1875–1955), novelist and antifascist exile, received the Nobel Prize in 1929 and became controversial politically with his public pronouncements in critical essays; after 1918 he offended the German patriots on the right, after 1945 he was distrusted by the left. His many novels and novellas reflect on the incompatibility of ordinary life and the life of the spirit or mind, especially as manifested in the artist's sensibilities. Refusing the blandishments of both postwar German states, he settled in neutral but German-speaking Switzerland.

remarked that she had had an errand nearby anyway and sent the book off for me. At my next visit on Saturday Dr. Meyer received me shaking his head and with *Buddenbrooks* in his hand. My father, he said embarrassedly, evidently did not know that literature was only a game. He took books and their authors too seriously. All of belles lettres was at home in the circus, as it were, and had a humorous side. The truth of his observation was underlined a couple of weeks later, when my father once again demanded the return of a book. This time it was Felix Dahn's *A Struggle for Rome*, which Heinz Steinki, the son of a tailor who lived in Blumenstrasse, had lent me.[21] My father disliked playing the censor, but he did not want such a politically dubious author as Felix Dahn in the house, either. "One ends up living with these people," he said, "they become part of the family." He shook his head. "Felix Dahn will never be a part of this family!" As a result, for years I had no idea how the Goths had got to Cosenza, and what had happened historically when they had sunk their king together with his treasure in the River Busento at night. What did become clear to me, however, was the depth of the wound that the demise of the Weimar Republic had inflicted on its supporters.

At around this time Sally Jallowitz, whom my mother still could not stand, turned up again. I told him about

---

21 Felix Dahn (1834–1912) was a professor of history and writer of historical novels focusing on the conquest of the Roman Empire by the Germanic tribes. In his *Struggle for Rome* he describes the burial of the Gothic king, Alaric, in the River Busento somewhere near Cosenza, a scene immortalized—and memorized by German schoolboys—in August von Platen's poem "Das Grab im Busento" (The grave in the Busento).

Dr. Meyer's residence theory, according to which the first generation of Jewish immigrants settled in the Scheunenviertel or nearby in Berlin's East End, and a hundred years later their grandchildren lived in Grunewald. That was unfortunately a thing of the past, Dr. Meyer had said, and he himself was an example of how lacking in energy even the Jews had become. In his irrepressible confidence Jallowitz merely laughed. He and his parents had occupied a basement on Andreasplatz near Silesian Station; he no longer lived in a basement but in a respectable apartment block near Spittelmarkt. Admittedly, he still went from one customer to the next with two heavy suitcases, but really he was past that. He had saved up a "pretty sum" and hidden it and a little silver under a floorboard in his small but nice two-room apartment: "The furniture, all of it the best modern, old-fashioned, fancy stuff!" And next he was going to marry. "But I swear to you"—and he pushed his hat to the back of his head, so that he could wipe the sweat from his face and neck—"my sons will live in Charlottenburg without any detour via the Seydelstrasse, and one of the three or four boys I'll have may even live in Grunewald! I swear to you!"

In early summer 1939 the founder and director of the language school at which my father was learning Italian and Russian offered to put him in charge of the Berlin branch. My father pointed out that he had been forbidden to give private lessons, but Dr. Hartnack brushed this objection aside, saying that after six years even the Nazis had become more accommodating. Nevertheless, he recommended my father apply to the relevant department to issue the necessary permission, and my mother went every morning to the rogation service to pray for a happy conclusion to the matter. After about three weeks the answer arrived: it had been impossible, it said in the letter, to agree to a permission, because the petitioner's behavior, "as known to the department," did not allow the conclusion that his political attitude had changed in the intervening time. He had not even concluded his application with the "German greeting," as had been officially required for years.[22] As soon as there was evidence before the department that the petitioner had come around to a positive assessment of the National Socialist order and of its leader Adolf Hitler, then it would be prepared to review the matter.

Throwing the letter onto the table with an angry laugh, my father remarked, "The bastards will wait a long time for that. They were all once colleagues of mine." My mother was unable to hide how desperate she was, but she was also obviously greatly impressed by her husband's intransigence. Occasionally, I saw her in the evening sitting in the easy chair in the drawing room, her face empty and exhausted by the long day; her eyes had fallen shut over her darning things and a kind of swoon, so it seemed, had overcome her. If she felt herself observed, she started up and said, embarrassed, that she hadn't been sleeping, but only thinking. Then she asked

---

22 The "German greeting" (*der deutsche Gruss*) was "Heil Hitler!" The Hitler salute was offered with outstretched right arm; most non-Nazis refused to use it on everyday occasions but had to comply at official functions and in government offices. It was also required in writing in official documents.

me to keep her company for a few minutes, but I failed in
the attempt to come up with an amusing piece of gossip.
So I talked about my most recent school essays, about
the agreement I had come to with Wolfgang, according
to which in future I was no longer supposed to support
Schalke 04, but Rapid Vienna instead, and finally that
recently one saw so many men with German shepherds.[23]
In the end my mother said, "Six or seven years and the
world and people in it are turned upside down!" It would
always be beyond her.

This was also when Walther Rosenthal and his attractive wife said goodbye. They didn't understand the Germans anymore, he said on the phone, and would leave
the country in three days, despite all the difficulties the
authorities were putting in their way. They had always
considered themselves to be Germans, but that had been
overhasty. Then Sonja Rosenthal came to the phone for
"one quick word of farewell." She just wanted to say, she
remarked, that the little bit of trust she still had in human
beings she owed above all to some Berlin friends. "Not so
few at all," she added. Then she said, *"Auf Wiedersehen!,"*
which almost sounded like a question, and hung up.[24]

On the whole, however, the summer of 1939 belonged
to my brother Winfried. One day he came running into

---

23 Schalke 04 and Rapid Vienna were professional soccer clubs playing in the same
league at the time within the unified German-Austrian entity created in 1938. The
German shepherd reference is, of course, to Hitler's favorite dog breed, now favored
by those who would emulate the Führer.

24 It was, in fact, a question whether they would ever see each other again, with
good reasons to doubt it.

the flat breathless with effort and happiness and shouted, "Done it! At last! I've managed it!" For two or three months we had watched him as in wind and rain, with youthful perseverance, he practiced the giant swing on the horizontal bar. Wolfgang, who was not a talented gymnast and only managed the knee circle, had soon given up, and after two weeks I had achieved nothing more than the much easier little giant swing. Only Winfried had gone on struggling and finally performed not only a rotation but two giant swings. The whole family, including my sisters, who had never shown any interest in our boys' world, followed him down to the garden. Because they were going on to a birthday party they had broad, colored ribbons in their hair, which my mother had been tugging away at before the beginning of the show, so that everything looked "neat and tidy." Then Winfried jumped onto the high horizontal bar from a chair, swung back and forth a couple of times, and threw himself into the giant swing. When he came down, even ending in a standing position, old Katlewski was so impressed that he offered to register Winfried in the local gymnastic club, Karlhorst Turnverein KTV 1900, and my father aroused our envy by giving Winfried one mark—as much as for ten poems!

The next day Hans Hausdorf, who often made considerable sums dealing in dental instruments and equipment, happened to call, and the giant swing was performed for him. He was so astonished that he took five marks out of his pocket. But when he heard how much Winfried had received from my father, he gave him only one mark. "I can't give you more than your father," he said, and Winfried retorted, "You can! You just don't want to!" After a brief hesitation, Herr Hausdorf added another seventy pfennigs. "But with that you have to buy an ice cream for everyone in the family!"

At around the same time the organist of our church declared himself willing to give me and my sisters piano lessons free of charge. My brothers had responded so negatively to the mere mention of instruction or (in Wolfgang's case) with such amusement that they were never asked again. Herr Tinz was a lively, charming Rhinelander with a bald spot and curly hair combed up at the sides. He taught me how to sit at the piano, the varieties of fingering, and an appreciation of composers I knew hardly anything about, such as Handel, Telemann, and Schütz.[25] More than that, his boundless enthusiasm (which in conversation could be quite trying) taught me that music demanded powerful emotions on the part of both performers and audience and that "without fire" it was nothing more than "blowing at a heap of ashes." Passion was more important than technique, he said in his high voice. In the course of the lessons our teacher was carried away by his own enthusiasm, and he frequently concluded them by playing a movement from a classical sonata, preferably one marked presto. When I asked my mother whether, after all the artistic thunder and lightning, she could play "Ah, vous dirais-je maman"[26] or one

---

25 These German masters of the Baroque were all primarily keyboard musicians who wrote many pieces suitable for piano exercises on any level.

26 Variations by Mozart on a French tune best known in English as "Twinkle, Twinkle, Little Star."—Trans.

of Brahms's dances, she looked at me from her stove with an almost pitying smile. With unusual curtness she said, "It would no longer be appropriate now!"

Then I would have to turn to my new friend, I replied, who was at least a year ahead of me on the piano. Wigbert Gans had only recently joined our class. He came from Halle and it so happened that his father, although only the previous year, had been "let go," as my father had been in April 1933. Wigbert's face under his long floppy hair expressed superior concentration, and Hans Hausdorf, who once met him at our home, said that Wigbert listened with a fervor which almost made one feel uneasy. Wigbert turned up at our school one day as if from nowhere and after five periods everyone knew that the class had a new top boy. He was not only ahead of us in all the natural sciences and, as it proved, of some of the teachers as well, he was also, contrary to every top-boy rule, among the best in foreign languages and even gymnastics. Since he wasn't a drudge or a show-off he was accepted from the day he arrived. Shortly afterward, when he visited me in Karlshorst for the first time, he introduced himself to my parents with the disconcertingly straightforward words: "I am Wigbert Gans and I'm from a family which is also 'genuine' or 'anti'—whichever you like."

We quickly became friends and managed to sit together at one of the double desks. We swapped stories of the most diverse experiences, complained about the ignorance of our form master Dr. Appelt, and read the *The Song of the Nibelungs*, Hölderlin's *Hyperion*, and Knut

Hamsun together.[27] Now and then after school we went the few stops to the city center, to Alexanderplatz or Friedrichstrasse, and found the piled-up hair, garish blouses, and green net stockings of the ladies on parade there more exciting than the women themselves. Sometimes we also strolled through the area between Hackescher Markt and Mulackstrasse and looked cautiously into the hallways and cellar homes of this musty world familiar from Döblin's *Berlin Alexanderplatz*.[28] At the entrances hung pathetic pieces of clothing, pots, or linen; from below there rose a sour, poor-people smell. There were occasional cigarette-butt sellers who had spread out their goods on an old tray, neatly arranged according to length and brand; three butts cost a pfennig, a half-smoked cigar three pfennigs. Here and there we passed a group of Jews deep in conversation, nodding their heads; even on hot summer days they wore dark coats and hats. They appeared curiously abandoned, and I felt attraction, dread, and sadness at the sight of them.

---

27 *The Song of the Nibelungs* is a medieval Germanic epic about the glory and fall of the Burgundian royal house among the Huns led by Attila; its oldest extant written version dates from c. 1200, but it contains much older materials. It became something of a cult item because of Richard Wagner's *Ring of the Nibelung* cycle and the Nazi interest in the Germanic past; both re- and misinterpreted the original epic and its ethos.

Friedrich Hölderlin (1770–1843) is often regarded as Germany's greatest lyrical poet; his *Hyperion* (1797–99) is a poetic novel written in epistolary form, expressing the author's deeply felt romantic yearning and his love for an idealized ancient Greece.

Knut Hamsun (1859–1952), Norwegian Nobel laureate (1920), was a novelist of the simple stark rural life; he was much admired by the Nazis and published in the Quisling newspapers, for which he was fined after 1945.

28 Alfred Döblin (1887–1957) was a neurologist and writer who left Germany in 1933 and returned in 1945. His novels, especially *Berlin Alexanderplatz*, paint a very dense and often depressing picture of the helplessness of the individual in both nature and modern society.

Leibniz Gymnasium was an establishment without any reputation, not to be compared to such legendary educational institutions as the Fichte Gymnasium, the Grey Cloister, or Canisius College, whose names were always mentioned with respectfully raised eyebrows. The somewhat unambitious teaching methods of most of the teachers were focused upon learning, and combined acquiring knowledge with a simple system of fair assessment.

The rector of the school, Wilhelm Weinhold, was held to be a crude Nazi without really being one. The military bearing that he was at pains to maintain, his chin determinedly pressed against his neck, made his authority look somewhat forced. The watery eyes with which he liked to stare piercingly when issuing a reprimand also betrayed what an effort it cost him to appear as "Sergeant Major Wilhelm," as he was called by the pupils. Yet was it really by chance that he entrusted timid Herr Pfaff, whose Swabian accent alone made all pathetic declamations sound ridiculous, with teaching ideological topics? In his lessons, as with a puzzled expression he interpreted Rosenberg's *Myth of the Twentieth Century* a paragraph at a time, we filled bags with water and hung them up above the classroom door; when they burst, to the howls of the class, he lapsed into completely incomprehensible Swabian.[29] His hands at his temples, desperate for help, he would open the door to Rector Weinhold,

---

29 Alfred Rosenberg (1893–1946), sometimes regarded as the chief ideologue of Nazism (although not by the Nazi leaders themselves), was the main publicist and developer of Nazi ideas; condemned to death by the Nürnberg Tribunal, he was executed in 1946.

who, in fact, did nothing more than enter the room with a firm step, his chin pressed against his throat, and order us a few times to "Stand!" and "Sit!," before conclud- ing the incident with a reference to the war and the good name of the school. He was a former theology student and at the annual Christmas service in the school hall, after the official part with Nazi choruses and political poems, he had the swastika flag removed from the room before giving a sermon between the reading of the Gos- pel and the Christmas carols.

Apart from that there was the history teacher, Dr. Schmidt, heavy and bald, who wore tweed suits and put- tees and liked to relate episodes from his life; also the almost delicate-looking Dr. Hertel, who was responsible for teaching German and Latin. Then there was the geography teacher Dr. Püschel, a gruff man whose eyes would flash when difficult questions arose and then, eyes shut, he would stroke his Vandyke beard with a clenched fist. If the class of smart, big-city boys understood his politically ambiguous remarks all too well, he would boisterously correct himself, though not without linking his correction to some new double meaning: an honest boor, who, in his advancing years, against his charac- ter and temperament, tried his hand at being a political tightrope walker.

Finally, one day when we were already in our sec- ond year, Fräulein Schneider turned up. She introduced herself as the new gym teacher and, unusually, asked to be addressed as Fräulein—Miss—Doris. She looked delightful and had a figure in which (in Gerd Donner's expert judgment) "all the right curves were in the right place." To the amazement of the schoolboys she came to lessons wearing trousers, which the class acknowledged with enthusiasm—her colleagues, however, with unconcealed displeasure. Fräulein Doris enjoyed thinking up new exercises on the box horse, horizontal bars, and climbing frame, on the vaulting horse too, of course, all with long take-offs after which, in support position, she caught the jumpers in a firm embrace. There were some who soon recognized that the bosomy beauty was good not only for keeping us fit, but presented far more exciting possibilities. Schibischewski was the first to grasp the opportunity. He walked back from a long horse jump saying, "Bull's eye!," while Jendralski expressed himself more coarsely, and Gerd Donner merely raised two fingers of his right hand, whatever that meant. Only a week later he went to see Dr. Weinhold with a "delegation" of three fellow pupils to request that there should be two additional gym lessons a week, as he understood from "authoritative sources" that they were "politically desirable." After lengthy negotiations this "exemplary request" succeeded in getting us one extra gym lesson.

In Gerd Donner, the third year of Leibniz Gymnasium had a born leader. He had had to repeat a year at elementary school and was therefore not only older but also more experienced than the rest of us. Apart from that he had a Darwinian instinct for survival, developed in the back courts of the working-class quarter of SO 36—North Kreuzberg. Always something of a dandy in his dress, he was constantly playing with his comb; at every break he would take it out and, his head thrown back, draw it through his long, unparted, wavy hair. A proletarian beau, he relished being admired as an authority on mysterious, all-night bars and exciting experiences with women. His motto was "Always use the back door"— that was the best way to get anywhere. On the way to the station he sometimes took me to see a classmate from his elementary school days. Harry Wolfhart's father had a collection of several thousand tin soldiers. Small, plump, and sporting a buzz cut, Harry's father, who was around fifty, spoke with an equal measure of melancholy and wistfulness about endless nights spent drinking long ago. He readily led us past the cabinets of a spacious double room and explained the accurate renderings of flags, uniforms, and cannon to us.

Then he left us alone. Harry explained that for days he had been trying to reenact the Battle of Jena and Auerstedt with almost two thousand soldiers. An account of the battle open at his side, he pointed out Napoleon's brilliant feints as units moved forward, then avoided contact or dissolved.[30] Gerd Donner had warned me on the way there: when a battle was in progress, Harry was sometimes overcome by a violent fit of temper and wanted to play fate; then he would take an old lamp chain from one of the drawers at the bottom of the cabinets and strike out

---

30 In the Battle of Jena and Auerstedt (October 14, 1806), Napoleon decisively defeated and destroyed the famed Prussian army, opening the way for a complete reorganization of the German Reich and Europe as a whole. It marked the end of the Holy Roman Empire and laid the groundwork for Prussian reforms leading to the Wilhelminian Reich of 1870.

blindly at the ranks of soldiers, until the whole beautiful order of battle was wrecked.

And that is exactly what happened on our visit. Gerd objected that the hitting out had come too soon today, but Harry had wanted to impress us. When I asked why he was so crazy, Gerd replied that Harry wasn't crazy, he was merely copying life. His father had been a successful businessman, who through a run of bad luck had lost everything, and from the leafy suburb of Dahlem had ended up in this dark corner of Berlin. Indeed, as Harry, quite beside himself, panting, his face bright red, had laid into the battleground, he had shouted, "I am Fate! No one can escape me! I am omnipotent!"

Gerd said that eighty to one hundred tin soldiers fell victim to each of his friend's outbreaks. Some could be soldered, stuck together, painted, and more or less restored. But almost half of the "seriously disabled" remained lost. And of the twenty or so buildings that were distributed across the battlefield of Auerstedt, all were gone. Harry's father, added Gerd, often stood by in tears when his armies were smashed. But he let it happen.

FIVE

•

Leave-takings

I have very happy memories of the summer of 1939. One glorious day followed another, and it was so blissfully hot for so long that the driver of the milk delivery cart at best handed out only small splinters of ice. Sometimes the water cart came up the street, always surrounded by a crowd of boisterous children, and I have never forgotten the smell of the water sprayed on the steaming asphalt. For long stretches we would wait for an unguarded moment, so that we could stand under the curving jet of water, until, as with the milk cart, the driver chased us away. In the heat it was too much effort to throw the heavy ball we used for dodgeball, so we usually played *Treibeball* instead, the point of which was to drive the opposing team as far as possible up or down the street with a smaller leather ball.

Despite the blazing heat we occasionally still played soccer. I know that when the legendary Breslau Eleven beat Denmark 8–0 (even today I can rattle off the names of the players, beginning with Jacob, Janes, Münzenberg, and going on with Kupfer, Goldbrunner, and Kitzinger), our Hentigstrasse 1937 lost 8–0 to Marksburgstrasse—a disgrace that over the years demanded revenge, which we managed a few times.[1] In that last summer of peace the fruit bushes were heavy with fruit, and we were busy the whole day carrying water for the garden and the hens. At the end of the summer holidays we went to the Walken Farm as usual, but hardly were we back in Berlin again— after mischievous scraps with my uncle and swimming in Packlitzsee Lake—when the skies darkened.

There would be war, my father reported from meetings with his circle, and it was imminent. Hardly anyone, however, to whom he passed on the information wanted to believe it. "You and your pessimism!" he was told, even by friends. Then, when the conflict did break out, he had yet another disappointment. He and his friends had been unanimous that Hitler was the "daredevil crybaby type": such people often went to the limit, but when faced with determined resistance their nerve broke, and with whatever malice was left in them they put a bullet through their heads. In that sense, they were all agreed, Hitler was a born suicide. Now the English and the

---

1 The Breslau Eleven was the German national soccer team, which defeated Denmark at Breslau in Silesia (today: Wroclaw in Poland); Fest recites the names of the players on that team.

French had held firm, but Hitler had still not killed himself. "The rules," said my father at second supper, "just don't apply to him."

After church on Sunday, September 3, 1939—as the two-hour British ultimatum began to run out—we went to our grandparents' for breakfast. My mother was very worried; a few days before I had heard her say to my father, "Now they'll take our children as well!" They had already been trying to do that for years, he had replied, but hadn't managed it. Then my grandfather had tried to reassure her by saying that Wolfgang and I were simply too young for this war; the technology would not permit the fronts to freeze into trench warfare again and the fighting would be limited to one or two years at most. In the early afternoon, when we set off home along Stechlin-strasse to the Seepark, past the tall rhododendron bushes and magnolias, it was striking how many of those out walking once again greeted my father; even those who had previously crossed the road to avoid him exchanged a few words. No doubt the majority of Germans were still "loyal to the Führer," but a few seemed, for the first time, to have an inkling that the country had entered on a dangerous adventure.

We first noticed the war because all the streetlamps were extinguished with one stroke. As night fell, black cardboard roller blinds were pulled down over the windows and, wherever they were forgotten, a chorus of "Lights out!" would sound from the streets below. There one encountered more and more pedestrians with a luminous patch on their coats or trying to find their way with a weak pocket flashlight. Instead of the water cart, a vehicle now came down the street whose driver called, "Firewood for potato peelings! Come on, people! Who's still got potato peelings, raw or cooked? I can give you best firewood for the stove!" And at the same time he rang a bell.[2]

Apart from that the war manifested itself in the acceleration of life. Passersby, among whom there were suddenly soldiers and nurses, seemed to walk more hastily down the street; the train conductors called out their commands more impatiently; the victory announcements on the wireless were louder than ever, interrupted by the so-called England song,[3] alternating with the Erikas, and of course all the proud women whose heart Heinz Rühmann had broken with his stolid charm.[4] A large winged bomb, which years before had been set up as a monument at the Rondeel, a circular flower bed, was one day given a floral decoration in the colors of the British flag, and many wondered whether the arrangement was intended for the brave German aircrews or their victims. Then again, from the open windows, the booming sound

---

2 This is an early indication of a barter economy which began to replace the official money economy. Farmers needed feed for their pigs, such as potato peels, while city dwellers needed fuel for their stoves, such as wood—in addition to the traditional coal at the time.

3 An anti-English song composed in 1939 to verses written in 1914 by the popular German writer Hermann Löns.—Trans.

4 Both the so-called England song and the one extolling the charms of a flower and girl named Erika were soldiers' songs much played on the radio stations during the war and sung by young and old. Heinz Rühmann was a universally beloved German comic actor of stage and screen who turned in some memorable performances in character roles after the war.

of speeches, rallies, shouts of *Heil!* from the radio receiv-
ers. A friend of my parents was supposed to have locked
her two maids in the radio room for the broadcast of a
Hitler speech, saying that since they had voted for the
man, they should also hear word for word what he had
to say. My father remarked one evening that he could no
longer bear the never-ending "pathetic howls"; the only
place pathos was still acceptable these days was when one
ordered pea soup at Aschinger's.[5] I thought that a very
witty expression. But Wolfgang was not impressed; he
thought the joke was itself pathetic.

At Christmas 1939 I found among my presents—
next to a pullover, three pairs of socks, and a shirt—a
book on English sea power written by a respected British historian. In explanation, my father said it was a
substitute, as it were, for *Buddenbrooks*, because books
on such topics were more useful than anything that
had been "thought up," and in this case it informed the
reader about the kind of opponent Hitler had taken on.
Close to tears, I insisted, when he tried to console me,
that the book had spoiled my whole Christmas. At first
my father thought he could change my mind with sooth-
ing words. But when I became rapidly more testy and
asked why it could not at least have been a book about
the Renaissance, he accused me of ingratitude and said
I was ruining Christmas for everyone else. Angrily and

---

5 Aschinger's eateries were a famous attraction to students and artists because
of their cheap and relatively plentiful fare, especially the pea soup with rolls or
Brötchen.

with a degree of childish contrariness, I replied that he should not talk to me like that. After all, we were "facing the world" together. My father gave me a searching look, and I was afraid he was going to lose his temper. But then he simply hugged me. This wordless gesture was an expression of both acknowledgment and self-criticism. The episode was never mentioned again.

We soon found support in "facing the world." For some time we had observed the new priest, Father Johannes Wittenbrink, saying his breviary on the paths of the church garden next door. Once my father had exchanged a few words with him, the two men found they had opinions in common and out of the almost daily exchange there soon developed a friendship. Aside from the services, which he conducted, with great liturgical earnestness, according to the Benedictine model, the priest turned out to be an educated man as well as one who laughed easily. Tall and with natural dignity, he had a face full of laughter lines.

Wittenbrink came from the coal-mining town of Waldenburg in Silesia, and he was very attached to the Austrian world. His wide interests in Habsburg history, the visual arts, and music he saw as being an inheritance from his mother, born a princess of Pless, the offspring of an ancient Silesian noble family that could be traced back to the twelfth century. He owed his comic talent, on the other hand, to his father, a veterinarian. Whenever the opportunity arose, he acted out comic situations for us. I still remember his imitation of a speaker at Hyde Park Corner in London who had a speech impediment, so that every *s* or *th* came out as a *sh*. Or he mimicked a lady in

the Café de Paris, who wanted to get rid of an annoying hair in her nose and at first sought cover behind the
wine list, then made use of a silk scarf and finally the big-
petaled flower in her buttonhole. But before she was successful, some of the customers sitting around her, after
first trying to suppress it, began to roar with laughter,
which gave the narrator an opportunity to imitate the
varied registers of hilarity that resounded throughout the
establishment.

A friendship arose first of all out of the bond of
Catholicism, as of religion altogether, which was something my parents took for granted. They were both—by
disposition and education—religious people. The family
went to church every Sunday and, of course, I and Wolfgang and Winfried were altar boys. In 1936, when the
new church was built, we had carried stones or building
materials, and with other children tried to make ourselves
useful in one way or another. For all that, my father was
not blind to the disastrous political decisions made by the
Catholic Church; for some time, however, he took them
to be an expression of ecclesiastical unworldliness.[6] At
any rate, he never wavered in his conviction that a human
being without faith was "incomplete." Neither reason

---

6 Many of those disastrous decisions were based on the erroneous assumption that
compared to the threat of socialism or Communism, Nazism offered the better alternative. Thus the pope handed Hitler his first diplomatic success by concluding the
concordat with him, while Zentrum leaders like Von Papen and others were core-
sponsible for the legal takeover of power by the Nazis, which provided them political cover. In short, conservative, Catholic politics were much closer to and forgiving
of Hitler's policies than of anything that might have aided the godless atheism of the
political left.

nor walking upright separated him from the apes; the difference between the two lay in the need for a Beyond.

What began as casual conversation became firm friendship when my father and Wittenbrink began to exchange political views under the chestnuts by the garden fence. When they realized they were of one mind about Hitler as the "mask of the Anti-God," trust grew and the range of subjects discussed broadened. Once, I came up to them as they were discussing whether resistance to a dictatorship was theologically justified or whether killing a tyrant was a sin, and for the first time I heard names like Althusius and concepts such as that of the two kingdoms.[7] On another occasion they were discussing the question that came up again and again: how could the creator allow evil in the world? Another question was whether a confessant could be given absolution if, while acknowledging his fantasies of hatred against a neighbor or a political regime, he continued to hate as he sat in the confessional and had no intention of summoning up the repentance required for absolution. I followed these sometimes passionate debates from my seat at the garden table, where I did my homework in the summer. On the question of absolution Wittenbrink was not to be moved. "There can be no absolution for those who con-

7 The references here are to Augustine of Hippo (354–430) and Johannes Althusius (1563–1638), whose theories of what constitutes legitimate earthly power, and thus whether there is a right of resistance to unjust power, are part of a Western tradition of political thought. The German resistance turned to such theorists in its search for an answer to a most important question: How could one justify, morally and philosophically, opposition to and possibly the violent removal of an unjust regime like that of Hitler?

tinue to hate!" he insisted, there was not the least theological doubt about that. My father's objections to the strict interpretation were in a sense right, but the church could not allow him that right. My father was silent for a while, then tried to come up with further justifications, and muttered as he walked away, shaking his head, that God would show understanding; at any rate, he trusted Him more than any theologian.

But nontheological issues were also discussed. For example, whether Protestantism—after the experiences of recent years, and given sermons like the one about the church as God's SA troop—had a future. My father argued that the German language owed Protestantism a great deal, thanks to Luther, music owed much to Johann Sebastian Bach, and the culture as a whole from Lichtenberg to Nietzsche was indebted to the Protestant parsonage. Protestantism was not yet so dead that it could be unhesitatingly written off. And the Confessing Church should not be forgotten either.[8]

Leaning on the fence, their arms folded, the two men agreed, in the further course of their conversation, that the Catholic Church, too, had initially not stood the test of the Hitler years without reproach. Once or twice the conversation lost itself in speculation, as, for instance, the question of whether there was music in the Beyond. Certainly not the "utterly heathen" compositions of Richard

---

8 The Confessing Church (Bekennende Kirche) was the name taken by those Protestant ministers and congregations who resisted Nazi state interference in church affairs.—Trans.

Wagner, Wittenbrink objected, almost in fright, but definitely Mozart, Haydn, and Schubert, above all Schubert. My father found such reflections quite misguided. Then what about the suicidal Heinrich von Kleist, he objected, the Goethe of *Elective Affinities*, or the Marquis de Sade with his obsession with sin? He granted a chance of heaven to all musicians, poets, and artists, because the foolishness which they thought up would no longer be of any significance in the Beyond. He personally hoped to hear Paul Lincke or Emmerich Kálmán as well as Schubert over there, and if he had any say in the matter Claire Waldoff would be allowed to perform, too.[9]

For all the shadows that lay over these conversations, they were tremendously varied and often playful, and years later my father still remembered them with affection. It had been one opportunity, he declared, of establishing a counterweight to the sequence of great impertinences which the Nazi regime had imposed on him. If, from the window of his study he saw the priest coming down the garden path next door, he often hurried straight downstairs to his "academy," as he sometimes called it, and Wittenbrink, likewise, seemed only too pleased at the opportunity to interrupt his saying of the breviary. For me at the garden table it was a kind of graduate school or at least the antechamber to it. For the first time I became aware of the wealth of topics, the absurdities of the world, and

---

9 Paul Lincke was a Berlin composer of operettas and popular songs. Emmerich Kálmán was a Hungarian composer of operettas, usually associated with the Viennese stage. Claire Waldoff was a famous Berlin cabaret and music-hall singer; she made no secret of her lesbianism and fell out of favor after 1933.—Trans.

beyond that of how many questions there were on which opposing opinions could be held. Furthermore, I discovered what pleasure there was in contradiction, as well as in the effort to develop grounds for one's own arguments and to present them as convincingly as possible. The most important lesson I took from those conversations, however, was that a discussion conducted between friends had certain rules. Sometimes I thought that these "garden-fence conversations" had such an unforgettable effect because no sentence was directed didactically at me. Admittedly, now and then, when it came to political or erotic topics, one or another of the two men cast a worried glance over at me. But I was never told not to listen or to concern myself with the black currant bushes in a remote part of the garden.

On one of those days, in spring 1940, just as I was going back up to our apartment from my place at the garden table, the telephone rang. At the other end of the line was a caller who was evidently speaking from a public phone box, and in a somewhat breathless and plainly disguised voice said, "You're going to have visitors!" The caller gave no name, did not use any form of address, and did not say goodbye. He simply hung up. From the window I called my father upstairs. "Give me ten minutes!" he replied, but I must have responded with considerable emphasis, "No, immediately! Important!" With a surprised look he threw the spade aside with which he was just digging a vegetable patch and came up. When he asked what was so important, I told him what had happened and wanted to ask what it meant, but my father

was already at the wireless in the living room and turning the dial from Swiss Radio Beromünster to the German Broadcasting Station, before rushing to his study
to put the first volume of Winston Churchill's *Marlbor-
ough*, which he had picked up somewhere, back in the
bookcase, and then going through each room to check if
there was anything "suspicious."[10]

Before he was even finished hurrying through the
rooms, the doorbell rang. Two men, who despite their
civilian clothes gave the impression of wearing uniforms, entered the apartment without a word of introduction, loudly giving the Hitler salute. Together with
my father they went to the study, and from the living
room across the hall I heard calm voices which only
rarely rose to a fiercer exchange. After about half an
hour the visitors departed unceremoniously, without
inspecting the radio. My mother, who had been sitting
on the bed in the bedroom, covering her eyes with her
hands, rushed to my father. But he was fairly vague.
They had nothing in particular against him. There was
no need for her to worry. Perhaps that was true. Perhaps
he only said it to reassure her. In any case, in the years
that followed, we received something like another fifteen warnings of this kind. The announced visit did not
always take place. Who the mysterious informant was
only came to light after the war, by chance.

---

10 Listening to foreign, or enemy, radio stations was illegal and punished by the authorities, sometimes by death; it was also best not to have books by foreign authors
or those proscribed by the Nazi authorities.

The first air-raid warning came at about the same time. Hardly was the wail of the sirens over when my father went up onto the roof of the house with my brothers and me to watch the attack. After an uneventful hour, in which we searched the sky for the signs of the zodiac, we could hear the initially distant hum of engines coming closer, without being able to make out anything in the beams of the apparently randomly scanning searchlights. Only where the fingers of light feeling their way across the sky came together did we see, at their point of intersection, individual silvery aircraft, and shortly after that fiery flashes. But the raid was taking place some way off, over Kreuzberg, Britz, and down as far as Rudow. When the all clear had already been sounded and we were still sitting on the roof duckboards, countless small black particles floated down, and Wolfgang said these were the shrapnel clouds that formed every time a gun was fired. The next morning lessons did not start until ten. And so it went on every few days.

At school the air raids became the dominant subject of conversation. Some spoke of houses close to theirs that had been hit, and everyone began to collect shell splinters. If there had been no air-raid warning for several days in a row, then Gerd Donner got increasingly annoyed. You couldn't rely on the "old Tommies" anymore, either, he moaned. He loved the air-raid warnings and went down to the cellar as he would to the cinema. Not only because for every hour on alert after 10 p.m. school began an hour later than normal in the morning, but because in his cellar he had made himself a "make-out corner" behind a stack of laundry detergent cartons, where no one else went, and where for two weeks he had been "having a bit of fun with beautiful Inge from five houses down." Beautiful Inge was just thirteen and a half, "but with everything in the right place," he emphasized, drawing curves in the air with his hands. A few days ago he had already got to the third button of her blouse, and just then the all clear had sounded. "But yesterday when I got to my little corner, beautiful Inge was already there, waiting for me, with her blouse already open down to the third button, inviting me, so to speak. 'Now you can just carry on,' she said. And what could I say to that? I carried on. Scouts' honor!" Another boy in the class wanted to show off, and told us that when his father withdrew to the bedroom he always locked the door. "Well, I ask, why does he do that?" he said with false innocence. Gerd Donner interrupted him: "Just stop boring us. I wasn't talking about my old man, but about beautiful Inge and me."

That winter my father brought back from his monthly meetings the news that the group of friends could no longer procure money or forged documents for those seeking help. They had destroyed the few pieces of paper with cover names, addresses, and the code. Only in cases of the greatest danger could they still provide help. The inspections were clearly becoming more stringent, the sentences more severe, and recently almost everyone in the group had reported cases of merciless persecution. Listening to "enemy radio stations" was now being punished with prison, and soon, no doubt, with the death sentence; likewise, the mere passing on of political jokes. Concluding his account with a serious warning to us, my father added that during the lengthy discussions it had been evident how despairing everyone was. In times like these the only thing left was the knowledge that there were a couple of friends nearby. Later, he also reported that—in order to make the law more "flexible" and more suited to "national needs"—leading legal experts were working on a new criminal offense of "conduct of life," which meant that merely keeping one's distance from the national community could be made a matter of criminal investigation.

It was about this time that I made a second twenty-five-pfennig deal with Wolfgang. He offered me ten nude photos of French origin, which he had bought from a street trader near the Admiralspalast music hall. As far as I remember, the pictures showed mostly plump ladies in calf-length laced boots, who, one foot resting on a stool, leaned out toward the viewer with lascivious smiles and sometimes also invitingly with outstretched arms. For every week I borrowed them Wolfgang demanded twenty-five pfennigs, so that I had to learn poems again in order to scrape together that amount. I did not find the naked women at all "wicked," but instead pretty "silly." Apparently, however, they were part of growing up, according to Wolfgang and all the other friends around me, from Rudi Hardegen to Helmut Sternekieker. Before we came to an agreement, however, I asked him whether with our deal we were not in danger of committing a "conduct of life" offense. He responded that we were enemies of the Hitler people and shouldn't let ourselves be intimidated by their laws.

*The third year of Leibniz Gymnasium, with homeroom
teacher Dr. Appelt. (1) Gerd Donner, (2) Wigbert Gans,
(3) Clemens Korner, (4) the author.*

Ever since Father Wittenbrink had heard that I
was going to see Mozart's *The Marriage of Figaro* with
Aunt Dolly, he called me to the fence with increasing
frequency when I was sitting at the garden table doing
homework. From a number of conversations I knew
that he loved art, especially music. He asked me what I
knew about Mozart, which operas I had already heard,
whether I knew the term "child prodigy," and then
related the well-known episodes of the composer's early
violin playing and tours through half of Europe with
his father and sister. He could not get over the fact that
Mozart had, as a child, composed a symphony, and,
at only a little more than ten years old, an opera, and
that he not only possessed the technical skills to do so,
but appeared to know everything about life, and even,

so Father Wittenbrink sometimes thought, something about death as well.

Wittenbrink returned to *Figaro*, which he talked about at greater length. He said that in the opera Mozart presents—in the incomparable manner of which only he was master—a merry amorous confusion. Yet at the end a deadly seriousness breaks through. In the "Italian" operas, at least, such as *Don Giovanni*, the plot of which he related in outline, a stone guest[11] always appears at some point and announces to the frightened characters, "The game is over!" In *Figaro*, he continued, that moment comes when the Countess pulls the veil from her face and the Count sinks remorsefully to his knees: it is the most moving scene in the whole history of opera. Before the performance, he advised me, I absolutely must read the libretto, otherwise the whole bustling plot, which only appears to be amusing, would be incomprehensible to me. And I should never forget that while the melodies of the Mozart operas, which thanks to their combination of grace and attractiveness have been whistled at every street corner, end in conciliation, every knowledgeable listener knows that happiness, even as it is being extolled in song, is already secretly announcing a hidden unhappiness.

The next day Wittenbrink invited me to his apartment. I remember that on the walls of the large room, as it was called, there were two Ruisdaels with their

---

11 An allusion to the statue of the Commendatore in Mozart's opera, which finally drags the unrepentant Don Giovanni down to hell.—Trans.

characteristic trademark of a tree trunk running at
an angle across the picture background, also a Jacques
d'Arthois, and one or two paintings of the second Italian and first European rank, as he added in explanation.
Then we moved over to his record collection, which filled
several cabinets and shelves. After lengthy explanations
he played me the conclusion of *Figaro* and, because he
could never stop when the subject was Mozart, that of
Così fan tutte as well. Of the supposedly bright finale,
he said it is the darkest ending of any opera; only Mozart
had the genius to make the C major of these bars sound
like cries for help. Could I hear that? he asked. I said no,
but that one probably had to have listened to Mozart and
much else all one's life; instead, I always encountered
only Herr Tinz and his thundering forte prestissimo.

In the midst of these days spent in the garden—and
just as we were finishing Xenophon's *Anabasis* and going
on to Homer's *Odyssey* at school, and in the history class
were hearing about the Turks at the gates of Vienna—
burst the already almost forgotten war: at dawn on May
10, 1940, the offensive against France began, which for
half a year had repeatedly been postponed.[12] Unlike the
First World War, the confrontation was decided within a
few weeks, and once again my father felt himself torn by
the same conflict as in the years before. At second sup-

---

12 The references to Homer and Xenophon indicate that the school is a traditional
Gymnasium where the classics are read in the original languages.

   In 1683 a pan-European army lifted the siege of Vienna by the Turks, ending—
once and for all—Ottoman expansion into Central Europe and beginning the southeast expansion of Habsburg influence over the next two centuries.

per, which now also included Winfried, he remarked that he was glad from the bottom of his heart at the French defeat, but could never be so at Hitler's triumph. Soon after, when he said at the garden fence that he had rarely felt himself so abandoned by the reason of the world as now, Wittenbrink responded that a "reason of the world" didn't exist. What we described as such was nothing more than what we retrospectively projected onto pure chance; it was obvious to anyone that for every ten examples of the action of world reason in history there were some tens of thousands of examples of the working of worldly unreason. I could tell from my father's face how true and depressing he found this statement.

This conversation was perhaps still on his mind when, shortly afterward, Dr. Gans, the father of my schoolmate, came to visit. Since the sky was overcast with dark gray clouds, the two first of all withdrew to the study. My father offered his guest a Boenicke cigar, while my mother made the coffee. I was asked to remain and learned that—with respect to the war against France, which had ended a few days before—Dr. Gans thought that as Hitler now controlled half of Europe, it was necessary for him to consolidate his power. Surely Hitler understood that; in any case, at some point even the greediest person is sated or at least needs time to digest. Hence at the moment there was no threat of a new campaign, Dr. Gans could predict that with some certainty. But the longer Dr. Gans talked and justified his reflections, the more skeptically my father listened. Meanwhile the weather had cleared up, and so the two of them went downstairs after coffee and sat at the table under the chestnuts.

What he was saying, my father began, resuming the conversation, sounded all very reasonable, but that was precisely why he was mistaken. One should never leave Hitler's unreason out of the calculation. He had always avoided the obvious. Consequently, there was only one quotation which adequately described the situation. It was from Goethe: "All comfort is vile, / and despair the only duty." That reflected our situation exactly. After some thought, Dr. Gans's features brightened and one could virtually see him changing his mind. "Quite right!" he then blurted out, if with some effort. "It may be that I didn't take sufficient account of the fact that this state is led by a madman." And after a short pause: "The quote, by the way, comes from the Paralipomena to *Faust* II. I know it, too." Then, shaking his head, Dr. Gans listened as my father said that he knew the source only as the "Fragments"; at once a kind of philological dispute was under way. Each insisted on his view, and since we were sitting at the garden table, it was too much of an effort to bring the volumes downstairs to look up the quote. They would, they agreed, talk on the phone. When I came home from school the next day it turned out that both my father and Dr. Gans had the same text in mind, even if they had noted it under different titles. The scene has always stayed in my mind as the quintessence of a difference of opinion among members of the educated classes.

That summer my father wrote to Roger Reveille (as the latter told me after the war) that he was glad France had been defeated; the country had richly deserved it. But the Frenchman should not grieve over it. Borrowing from a German poet, only with a different empha sis, he wanted him to know, "*We* are on a ship of the dead."[13] When I asked my father at the time whether it had not been altogether thoughtless to send such a letter to France, he replied that he had given neither a sender's name nor a signature, and had posted it miles away in Lichterfelde. Roger had let him know through a third party that he had received the letter. And what, I asked again, if in a difficult situation—that is, under threat of torture—Roger had, after all, revealed the sender's identity to the Gestapo? At that my father said one would not get anywhere without taking risks, adding, with a smile, that danger had its charms, too.

Perhaps I had taken this and other similar remarks all too literally. At any rate it was about this time that I established a new record in "platform jumping." Gathering all one's courage, one jumped from the train as it was coming into the station and allowed oneself to be carried by the momentum the thirty steps past the little stationmaster's office and as close as possible to the stairs leading down to street level. But I soon got around to more reckless—in fact, foolish—ventures. At some point in autumn 1940 I began to scribble Hitler caricatures on fences, lampposts, and front doors. They consisted of an elongated circle, a line sloping a little to the right, and a hatched smudge: it was always Hitler's face. As far as I was aware only Wigbert

---

13 Spoken by Hagen in Hebbel's dramatization of the *Nibelungenlied*.—Trans.

Gans, who even joined me a few times, knew about it; later I heard that other schoolmates had also engaged in such foolhardy activities, some even with a sketch of a hammer and sickle dripping blood. It helped that recently classes lasted until dusk and were conducted in the morning or the afternoon on alternate weeks.

Our homeroom teacher, Dr. Appelt, was a ponderous man with a flat-featured face, who was permanently sweaty seldom entered the classroom without the party badge. The dark shadows under his eyes testified to the toil of the night hours in which he pored over the syllabus, without ever quite getting on top of it. At any rate, Wigbert Gans several times pointed out mistakes in his calculations in the application of the laws of physics, at which the class jeered and stamped their feet, while he ran to his lectern and handed out black marks and detentions by the half dozen. For reasons which I never understood but may have had to do with my father, he entertained an unconcealed dislike of me, to which I responded with all the impudence of my thirteen years. Usually, it was no more than the obstreperousness of an adolescent talking back—accompanied by the laughter of my classmates— that got me a black mark in the register. More serious, however, was the following piece of recklessness. One morning, quite by chance, I was in school a quarter of an hour before lessons began. Sitting around in the classroom and staring out at the dingy winter morning, I took out my pocketknife and without thinking carved the same Hitler caricature, which for some time I had been scribbling on walls and fences, on my desk.

Luckily, Gerd Donner was the first to come into the classroom after me. Taking one glance at the desk he hissed quietly, and with the instinct for survival of a boy from the back alleys of the East End of Berlin, "Get rid of that immediately!" Without waiting for my reaction, he took out his own pocketknife and began to remove small splinters of varnish from the surface of the desk. Meanwhile, the rest of the class arrived, the room filled up; some came up to the desk and in what was left could just about discern the outlines of the familiar caricature. In the commotion that arose, Gerd Donner threatened that anyone who reported anything would be in big trouble.

Dr. Appelt had barely entered the classroom when, to everyone's astonishment, one of the pupils rose to his feet and reported me "as duty required" and as he had learned as a leader in the Hitler Youth. When he had finished, the teacher came over to me, shaking his head in disgust, bent over to inspect the desk, was aghast at what he saw, shook his head once more, and finally told me to follow him to the rector after the lesson. There I was subjected to a brief interrogation and the next day questioned by a policeman called to the school for that specific purpose.

It was indeed, as my parents reproached me that evening, an unbelievably foolish thing to have done, and they rightly asked if I had not thought about the consequences the incident could have for our family. Some classmates also conspicuously withdrew from me. For the first time I had an inkling of what it meant to be excluded. Dr. Appelt clearly agreed with the disrepute into which I had fallen, and from then on he seemed to regard every moment of inattention and every disruption for which I was to blame as the action of a good-for-nothing, who was politically and humanly a bad egg. Soon I had an unbeatable lead over everyone else in my class when it came to black marks in the register and detentions, and when this unhappy course of events showed no sign of coming to an end, my "unfortunate father," as Dr. Weinhold put it to me, was summoned to the headmaster's office. Once again there was a stern-looking gentleman present, who evidently represented the school authority and immediately turned the proceedings into a kind of interrogation. I denied any kind of political motive, but admitted the damage to property and asked to be shown leniency, as I had been advised from various sides. After lengthy discussion—in the course of which I got to know my father's negotiating skills—it was agreed to refrain from the *consilium abeundi* (expulsion) that had originally been decided. But the condition was that I should voluntarily leave the school at the next possible date, Easter 1941; that is, in about three months. "It would be best if you took your other two sons away at the same time!" the gentleman from the education authority advised my father.

After the conference, which had taken place during the last school period of the day, my father embraced me, which was unusual for him, in front of all those present and left the room, tight-lipped, to go back to Karlshorst, while I returned to my class. Among the friends who stood by me were, of course, Wigbert Gans, Clemens Körner, and Gerd Donner. At the end of lessons, Gerd Donner was waiting for me outside in the corridor and, although

I would not be part of the class for much longer, he now frequently accompanied me on the half-hour walk to the station in what was an extremely cold winter. On the first day he had me tell him what happened in the headmaster's room, and concluded, "So, nevertheless, expelled!" and after a few more steps, "But lucky, too. You should be pleased!" From that time on I counted my relation with him as one of those belated friendships, which turn up in everyone's life now and then. Whatever we talked about we found those points of agreement that every friendship needs, and the differences that enliven and keep it going, whether the subject was football or film stars, books or radio detectors, friends or many a "beautiful Inge."

Inevitably, I've forgotten the content of almost all of our conversations. But one from just before Christmas 1941 has stuck in my mind, because in the course of it we interrupted our walk and, despite the cold, stopped on the dark bridge over the Spree. Snow was falling heavy and sticky from the wet cold sky, collecting on the railings and melting on the ground. The pedestrians who hurried past, muffled up and often carrying a Christmas tree under their arm, seemed shrunken. We shifted from one foot to the other. A couple of times one of the carts that had recently been pressed into service again came by, the horses slipping and kicking out with billowing clouds of breath.

What kept us there was a conversation about the ultimate questions of life and death. Gerd Donner said that— as an intelligent person—I surely couldn't believe everything that was said in church. He had nothing against

Father Lauen, our "snappy" religious education teacher, but the fairy tale about the Dear Lord with the curly beard, together with the Resurrection and the "immaculate conception"—he could only laugh at it. And he knew for sure that secretly I was laughing, too. Ice floes drifted past under the railings of the bridge as we talked with steaming breath. Finally, I replied that I even liked to believe what he described as a fairy tale. Perhaps it was all invented. But that just dressed things up for unsophisticated minds, and I was a little surprised to discover that he was among them. What faith, in essence, gave me, was the feeling of having a kind of second, dependable home and of being a match for everything. He would be wise to wait and see! Gerd Donner made a dismissive gesture with his hand and replied that some people needed something like that; he had not suspected I was one of them. At any rate he did all right without the "old beardy up there." And when, frozen through, we finally set off again, he said, "The people from my street, which you've never even seen, don't need the Dear Lord of the Catholics." They got the conviction to cope with the world not from the Dear Lord, but from their mother's milk; or else they were lost. When we parted at Silesian Station we had not moved one inch closer.

One Sunday at the beginning of February 1941, shortly after we had come back from church, two senior Hitler Youth officials entered the building, banging the street door and demanding to speak to my father. They had just found out—one of them shouted from the bottom of the stairs—that none of his three sons had joined either the junior Jungvolk or the Hitler Youth. There had to be an end to it. "Malingering!" barked the other. "Impertinence! How dare you!" Everybody had duties. "You, too!" the first one joined in again.

My father had, meanwhile, gone down to the pair. "Whoever you are," he responded, frowning in annoyance, "I have no intention of allowing you to come here, on a Sunday at that, with a lie. Because we have several times been pestered, likewise on a Sunday morning, by your lads. So you haven't just found out something." And getting ever louder, he finally roared at them, "You accuse me of malingering and are yourself cowards!" And after a few more rebukes he shouted from the second step over their army-style cropped heads, "And now, will you leave my house? Get out! This minute!" The pair seemed speechless at the tone my father dared to use, but before they could reply he drove them back, so to speak, through the entrance lobby and out the door. The commotion had initially startled the whole building, and several tenants had appeared on the stairs. At the sight of the uniforms, however, they quietly closed the doors to their apartments.

Hardly had the street door closed behind the two Hitler Youth leaders when my father raced up the stairs to calm my mother. She was standing in the door as if paralyzed and only said, "This time you've gone too far!" My father put his arm around her and admitted he had forgotten himself for a moment. But first the Nazis had stolen his profession and his income, now they were attacking his sons and Sunday itself. One had to show these people that there was a limit. "They know none," said my mother in an expressionless voice. It was all the more important, objected my father, to point it out to them. It wasn't he who had gone too far, but the Hitler rascals. It was virtually the definition of a Nazi that he was someone who always went too far.

To everyone's astonishment this incident had no consequences. Except that two days later Fengler, the block warden, called and warned my father in front of the whole family—we were just sitting at table—"Behave yourself! You're not alone in the world! Will you finally realize that? And, after all, membership in the Hitler Youth is the law!" My mother told my father to remain seated, and accompanied the hated block warden to the door. "My husband isn't usually like that," she said, making an effort to be friendly. "But on Sunday we go to church. We won't let anyone stop us doing that!"

At the supper table Fengler's visit brought us back to the incident again. My father was at once angry and amused: "National community—my goodness! I feel disgust, nothing else!" After the unbelievable things that had been imposed by law—the exclusion of all Jews from the liberal professions, even doctors and pharmacists, the termination of all telephone connections, and the "yellow star"—now, he said, the man in the street was taking a hand and thinking up ever new forms of harassment for the authorities.[14] Jews were no longer allowed to sit on

14 The author here refers to the restrictive legal measures introduced by the Nazis against Germany's Jewish citizens, including the order for all Jews to wear a visible yellow star on their clothing, marking them as social outsiders. After 1945 Germans were made to wear white armbands, for the same reason, in the Sudetenland, before deportation from Czechoslovakia.

park benches or to "pollute the good air of German forests by walking in them." They were no longer allowed to
subscribe to newspapers and magazines, and Dr. Meyer,
who had until recently ridden a Wanderer bicycle, had
had to hand it in, along with his typewriter; Jews were
also not allowed to keep pets such as dogs, cats, canar-
ies, or hamsters. When a Jewish friend of Hans Hausdorf wanted to buy flowers for the grave of his wife, who
had died recently, the sales assistant snapped at him that
flowers were a decoration of a German character. Jews
had no claim to them. He should get out. And Germans
themselves had to answer the question of the marriage
registrar, whether they were ready to pledge themselves
for life, not, as had been usual for generations, with a
simple "Yes," but with a "Yes, Heil Hitler!" What on
earth had become of the country?

At the end of March my brothers and I began our
farewell calls. With the help of a friend of my parents
it had been possible to place us in a Catholic boarding
school in Freiburg, whose pupils also took classes at one
of the city's two municipal Gymnasiums. I called on the
Gans family by Treptow Park and walked once with
Gerd Donner through his quarter behind Görlitz Station: shabby, dark streets, where big cakes of plaster had
fallen from the facades of the houses. Around us there
were yelling brats; handcarts with potatoes, chopped
wood, and other small goods were being hauled along;
bawling children leaned against the walls of some houses
as if they had been dumped there, and in one entry-
way boys were trying to drag a stubborn billy goat out

onto the pavement. I took my leave of the parents of my Karlshorst classmates and from Father Wittenbrink, who made me promise to write regularly. I called on Dr. Körner, the senior physician of Karlshorst Hospital, who was one of my parents' close friends and whose son had for a long time shared a desk with me, and also on Gerd Schülke and Ursel Hanschmann. Wolfgang thought it all very overdone and remarked, "What's the point of it all? We're not going to a penal colony! Or are we going into exile?" "In part, yes!" I replied. On the day before our departure I went to see Dr. Meyer.

When he opened the door of the apartment, he stood in front of me wearing, as always, the light suit with a brightly colored neckerchief, and this time he had a circular summer hat on as well. From the hallway came a smell of cabbage soup, poverty, and old age. As he greeted me a smile passed over his features, which could often appear frozen. He said no more than "Come in!" and went ahead of me into the library. There was already tea on the side table. Dr. Meyer had even got biscuits from somewhere. He asked how my parents were, my siblings and friends, then asked me to avoid political topics, and suggested I read him some of his favorite poems. While I was reading one he was already choosing the next: I still remember that I began with Goethe's "Welcome and Farewell," then his "I Think of You" and "The Sorcerer's Apprentice," followed by Schiller's "Nenia," and after that I read some verses by Heine, Lenau, and Chamisso. When I wanted to go on with Stefan George, Dr. Meyer abruptly asked me to stop; he was not in the right mood.[15] After a few sips of tea, he said it had probably not been a good idea for me to drop by. He was distracted and was asking himself countless things to which he had no answer.

I made a remark about the future, to which no one has an answer, but Dr. Meyer went on talking without paying attention to what I had said. The worst thing was that the great poets, from whom I had read something just now, bore some of the blame for his misfortune: Goethe and Schiller and all the rest . . . How often had he—when his wife was alive—considered emigrating and been close to making the decision to leave? But then trust in the culture of the Germans had always won out . . . A nation, they said, that had produced Goethe and Schiller and Lessing, Bach, Mozart, and so many others, would simply be incapable of barbarism. Griping at the Jews, prejudice, there had always been that, they thought. But not violent persecution. They wouldn't do anything to us . . . "Well!" he interrupted himself. "You know how mistaken we were . . ."

---

15 Born in Hungary, Nikolaus Lenau (1802–50) is best known for many lyrical poems that have been set to music; he tried to live in the United States (1832–33) but returned to Europe and an unhappy love relationship. He also wrote many political poems.

Born in France, Adelbert von Chamisso (1781–1838) circumnavigated the globe (1815–18); some of his poems were put to music by Robert Schumann. The best known of his stories is "Peter Schlemihl's Miraculous Tale."

Stefan George (1868–1933) tried to create a new idiom for German poetry in order to renew Germany spiritually; his uncompromisingly formalistic poetry and his powerful personality made him the center of an influential circle, the George Kreis, of intellectuals who would become prominent in a variety of fields later. Always peripatetic, George left Germany in 1933.

Then came one of many pauses. His wife—Dr. Meyer resumed his train of thought—had been cleverer than him. Unlike her, he had adopted the admired Germans' credulity and political naïveté. Men were just blockheads. But now it was too late to moan. We should stop lamenting! So, he said, with an audible change of register in his voice: he envied me. For example, because I could travel to any place I wanted; because the opera houses were open to me; and, above all, because reading *Buddenbrooks* was still before me. I should know that hardly anything in life was comparable to the pleasure of reading a book like that for the first time. We sipped awkwardly at our teacups. After a few minutes Dr. Meyer stood up determinedly and put his arm around my shoulders: "It's better you go now!" When we had come to the apartment door, I tried to think what I could say to him, but felt paralyzed and involuntarily remembered my father's words that at times like these one should avoid all pathos.

Back in Karlshorst I could already hear at the entrance from the street Frau Bicking singing in her wailing tremolo that she was going to dance into heaven with someone, where she (as she went on singing with hardly a break) would do like the swallows and build a nest with her dearest. But in a moment she was back to her favorite song, according to which everything happened long, long ago.[16] Frau Dölle, who so much liked to play

---

16 These are all allusions to well-known lyrics of popular songs called *Schlager* (hits).

the stool pigeon, asked me whether "Old Bicking's yowling could still be considered singing or whether it was
a nuisance already." Since she didn't expect an answer
from me, she said she would let the crazy old woman go
on warbling just one more time, adding, while pointing
at the ceiling several times with her broom: "But everything has to stop sometime!" And finally: "Soon, soon is
the time!," imitating old Bicking's yowling.

My parents were shocked by my report about the
visit to Dr. Meyer, and my mother interrupted me to
ask what could be done to help. When she insisted on
the support of my father's group of friends, he shook his
head vigorously: he had urged emigration after the boy-
cott of Jewish shops and businesses in April 1933, then
after the Nürnberg Laws of 1935, and again and again up
to Kristallnacht, when the halfway favorable point had
already passed.[17] But no one had wanted to listen to him.
Everyone had mentioned countless reasons for staying,
and he had even been accused of wanting, just like the
Nazis, to make Germany *Judenfrei*—free of Jews. After
he had calmed down, he nevertheless promised to do
whatever was possible to help his friend.

The following morning Albert Tinz dropped by. He
said a few words to my mother, then went into the living room where the piano was, sat on the stool, and, after
a mighty sequence of chords, led in to an improvised

---

17 Fest here refers to a series of laws, promulgated since 1933, aimed at systemati-
cally excluding Jews from public life in Germany. Some of the provisions could and
were actually also used against non-Jewish Germans regarded as politically unreliable, i.e., anti-Nazi, such as Fest's father.

andantino, which charmingly blended some melodies from my mother's favorite Schubert songs, from "Night and Dreams" to "The Carrier Pigeon." Then he played one of the early Beethoven sonatas, which was also one of my mother's favorite pieces, and after he had waited, eyes closed, for the last note to fade away, he said, "Once again, what I always say is don't drag things out, even when they are sentimental! Otherwise you just end up blowing at cinders. Without passion there's nothing! Not even a pianissimo! No music at all!" The small man with the artfully twirled-up hair rose and said that he had really had no great success here, except for me. Perhaps someday we would understand where all music began and ended. That would make him happy, and he wasn't giving up hope. After these words he shook his mane of hair and, as always, hurried out.

The last person to whom, together with my brothers, I said goodbye was old Katlewski. We came upon him beside the herb garden and, when he asked whether we were really leaving tonight, we answered as if with one voice, "Yes, at twelve past eight!" Since we were saying goodbye, he was, for once, going to be generous, he said, and tell a joke just like that, without the usual urging. "But as always, not a word to anyone . . . Well, how does it start? So there's one of these guys from People's Welfare[18] collecting money and he's shouting, 'Come

---

18 The People's Welfare was one of many organizations created by the National Socialists to distribute social and economic benefits as broadly as possible. Ironically, this makes them, after Bismarck's introduction of social welfare programs, major progenitors of the universal welfare network now enjoyed by the German population.

on, people! Everybody gives a dime! Everybody's got
that much, national comrades! Don't be shy! It can even
be a nickel! Come on! Do it now!' And as he's taking in
the money there's a man standing there with both hands
in his pockets who says calmly, 'Not givin' nothin!' And
when the guy from People's Welfare replies, 'What
d'you mean? Giving nothing! Come on!' the other says,
'Because I'm not a national comrade!' Says the one collecting money, 'That's crazy! Not a national comrade?
Have you ever heard the like of that?—And why, if I
may ask?' The one questioned grins and says, 'Why?
Because I'm a Jew!' For a moment the guy from People's
Welfare is quite dumbfounded. Then he says, 'A Jew
are you? A Jew—anyone can say that!' "

We laughed out loud, but Old Kat put his finger to
his lips and warned us once again: "Don't repeat it! You
remember! As always!" And at the very end he wanted
to tell us another "bommot," which was really fresh, just
from yesterday. "Hitler," an old Socialist friend had con-
fided in him, "is such a brazen liar that even the opposite
of what he says is untrue." Then he took his leave with
"Take care, lads! It was really good with you! With each
of you!" He turned on his heel and left.

At school the only teacher to whom I did not say
goodbye with some degree of courtesy was Dr. Appelt.
At the end of his last class, which he concluded with a
relieved reference to my departure, I walked about three
yards toward him and bowed very slightly, which was
supposed to be ironic, but ended up only as somewhat
stiff. At any rate, I did not give him my hand.

In the evening the family accompanied us to Anhalt Station. The train was already there. When our luggage had been stowed away and we were exchanging farewells on the platform, none of us had the feeling that a period of his life was over. My father called each of his sons in turn and walked with him along the platform to the end of the glass roof. He was a proper teacher, after all, said Winfried, and couldn't help it. We would get a few encouraging—or at worst admonishing—words. No schoolmaster misses such an opportunity. In fact, we were each sent on our way with a kind of rule of life. To me my father said that he often divided people into those who asked questions and those who answered them. The Nazis, for example, were the kind of people who always had the answer to every question. I should take care always to remain someone who asks questions.

A little later, with bursts of steam, and to the accompaniment of shouts and the waving of handkerchiefs, the train started to move off. The times—given the plunge in 1933, the uncertainties and countless worries—had made things difficult for my father, as for my mother. For us, however, they had been happy years, on the one hand because our parents had let us feel their fears as little as possible; on the other, I told myself later, probably because such fears, if they have anything like a happy ending, not only detract from life, but also make it more dense and complete.

SIX

·

Alien Worlds

When dawn broke we could make out the shadow line of the Black Forest through the compartment window, and later, as villages appeared and Freiburg came closer, Kaiserstuhl, caught by the early light.[1] While we tried to find out the names of the towns, valleys, and stretches of land that rushed past, Wolfgang, half of whose mind was still in Berlin, said he regretted that he would now never be able to take part in one of the "secret society meetings," as my father had recently promised. So he would just have to make do with the "noble and irresponsible Raskolnikov," whom he had almost finished reading about.

---

1 Kaiserstuhl is a group of volcanic hills northwest of Freiburg, whose slopes have been terraced for vineyards.—Trans.

Such ideas were very remote to me and I had only heard of Dostoevsky from my father, and recently from Wolfgang. In contrast to my brother I spent the largest part of the journey reading the plays of Friedrich Schiller, which, after the ballads and poems, were for me the great discovery of that spring. At the station in Freiburg my parents' friend was waiting, the one who had undertaken to pay the costs of our stay. In two taxis, for which we had to wait an endless length of time, we drove with cases and boxes to the boarding school in Adolf Hitler Strasse.

The front of the long building, several stories high, faced the street; I ascended the broad central staircase with mixed feelings. In an instant I grasped the strange world which opened up behind the heavy double doors. The nun who sat in the porter's room at the top of the flight of stairs, and gently and devotedly nodded three times at our arrival, already seemed to me to be pulled by strings, but when I whispered a remark about it to Wolfgang, he hissed back indignantly, "No silly jokes! It's only a bit provincial!" There was a strong smell of floor cleaner and polish in the quiet corridor leading to the rector's office. The rector, Dr. Hugo Hermann, at whose door we knocked, was an impressive figure: a clergyman with a sharply defined priest's face, tall, thin, and with a winning manner. Behind the lenses of his rimless spectacles one looked into narrow, somewhat slanting eye slits.

When we entered the room he was reading a book, but, hardly looking up, he continued reading. "I'm the boss here, that's what that means," I whispered to Winfried this time, who laughed out loud, causing Dr. Hermann to acknowledge us at least. He came over and talked to the person who had accompanied us, the conversation also touching on our parents, their political difficulties, and our characters. Only then did Dr. Hermann turn to us. From me he wanted to know—probably alluding to my near-expulsion from Leibniz Gymnasium—why I had such trouble with discipline, and I replied with the quick wit that was my Berlin inheritance, that it always depended on the person who was demanding it of me: my father had never complained. Smiling ironically, Dr. Hermann shook his head; it was evident that he regarded my response as uncustomary, even impertinent. Already at this first meeting it became clear that he was clever, sensitive, and, in a natural way, more than a match for me. But at the same time there was a noticeable tendency to inflexibility, which, with his clerical haughtiness and his ascetic energy, and despite all the attractive aspects, combined to form a rather disconcerting character.

Very evident—as we discovered soon after the introductory interview—was his keen if limited knowledge of human nature. In later years I was convinced that Dr. Hermann knew immediately what a disruptive effect we North Germans from the big city, which by his lights was profoundly heathen, must have on the calm course of his establishment.[2] Apart from that he grasped how altogether

2 Here Fest alludes to a number of German social and regional stereotypes which influenced his stay at the new boarding school. There is a firm cultural divide between the South and the North in Germany which reflects German history: the West and South, i.e., the regions that once formed part of the Roman Empire, have a longer cultural tradition, are predominantly Catholic, and often anti-Prussian; the North and East were civilized later, are often Protestant, and think of themselves as

subversive we appeared in his clerically saturated Black Forest world. "The Berliners," he soon called us, showing a lack of insight and setting us apart. "And no politics!" he warned us at the end of this initial encounter. "That can lead to difficulties for the whole institution!"

On the evening of the first day, which I largely spent with Wolfgang and Winfried looking at the charming little city from cathedral to St. Martin's Gate, Dr. Hermann called me over to him and the group of star pupils talking under one of the big leafy trees in the school playground. Not least, it was probably his intention to make amends in public for the morning. I was not the only person for whom understanding had to be shown—he, too, he said, had that right. He smiled in an effort to appear gentle, but the effect was artificial. Only a few weeks before, he had been in Berlin for the third time in his life, and again just for two days. He had felt very strange there, he went on in a spuriously lighthearted tone, evidently because he already found his half-apologetic introduction excessive. At any rate, in this monster of Berlin he had felt himself to be as far east as Brest-Litovsk or Minsk, where he, however, thank God, had never been. And the people there! An alien race that he found quite frightening! Then, as those present laughed, he adjusted his soutane with a hint of amused smugness in anticipation of my response. Without waiting for the obsequious

---

superior—because of recent Prussian domination of German history. Add to this the universal disdain of all Germans for loudmouthed Berliners, of which Joachim is successfully trying to be a prime exemplar, according to his own account.

laughter to stop, I cut in, saying that now I understood why Freiburg is the way it is! So close to Africa! Because wherever one walks or stands in the town, as we had done this afternoon, one's constantly "running into blacks."[3]

At a stroke Dr. Hermann's expression froze, and even today I relish the utter shock this remark caused among those standing there. The rector abruptly turned his back to me and, shaking his head, disappeared into the building through the nearest swing doors. "You can't talk to the rector like that," one of the pupils snapped at me. "Have you no manners?" I certainly did, I retorted, but only where there was mutual respect. And what did he have to say, I would like to know, about the rector's remark? Had that been acceptable? As I looked around the group, one after another walked off, and soon I was standing there alone, leaning against the brick wall. Wolfgang and Winfried came up. I explained the incident to them, and Wolfgang concluded: "So the start is a complete mess! It'll be hard for you to make it up. But don't worry. We'll stand by you, no matter how dumb or how right your behavior has been."

Despite all the criticism then and later of my "Berlin mouth," I never tried to distance myself from it. I was no doubt too indifferent to figures of authority and possibly influenced by my father's example. Apart from that, even just a few years later, I suspected that at that first meeting

3 A pun: "blacks" here stands both for black Africans and for priests in their black soutanes and others in holy orders. More generally, "black" in German denotes Catholic (in the same way as "red" does socialist or Communist).—Trans.

there had been an intention to hurt or offend in Dr. Hermann's rebukes. Only later did I hear from someone who knew him better that the rector had for some time reproached himself for his clumsiness, yet any other response had been impossible for him. Because, despite a "family history that demanded respect," he thought he recognized in us "Berliners" an aspect of that spirit of the times which he saw embodied above all in the Hitlerites he hated.

Even given greater understanding, I would not have been able to come to terms with the lifestyle of the boarding school. I missed the freedom of Berlin every single day. The division of the hours, with a bell rung for waking, praying, eating, silence, and so on throughout the day until it was time to sleep, the jostling in the refectory (as the dining room, following the monastic model, was called) and in the classrooms in front of the twenty or so desks with their tip-up seats, as in the bare, whitewashed dormitories: I had a deep dislike of all the lining up and falling in, as if it were a cadet school. *I have left Berlin, which everyone likes to insult,* I wrote in one of my first letters home, making an effort to be ironic, *and yet it's here that I have for the first time really got to know Prussian drill. I used to love it, now I hate it.* My father wrote back, as we later recalled, that I *shouldn't sound off like that.*

Nor did I find anything in common with my roommates. They were mostly sons of peasants or farmers from the Black Forest or the Upper Rhine, for whom the establishment was an opportunity to go to a Gymnasium. The majority were talented, ambitious, and astonishingly hardworking, but from a narrow village life incompatible with the Berlin world. Aloof and always a little irritated, as Wolfgang accused me of being, I listened to their conversations in an idiom which was hard to understand and radiated so much obtrusive sentimentality.[4] I longed for Berlin, for the area around Silesian Station, the platform jumping, and even the splendid disreputableness of Friedrichstrasse. Apart from that, it was the conversations at the garden table which I increasingly missed. And playing the piano. The places with the three or four piano teachers at our boarding school were taken long ago, and I achieved no more than to have my name put on one of the waiting lists. I could work out that there was a small chance for me in 1944, I was informed, when the sixth formers of that year left the boarding school; in the meantime there was only one place available with each of the elderly ladies who gave instruction in recorder and lute. After a few lessons with the lute teacher, who (as far as I remember) was called Fräulein von Neuenburg, or something like that, I decided, with great regret, to give up playing music.

I made contact with others and soon acquired new friends at the Gymnasium I attended. Even Dr. Brühler, the director—to whom we had to introduce ourselves before the beginning of the first school day—made a

---

4 The local boys speak Alamanian dialect, which, in this region, retains medieval words and grammatical constructions; this language has been spoken there since the third century A.D. and is used in all Alamanian regions, which include Baden-Württemberg and Bavarian Swabia in Germany, Vorarlberg in Austria, all of German-speaking Switzerland, and all of Alsace and portions of Lorraine.

cosmopolitan impression, and one involuntarily asked oneself what circumstances could have brought him to this place. In his light gray, double-breasted suit, often with a flower in his buttonhole, he appeared almost exaggeratedly elegant. Although only in his mid-fifties, he had white hair brushed severely back, which curled a little at the neck, and with it an apoplectically red face, which went with an old-school gentleman of his sort. In a high voice, demonstrating a charming self-confidence, he explained to us that it was his ambition as headmaster of the Friedrich Gymnasium to make it the best in Germany, and he very much stood by this aim, despite all the difficulties of the present time. He expected high standards and discipline to be taken for granted. But it was just as important that his pupils understood something of the humanist spirit, without which all learning degenerated into meaningless drill. And—as if he wanted to indicate that he had heard something at least about the reasons for our change of schools—he added that everything else was a matter of complete indifference to him. No doubt we had some catching up to do, as was inevitable because of the air raids on Berlin and the frequent cancellation of lessons. After one year he would decide whether the school wanted to keep us.

Yet catching up with the pupils of the various classes was not very hard for us. Other differences were more evident. Above all, in contrast to the obsession with getting through the curriculum at the Berlin school there was something scholarly about the Friedrich Gymnasium. In almost every field the knowledge we acquired

served simultaneously as material to make connections
visible and to test the attraction and difficulty of intelligent questioning—that is, to get to know methods, the
rudiments of which I had learned during the garden-
fence conversations. An example of that was provided by
our Greek teacher Dr. Breithaupt, a tall, hook-nosed man
who practiced his profession with enthusiastic earnestness. He had known old Dörpfeld, who had excavated
Troy, Pergamon, and other sites of ancient Greek culture.[5] On occasion, he brought into class a letter from the
scholar, which he held up with his fingertips like a relic
of the age of the Apostles, while with glowing eyes he
basked in the admiration he read from the faces in front
of him. Then he quoted some of the issues raised in the
letter, which concerned Dörpfeld at the time, and asked
to hear our responses. He also knew Karl Reinhardt and
other great names in the scholarship of antiquity,[6] names
which he pronounced with whispered awe, as soon as
he acquainted us with the various scholarly opinions of
Minoan or Spartan culture, the route of the wanderings
of Odysseus, or the dispute about the applicability of
Plato's ideas of the state.

A further difference was that the political views of
the teachers were expressed much more frankly than in
Berlin. That was not only due to traditional Baden lib-
eralism, but also to the self-confident Catholicism of

---

5 Wilhelm Dörpfeld (1853–1940) was famous as a pioneer of archaeological method
and for his excavations.—Trans.

6 Karl Reinhardt (1886–1958) was an influential scholar of ancient Greek philosophy and literature.—Trans.

the region. Our natural history teacher openly made
fun of "Aryan physics." In the English class, Dr. Brühler (who would later become a member of the Deutsche
Partei in the Bundestag) imitated the actor Otto Gebühr
in the *Fridericus* films about Frederick the Great, and,
by simply transposing individual sentences into English, exposed the hollow pathos of these performances.
After viewing one of the great king's military defeats he
would sigh in English, rolling his eyes, "I am so lonely,"
or, blowing up his cheeks, he would say, "But now I am
going to victory! Who would hinder me? Me the one
and only Frederick—oh no, Otto Gebühr!" In religious
instruction, following Bishop von Galen's pastoral letter,
the "euthanasia murders" were discussed in plain terms.[7]
These were things which were thought of by many of our
teachers in Berlin, but hardly spoken out loud.

Only the gym teacher, a man with exaggerated mus-
cles and a low hairline, and even more Dr. Malthan, who
taught German and history, were considered supporters
of the regime. Yet whereas the former did so in a pig-
headed, pompous way which transformed every chin-up
and every improvement in the high jump into a contribution to the national physical training program, the other
embodied the type of intellectual who had absorbed all
the measures of the state into a system of cynical justifications exemplifying the idea of power. Tall, with

---

7 Cardinal Clemens August, Count von Galen (1878–1946), publicly opposed
the Nazis' racial policies, especially their attempts to euthanize severely disabled
children and adults. His protest and that of others helped stop these extermination
programs.

thinning hair and a slight squint, he held forth on Lessing's Philotas, on the German emperors and Prussia's Frederick, Kleist and Napoleon, Görres and Metternich, and so on to the greater German struggle for freedom—heroism and sacrifice included. He liked to describe the pupils who didn't measure up to his standards as "poor souls," before entering a five in his notebook and jeering, "Don't make such a miserable face!"[8] On the red-letter days of the National Socialist calendar one sometimes saw him in the light brown uniform of a political officer. He walked along the corridors with small, fast steps and, because he held his arms stiffly by his side, looked strangely wooden as he did so.

However, Dr. Malthan was very far from a comic figure. He was feared by all because of his scholarly and ideological demands; both our religious instruction teacher and older schoolmates repeatedly warned us about him. One day, as if I had to put his dangerousness to the test, while he was talking about the meaning of the Russian campaign as taking possession of a living space promised to the Germans since ancient times, I asked him a skeptical question. But instead of the anticipated thunderous outburst with which he usually silenced anyone and everyone—often with the despairing but practiced-sounding exclamation "What is that supposed to mean? What on earth?"—Dr. Malthan was merely dismissive in a friendly way, and gave me as an

---

8 The German grading system at that time went from one (the highest grade) to five (the lowest). A five still equals a failing grade in the American system today.

assignment an essay on "The Economic Importance of the Donets Basin for the Reich." "When you know that," he added, "you will understand once and for all how necessary living space in the east is for us."

Perhaps it was simply the thoughtless folly that had already got me into trouble in Berlin, perhaps also an attempt to make the subject a little more interesting for me: at any rate, I wrote the essay, which carefully noted all productive raw material deposits and the industrial capacity as well as the agricultural acreage of the huge area in a single, tightly structured sentence of about four pages. I was called upon by Dr. Malthan to read out my essay, so I tried to make the text clear and put in a period or a semicolon, where on the page there was only another comma. When I had finished he eyed the class suspiciously. When nobody stirred, he said tersely, "Fine!" and even managed some plain praise: "You are well able to give a talk! Perhaps at some point in future you will be called on to speak publicly in school." In any case, he would inform the rector's office about me.

My refuge from the irksome features of the boarding school remained Friedrich Schiller.[9] I had taken the volume with the early plays with me to Freiburg, and during the journey had read *The Robbers*, and then the beginning of *Intrigue and Love*. But the absence

---

9 Not only was Schiller at the center of German culture for educated Germans at that time, his youthful enthusiasm for rebellion in his early plays and his heroic grandeur of language and sentiment have endeared him to generations of schoolboys dreaming to be heroes. Moreover, he also looks the part himself in all his portraits and busts.

of peace and quiet in the compartment—the constant succession of passengers and the conversation starting up anew each time about the little turns of events in their lives thanks to the intervention of a greater fate—hindered my reading. As a result, I started from the beginning again after my arrival in Freiburg, most often in the evening under the blankets in the dormitory, when everything was silent.

It was the elevated tone and the beautiful exaltation that gripped me from the very first line, as it had during the journey. Against all the dark formulations which Schiller often granted his base and vicious characters, at the end bright light or at least its first rays irresistibly forced its way onto the stage. Even today I recall some passages with a feeling of emotion—of happiness and enchantment—such as otherwise only music is capable of arousing. It's not the almost proverbial lines—with which in those days practically everyone was still familiar—that produce this effect. But the words with which Thekla—who (to her mother's dismay) has fallen in love with Max Piccolomini (in the drama *Wallenstein*)—explains to a friend why she is late, I find unforgettable, because they sum up the hopeless conflict of emotions in only two lines: "My mother wept so again, I see her suffer / and cannot alter my own feeling of happiness." Or the outburst of old Miller (in *Intrigue and Love*), with his constantly repeated court toady's phrase of mocking subservience, "At your service!" And, of course, Wallenstein's monologue and those passages which stay in the mind because of Schiller's laconic brevity—most famously perhaps the conclusion of *The Robbers*. Or Lady Milford's unaffected but all the more overwhelming retort to Ferdinand's disparaging torrent of words (again in *Intrigue and Love*): "I did not deserve that, Major!" And so very much more.

And then the pictures of the writer in which (as I thought at the time) he appeared both noble and at ease; and his idea of freedom or his psychological astuteness, which we—as Wolfgang (always one step ahead in his education) explained to me—involuntarily translated into political terms. Who, he said, does not think of the "fat fraud Göring" when he hears the line about the "apes of God"? Or of a gangster figure like Goebbels when the talk is of the "lodgings by the gallows"? And, finally, of the lot of them when the poet talks of the spectacle of strength, which is only despair? Where had Wolfgang read that? I exclaimed, half in annoyance that he already knew that, too. How did he find the quotations with which he was always ahead of me?

At any rate there is a skepticism of human nature in Schiller that also runs through almost all of his plays. The Germans tend to think of him as a somewhat naive and pathos-ridden advocate of freedom; they think of Beethoven's Ninth Symphony and the embrace of the world in the final choral movement. They think about the limits to the power of tyrants, against whom mankind will reach up into the sky to pull down man's "eternal rights," which "are affixed up there as are the stars themselves." Yet I soon recognized that Schiller was politically much less naive than the nation as a whole.

Certainly, he could praise the dear Lord above the starry canopy, and write the village idyll of the "The Song of the Bell"—but also an essay like the one "On Naive and Sentimental Poetry," which has hardly an equal in German for its acute perception.

I sensed at least that on the whole, in the more general texts—that is, the poems—Schiller held on firmly to his optimism about mankind. In the plays, on the other hand, which are closer to reality—in *Intrigue and Love,* in *Fiesco,* or even in *The Maid of Orleans*—the dark hostile powers retain the upper hand. *Wallenstein* is a broadly conceived train of base intrigues and, as I read many years later, Hegel discovered an "abyss of nihilism" in his fellow Swabian: a vast world of treachery, deceit, and broken oaths, of dirty tricks, spite, and cynicism. Schiller has Franz Moor (in *The Robbers*) exclaim that man emerged from the mire, waded through the mire for a while, and created a mire, before fermenting in the mire again: as an image of man it could hardly be more pessimistic.

I read these works throughout the autumn and into the early winter of the Russian campaign, so that for me the name "Freiburg" is always associated with Schiller in an absurdly contrasting fashion to the ice storms and blizzards outside Moscow. In between I read whatever came to hand. As a mark of respect to my father I borrowed Jacob Burckhardt's *The Civilization of the Renaissance in Italy* from his library; it greatly impressed me and stimulated further reading about the Borgias, the Sforzas, and the Malatestas, about Federico da Montefeltro,

Michelangelo, and countless others.[10] It was an escape. At the same time, in a muddled alternation I read Rilke, who for a while supplanted everything else; at the time I could recite by heart the wondrous language of *The Lay of the Love and Death of Cornet Christoph Rilke.*

At school it continued to be the *Odyssey* that took the place of this "leisure reading," as my brothers mocked, but also Virgil and Horace. Even the unloved mathematical exercises were for a while coveted material, but once or twice a week I spent the afternoons with the class in Dreisam Stadium just outside the city. As before in Berlin, Winfried excelled at the short distances and several times ran the four hundred meters in under a minute, which I never managed. And to my own astonishment I discovered a talent for the high jump, at which I got to 1.67 meters, whereas Wolfgang, averse to physical education, as it was called, frequently dodged it and showed an admirable degree of imagination in inventing ever new excuses. Our feeling of solidarity proved itself against our "penal colony," even if it was no longer "us against the world." From time to time we went on our "small town walks," climbed to the top of the cathedral spire—from which on clear days one could see as far as Alsace and the Vosges—and made off for longer than permitted to the Castle Hill or to Günterstal on the southern outskirts of the town, in

---

10 Fest here lists some of the major political and artistic figures of the Italian Renaissance, a period to which he was always drawn; this subject and Italy will continue to exert a major pull throughout his life.

order to spend a couple of hours by ourselves or with a slowly growing circle of friends.

In late autumn I read Schiller's *History of the Thirty Years' War*, as well as, in one go, his *History of the Revolt of the United Netherlands*. Unlike Goethe, Schiller was a kind of "cultural hero" of the Germans, and Christian Daniel Rauch's statue portrayed him as an idealized youth in whom the nation liked to recognize itself. After the first attempts at rapprochement between the two, which ended in ill-humor, Schiller concluded that Goethe "generously declares his own existence, but only like a god, without giving of himself." Mankind should not allow someone like him to emerge among them, he added, in a sentence which was a mixture of awe, admiration, and, admittedly, jealousy.

But then suddenly Schiller wrote (as I discovered somewhere in the small print) the admiring letter to Goethe with—as I judged in my own preference for the former—an utterly mistaken sentence: "You have a kingdom to rule, I have only a rather numerous family of concepts." I was then completely convinced that rather the opposite was true: Schiller was the regent of the poetic kingdom, while Goethe stood at the head of a large family, but because of countless half-finished life projects, one that included a considerable number of bastards. And to me Schiller possessed a tone, like that of Heinrich von Kleist in *Prinz Friedrich von Homburg*, which Goethe maybe only came close to in the early poems with their warm natural sound and wholeness: the harmony of an ever-greater idea with impulsive emotion and incomparable beauty of expression. Initially, when the Schiller fever broke out in me again after a few weeks, I had a bad conscience, because I found the *Cornet* and also some of the Rilke poems merely elegant. They were no doubt more than that and even today I am grateful for the various circumstances that blessed me, if even for quite a short time, with a "Rilke fever," which I never quite got over.

At the beginning of the long holidays we traveled to Berlin. Our stay began with a kind of horror story. Late in the evening, two days after our arrival, there was a sudden shout of "Fire!" from several quarters. Fire engines shot up the streets with screeching tires and all around sirens began to wail, even though there had been no air-raid warning. A fire had broken out in Junker Jörg Strasse, a few houses away, and within a short time the flames had taken hold of the whole building. When we came to the scene, having jumped out of bed as fast as we could, the roof truss was just crashing through the four stories of the house, and the crowd of onlookers standing there, open-mouthed, let out a gurgling groan. At that moment, as if from nowhere, an elderly couple appeared at a window, looking for something to hold on to, but finding nothing; after agitated shouting from the crowd, they jumped, hand in hand, into a safety sheet held out below. Weeping, their feet shuffling, they were led away by first-aid men. Wolfgang, never short of an ironic remark, called out at the circle of onlookers illuminated by the flames: "Why doesn't anybody shout 'Lights out!'? And where's the air-raid warden, dammit?!" A

passerby beside me said, "Brat! He shouldn't be allowed
to say that!"

We remained until, despite every effort, the building
had burned down almost to the foundations, and we left
only after several summonses from my father. "Come
on home!" he said. "You'll have plenty of opportunities
to see something like it." When Winfried asked what
that was supposed to mean, he replied, "That was just
a prelude." A little later, back in our apartment, he took
us boys aside and said, "That wasn't an air raid. So far
we've been spared that. But at some point they'll come to
Karlshorst, too. That was a portent. Perhaps a guardian
spirit wants to tell us, we should get used to it." When
my mother heard that, she stood up and left the room. At
the door she said, more to herself, "If only there weren't
these dreadful politics! They simply destroy everything!" And when Wolfgang followed her, she remarked
to him that father was only capable of thinking in apocalyptic terms now. "Please tell him, he should at least keep
it to himself."

In order to leave time for some visits, we did not
travel to Walken Farm until three days later. As usual,
Uncle Berthold was waiting at the railway station with
the horse and carriage, but this time we interrupted the
ride in Schwiebus to see relatives. Among them was the
"other Franziska" (as we called her in memory of our
maid) Aunt Cilli, and other relations on my father's side.
After that we drove, as usual, over bumpy village streets
and deep sandy tracks to the farm at Packlitzsee. This
time I regretted from the day we arrived that my parents

left us behind, as always, after a brief stay. Because in Freiburg I had discovered that, more than anything else, I missed someone who was sympathetically prepared to explain, reply, and contradict. For a broadminded response to even naive or apparently far-fetched questions there was no substitute for my father, and only now did I become aware of the lack. Wolfgang, annoyingly smart as ever, remarked, "You can't always have clever people around you." He also added, unnecessarily, as I thought, "You've left father's apron strings behind—or, if you prefer, second supper. Get used to it!"

Back in Freiburg there was an unpleasant surprise in store for us. On the Wednesday—the first so-called *Heimabend,* or home evening, as it was called, after the beginning of the semester—the deputy rector of the boarding school discovered us in the lectern corner of one of the study rooms, where up to then we had passed the Hitler Youth sessions talking quietly or reading.[11] With every sign of dismay he established that we were not complying with a "legal obligation," and he appeared even more astonished when he heard that we were not even—nor had we ever been—members of the Hitler Youth. He accused us of "irresponsible behavior" and so of endangering "the existence of the whole institution." That same evening "the Berliners" were summoned to Dr. Hermann, and at the end of the week a

---

11 *Heimabend* (home evening) was the Nazi term, borrowed from the Youth Movement of the 1920s, for compulsory gatherings of the Hitler Youth for a combination of indoctrination, sports, and singing.

youth leader of about the same age as me turned up and handed us our membership books for the Compulsory Hitler Youth, with the words that no "decent German lad" could be expected to do service in a unit with us.[12] "So no need to worry!" he exclaimed. "You'll be with people like yourselves! But wrap up warm," he tried to joke. "We make the dandies go barefoot through hell!"

Like Wolfgang and Winfried I wasn't unhappy in the Compulsory Hitler Youth. While the "decent lads" in the basement of the Friedrich Gymnasium were singing "From gray city walls . . ." or "The bells rang out from Bernward's tower . . ."—and in between listened reverently to the beating of a drum, a so-called *Landsknechtstrommel* which punctuated not only the addresses given and the songs, but also the heroic passages of the war stories that were read out—we had to march around in a circle in the school playground in wind and rain, crawl on our stomachs, or hop over the terrain in a squatting position holding a spade or a branch in our outstretched hand.[13]

In our group there were, without exception, likable, rebellious boys who undauntedly stood by each other, wore their hair long on top, and described the "swing

---

12 Membership in the Hitler Youth proper was by application and selection; the so-called Compulsory Hitler Youth was for those not taken or who had not applied. But every German boy was expected to be exposed to the organization at some point, just as the *Reichsarbeitsdienst* (Reich Labor Service) and military service were expected of all males over eighteen.

13 The drums were replicas of the large drums used by the mercenaries of the fifteenth and sixteenth centuries; the Hitler Youth fostered something of a cult of the *Landsknecht*, German mercenaries who fought all over Europe and sacked Rome in 1527.

sessions" that they organized in parents' homes as
"house music evenings," in order (as they joked) to carry
the Führer's claim to cultural standards into the world in
their own way. Himmler had recently threatened to put
the "Swing Youth"[14] into concentration camps, but he
just didn't know what "German" meant, one explained
to me. After two hours of "messing around," as we called
the mindless exercises in the dirt of the schoolyard, we
waited for the Hitler Youth leaders, and ostentatiously
demonstrated that we were in the best of moods; each
time two of our boys were told to have a joke ready, to
which the rest of us standing around had to respond with
a roar of laughter. In contrast to the boarding school or
the school class, no one here took exception to the usually
silly adolescent jokes from Berlin, which Wolfgang and I
contributed. But no matter how feeble the punch lines,
when the Hitler Youth leaders approached we laughed
uproariously, and enjoyed their surprised annoyance as
they walked past.

At Christmas we were home in Berlin again. After the
initial exchange of family news there were long evenings
under the tasseled chandelier with endless stories from
the neighborhood. Separate suppers had meanwhile been
done away with and my two sisters were allowed to be present until their bedtime. We heard the latest gossip about
Hausdorf, about the Goderskis, about old Katlewski,
who seemed to have faded away since we left, as well as

---

14 This term refers to those rebellious youth groups and individuals who preferred
jazz and other modern music to the marching and hiking songs of the Hitler Youth.

about the Schönborns; and my father complained that despite repeated invitations Dr. Meyer didn't come to see them anymore. Via friends the Rosenthals had passed on news that they had reached England poor but more or less safely—alive, at least—and they intended to move on to the United States. "As far away as possible from this terrible Europe!" Herr Rosenthal had said.

Later my father got around to Sally Jallowitz. Recently, after nightfall, they had together buried two suitcases with silver, jewelry, and fine cloth under the garden shed. The ground had been frozen solid, so it had been hard work. It wasn't everything, Jallowitz had announced, and he didn't have a wife yet, either. Then he said that he would leave Berlin if he had to, but just for a couple of weeks, and would return on the first train as soon as this Nazi madness was over. And he would return in a first-class compartment, he added, on "thick leather upholstery," a good wine in front of him and a cigar in his mouth. "And peace at last!" he concluded. "And nice people everywhere. Everything that dominates today will then be far in the past. I can hardly wait!" He had given my father cloth for a suit—"for good services," he said, "dark blue pinstripe, vest included." And at the end: "You can wear this stuff in the Hotel Esplanade when we celebrate the end of the war, you and I."

Dr. Goldschmidt, too, had turned up one day, my father went on. He, however, came with only a small bag, which (again after nightfall) they had buried about three feet deep under the table tennis table. He had acquired only valuable objects, Dr. Goldschmidt had said, but ones that didn't take up much room. During his explanations, which gave my father the impression of being a final "testament story," he kept twisting his smoothly combed-back hair, so that by the end his large head looked quite ravaged. With all that they had lost all sense of time and Dr. Goldschmidt had to spend the night in our apartment, because he was not allowed to be on the street after the curfew hour for Jews; he was now worried that one of the fellow occupants of his house might have noticed his absence and, so as not to make himself culpable, reported it.[15] To the delight of both my mother and father Dr. Gans had been in Karlshorst again recently, very downcast, because even in his Russian adventure Hitler appeared to be favored by fortune. He at any rate was not ready to say that the obviously failing winter offensive was a turning point in the war. And so on, through the whole familiar *tour des personnages*, as my father put it.

For Christmas my father had come up with a little atonement. Among my presents was Ernst Jünger's *On the Marble Cliffs*, which had been published a couple of years before.[16] My father said that while it wasn't *Bud-*

15   In other words, Dr. Goldschmidt was confined in a "Jews' house" with other Jews, effectively as a prelude to deportation, hence the desire to bury valuables. Fest doesn't say so, but at this time, under Nazi decrees, both Dr. Goldschmidt and Fest senior were risking punishment, the former for spending the night away from the house, the latter for putting up a Jew for the night.—Trans.

16   Ernst Jünger (1895–1998), German novelist, memoirist, and highly decorated soldier in World War I. His early novels celebrated a so-called heroic nihilism, while his later work turned more toward the creation of a new man and an individualistic humanism. *On the Marble Cliffs* (1939) was read by some as a covert critique of the Nazi regime, while many other critics thought he helped prepare the intellectual ground for militarism and fascism in Germany.

denbrooks or *The Magic Mountain*, it wasn't a book about sea power, either. Even if it was a novel, it was one with "a great deal of hidden reality"; the empty space between the lines was what one really had to read, it was there that one discovered things one knew. He hoped it would please me. This time it was I who gave the hint of an embrace.

Naturally, I went to see Father Wittenbrink shortly after my arrival. He invited me to his home on one of the days between Christmas and New Year's to listen to music. One day then turned into three. I told him about my aversion to the boarding-school system, the narrow-minded "barracks world" made no more bearable by its Catholicism, and he replied, probably not without reason, that with my sensitivity to discipline I was only making life difficult for myself. Instead of complaining about being unable to find friends, I should think of steps that would make friendship possible in the first place.

I quickly changed the subject and, since we were sitting in front of the gramophone and piles of records, I steered the conversation to Mozart. I had recently read a remark by Leopold Mozart, who said that he had never met anyone, including Haydn, who had not described his "wondrous son" as being "beyond comprehension." Surprisingly, Wittenbrink did not stick to Mozart, but soon moved on to Rossini and talked enthusiastically about the unique structure of the latter's ensemble scenes, which, as he roughly explained, created towering and enchanting palaces of music by combining crescendo and accelerando. The conclusions to the acts, as in *The*

Barber of Seville, had always taken his breath away, he said, and he played me one of his new club records with passages from *La Cenerentola*. But, he added, as if suddenly returning to the world, if after all the tumultuous joy one explores the halls of these musical palaces more carefully, then for all their grandiose scale they are curiously empty: the most marvelous earthly pleasure in the middle of nothingness. The Department of Spirituality, Consolation, and Profundity was to be found next door, with the German composers.

Until then, of Rossini's works I had known only *The Barber of Seville* from the performance to which Aunt Dolly had taken me, and I had hardly anything to say about it. In the meantime, Wittenbrink had moved on to Beethoven. Goethe had remarked that there is no dying in comedies, their aim is always love, marriage, and happiness. But the great exception was Beethoven's *Fidelio*. For all the jubilation of the union at the end, there was nothing comic about this opera; here, someone whose head is full of the Enlightenment's trust in the world believes that all suffering and oppression end in pure bliss. That, of course, is not the way things are. Deliverance is the rarest thing in the world. It didn't even happen in dreams. Not in Father Wittenbrink's, at any rate. One only had to look around! Then he was on to politics, the war, and the countless horrors everywhere.

For the return journey to Freiburg I had taken Jacob Burckhardt's *The Cicerone*, from whose chapters I tried to put together a necessarily inadequate picture of the arts in Italy. Later I leafed through *The Greeks and Greek*

Father Johannes Wittenbrink, a neighbor and friend
of the family, in a photo taken in the 1950s

Civilization, but my fellow travelers were so bothersome
that from time to time I dozed, apathetically. "All Berlin is in flight," whispered Wolfgang with a glance at
the crowded corridor and the piled-up luggage racks.
"That business in the winter before Moscow seems to
have shown everyone what difficulties we're in." Then,

seemingly unaffected by the commotion, he went on reading Dostoevsky.

Around this time, I decided on my future profession. In Greek class Dr. Breitscheid was reading out a poem written in a classical style. Its title, as far as I remember, was "The Tears of Nausicaä" or something like it. The author's name was Eckart Peterich, added our teacher, and the poem described a maiden gazing after a longed-for or vanished happiness. When I asked what kind of poet Peterich was, Dr. Breitscheid talked about Peterich's publications, his origin in a German-Italian family of scholars in Florence, and his marriage into a wealthy patrician family, so that he was able to live in aristocratic circumstances. All of these factors permitted him to lead a life as—yes, as what (he said, looking for the right word), well, let's say, as an independent scholar.[17] The term, mentioned in passing, was like an inspiration to me: Florence, the wealthy lifestyle, and the propertied patrician wife included, of course. Apart from that my second thought was that as an "independent scholar" I would evade, as my father put it, the wretched impertinences of the Nazis, and so freely dispose of myself and the objects of my interest, as no university teacher far and wide was able to do. My preferences were anyway all for the remoter past, whether Athens or Florence. As my

---

17 Private scholar or *Privatgelehrter* was the term for scholars, normally financially independent, who devoted themselves to the study of some topic in the humanities, less often the natural sciences. Their contributions ranged from the amateurishly negligible to the academically highly significant, as the example of Heinrich Schliemann (1822–90) shows. His excavation of "Troy" essentially founded modern archaeology.

mother often reminded me with amusement years later, I wrote to my parents on November 22, 1941, in a flush of clever Dick excitement: *I have a profession.*

In a lifetime one probably never again reads as one does between the ages of fifteen and twenty-five. The feeling was intensified by the circumstances of the war, which ate into our minds and made us fear we might miss one of the important works. This fear was even more marked when it came to music. Whenever I played with the crystal radio set which Wigbert Gans had given me on my last Berlin visit, I heard through all of the abrupt whistling and intermittent interruptions a basso continuo, which told me that this very performance of Beethoven's Fourth Piano Concerto with Edwin Fischer or that Haydn symphony conducted by Eugen Jochum might be the only or indeed the last chance to become familiar with these works.

The feeling was so powerful that I passed hours turning the dial of the set without picking up more than a few distorted bars of a never-to-be-identified piece of music or spent my time over books of which in less threatening times I would have read at most a couple of dozen pages. Since I read mostly after lights out under the blanket in the bright cone of a pocket lamp, I had for the time being to do without Dostoevsky's *Crime and Punishment* and *The Idiot*, which Wolfgang had brought from Berlin. Both were too heavy and bulky. More for lack of anything else I then turned to Robert Graves's great book *I, Claudius*, and after so many detours at last once again read a book that not only had one of my favorite themes as its subject, but was also a work of literary stature, which combined linguistic sparkle, excitement, and instruction.

My problems with the boarding-school regulations continued throughout the first year, and forever led to ever new, sometimes absurdly difficult situations. I never found out how my two brothers coped with it— and Wolfgang even seemed to take liberties without suffering any consequences. He was soon giving talks to the top three classes on "Goethe's *Faust* in the Light of Modern Experience," as I remember one title, as well as "The Romanticism of Sturm und Drang" and "The Battle of Tagliacozzo in 1268," where the power of the Hohenstaufen imperial dynasty came to an end. Once, when Dr. Hermann tried to turn Wolfgang against me with remarks of feigned concern for me, boarding-school rumor had it that he had refused to listen, and had expressed himself in his "impertinent Berlin accent." He wouldn't tell me anything more. "It was nothing!" was all he said. "There's been worse!"

During the winter I went to the theater several times, but not until spring did I get to the opera. On the program was Wagner's *Die Meistersinger von Nürnberg* under Bruno Vondenhoff, who conducted the municipal orchestra. The production conveyed to me the engaging and often rousing side of Wagner. At the same time, stimulated by conversations and reflection, I discovered in it—in addition to medievalizing Old Nürnberg romanticism—a lot of Neuschwanstein and pretentious, pasteboard scenery. Nevertheless, what was, on the whole, a strong impression was blurred by my return to the boarding school. Since, out of some crazy adolescent boy's pride, I didn't want to request special permission to be out late, I had asked Winfried to arrange my bed for the usually cursory evening inspection, so that it looked as if it was occupied. The greater difficulty was climbing over the high metal fence around the school and then getting past the porter's lodge. But everything went without a hitch, so that soon after, at the invitation of a grammar-school friend, I undertook my second opera excursion.

The friend's name was Willibald and his father was a respected publisher in Freiburg; the latter had suddenly and unexpectedly been prevented from going to the opera that evening. I would most like to have seen one of the Mozart operas I knew, but the performance was

Last photograph of the family together before the three sons left for the boarding school in Freiburg in 1941. Back row from left: Winfried, Hannih, Wolfgang, the author; front row: their mother Elisabeth, Christa, and their father

Beethoven's *Fidelio.* When, shortly beforehand, Father Wittenbrink called me by chance to answer one of the "interrogatory letters" with which I tried to continue our Berlin conversations, he was as if electrified by the news of my opera invitation. *"Fidelio!"* he exclaimed, and there followed a jumble of words. He talked about parts, climaxes, the finale, and in between always something like, "The conclusion: pay attention to it! That's when the signal comes!" Then he lapsed once more into confused enthusiasm until I understood nothing more of the story. After a question which, though esoteric, seemed quite comprehensible amid his flood of words, he urged me to read the libretto.

I found it quite an effort to read the text and I told my friend that it was a shame Schiller hadn't written the libretto to *Fidelio,* but (as I had read) an unknown Frenchman and somebody else. On the evening before the performance, Wittenbrink called again and urged me, even if this time in a more controlled voice, "Watch out for the trumpet! That's what I wanted to tell you. That's the signal! The trumpet is everything!" And so on, for a while, till at the end, throwing all political caution to the winds, he added, "The belief in the trumpet signal, one must never lose that, not even today!"[18]

---

18 In Beethoven's opera, the trumpet signal in question heralds the arrival of the Prime Minister who will free the prisoners, including Fidelio, and punish the evil governor of the prison, Pizarro. Fest and his friends read this as an analogy to their situation, with Hitler in the role of the jailer. It is not clear who the outside force is supposed to be that will rescue Germany from Hitler, or who will sound the clarion call. Schiller's "Ode to Joy" in Beethoven's Ninth Symphony and *Fidelio* are seen as symbolic exaltations of freedom.

It was then noticeably not Schiller, but indeed "an unknown Frenchman," whose words began the performance. After the overture I did my best to adopt the expression of interested boredom which I saw on the faces of everyone sitting in the semidarkness of the orchestra seats. But with the appearance of the prisoners, the dungeon, and the entry of the prison warder accompanied by Leonore and the Commandant, the scene, in my understanding at the time, visibly grew in stature and was soon overwhelming. I can still hear the singer of the Leonore part as she stood in the way of Pizarro, who was brandishing a dagger, and with a shrill "First kill his wife!" drew a pistol. And then in the shocked silence it really did come from far off: the trumpet signal. One hears and never forgets something like that, or one has never, in any sense ever heard it in the first place.

That more or less was the impression made on me. Of course, the opera's power, apart from the truly overwhelming music of Beethoven, had to do with the political circumstances which dominated all our thoughts and feelings. At the beginning of the year news had come that one of Uncle Berthold's sons had frozen to death in the Russian snow. Now we learned that his other son had also been killed. Under the impact of such events, it occurred to me that the trumpet scene with "Our gracious majesty's will and pleasure," with the joy of liberation and the jubilation of reunion at the end, would never again be so well understood as by us in the Hitler years. Because where has that ever happened—at a mere trumpet signal the prison gates spring open, those sentenced to death are freed and the oppressors led away? Even during the applause at the end, I assured my friend Willibald that really everyone must see it. Yet, as they left, the audience talked about how strained top notes of the Florestan sounded of late, about the latest news from the front, and, a moment later, again that Marzelline's voice was not quite mature. On the other hand, I said it had all been a fairy tale to me, a German fairy tale at that, and really it was very foolhardy of the regime to permit performances of *Fidelio*. At the boarding school Willibald helped me over the fence.

About a week later we traveled to Berlin for the long holidays. On the journey Wolfgang, sighing frequently, was absorbed in reading *War and Peace*, while I, once again, concerned myself with the Italian Renaissance. What I had in front of me was a book about—as it literally said—the "most glorious" and "kindest tyrant in the world," Lorenzo the Magnificent. In a colorful, somewhat arbitrary collage, the richly illustrated volume described the great days of Florence, its radiance and its dark sides. Immediately after our arrival in Berlin the family came together for supper at the garden table; soon after that Father Wittenbrink was at the garden fence to ask me about the *Fidelio*. I still remember that I replied that I had seen "the German fairy-tale opera," more of a fairy tale than Aunt Dolly's beloved *Magic Flute* or *Il Seraglio*. Then he wanted to know details of the production, from the duet at the beginning to the "nameless joy" at the end, whether Don Pizarro had been dressed up as somberly and with "trimmed side whiskers" as the

part demanded, and whether Rocco, although he sang
with the mighty bass of a ruler, had embodied the poor
wretch that he was.

Naturally, he also got around to the trumpet signal and had questions about that. I expressed reservations about Beethoven's missing theatrical sense and
referred to Schiller, mentioned some inconsistencies in
the libretto that the latter would never have allowed,
and was finally on to the outburst of joy at the finale.
At the end Schiller would no doubt have added, simply
as a warning, the nuance of a few countervailing voices,
because, according to everything I had learned from
him, the world spirit never—or only in political verse—
appears in the gallery as the herald of freedom. Instead
of overthrowing the scoundrels, the opera instead helps
them to an unexpected opportunity, I said. Wittenbrink was shocked. But that was just what he had once
told me here at the fence or on the telephone, I objected.
He said I was dismissing a great parable by calling it a
fairy tale. With many words, haltingly pieced together,
I replied, more or less, that it was certainly the most
beautiful but at the same time most unlikely fairy tale
in the world. "But a fairy tale, nevertheless. That's
not how freedom comes about! And perhaps precisely
because of that it's a particularly German fairy tale! An
operatic notion, that's all!"

That at any rate is what, over time, I was repeatedly reproached with having said. Before we went to
the Walken Farm that year, I was annoyed at the lack
of comprehension of those around me whenever the

conversation touched on *Fidelio*, especially as even my father went over to the other side. He couldn't do that, I told him. He was, after all, in my mother's words, someone who only uttered apocalyptic warnings. "Yes, yes!" he said, reluctantly, but with my remark about a fairy tale I was trivializing a great hope. After a few days under Uncle Berthold's rod, however, I began to miss our disputes.

SEVEN

•

Friends and Foes

On the return journey to Freiburg I read Gobineau's *Renaissance Studies*, which the Schönborns had lent me. But this time I was disturbed by a woman who got on at Kassel and didn't stop talking. She was afflicted by marriage problems because of the war, by her sons "Plisch" and "Up-to-No-Good," who were about ten, by annoying neighbors, and by more besides. Recently in Berlin, in Pariser Strasse, her attention had been caught by a passerby with worn-down heels; after a short pause for breath, she said that had reminded her of a remark by her father that it was a characteristic of Jews to tread down their heels. Crossing Güntzelstrasse she had pushed close to the man and seen that he wasn't wearing the Jewish Star. "But he was one of them," she continued. She had followed him a couple of streets farther to a house into which he disappeared and had reported the address to the nearest police station, without a name, unfortunately, but she had a "good nose" for everything Jewish. Lowering her voice, she added, after glancing around the compartment: it was said that the Jews hid gold and jewelry in their heels; someone who kept a lookout for it could get "a tidy sum."

Neither of the other two passengers in the compartment said a word. Winfried was asleep. Wolfgang muttered something about "Stretch my legs," and told me, "Come on! It does you no good to sit there all the time!" Hardly were we in the corridor when he exclaimed in an incautiously loud voice, "Revolting! National comrade!"[1] I asked him to speak more quietly, but he snapped at me, "Shut up! Father really is right: I don't want to belong to something like that. National community makes me sick!" At Mannheim Station, the next stop, the older of the two men in the compartment left without saying goodbye. At Offenburg I saw him standing in the corridor in the next carriage. He looked through me, although until Kassel, where the garrulous woman had joined us, we had several times talked animatedly and he obviously recognized me.

When I called my parents to say we had arrived safe and sound I hinted at our experience and then asked

---

1 "National comrade" is the translation for *Volksgenosse*, a term coined by the Nazis, who were fond of linking all their ideas to the word *Volk* (folk) in some way or other; thus society became a *Volksgemeinschaft* or community of all belonging to the same folk. These terms applied only to those whom the National Socialists deemed worthy of their new state; outsiders, like non-Aryans, could not gain acceptance. You were either born into the *Volksgemeinschaft* or forever remained excluded; there were no conversions.

after Dr. Meyer, because during our stay in Berlin I had several times tried to visit him without success. "Probably doesn't answer the door anymore," remarked my father, and incautiously added, "to give the most favorable explanation." In the background I heard my mother cry out her "Heaven have mercy on us!" My father promised that in the next few days he would once again go to Halle Gate and not take his finger off the bell.

At the boarding school it was "monastic rules" again, as we put it. At Gymnasium it was still the *Odyssey* and Virgil, while in the German class Schiller turned up for the first time with *Intrigue and Love,* and my prior knowledge was shown to advantage. A few weeks after that the class received a kind of call-up to basic military training in air-defense gunnery or flak.[2] The camp to which we had to report was around a former Nazi Party building in one of Freiburg's southern suburbs.

It was the same institutional world as the boarding school and yet I felt liberated. Later, I often asked myself why I found the much less flexible regulations of the military so much more bearable than the house rules of Dr. Hermann. What was probably important was that now I was no longer living exclusively among Black Forest peasant lads, who, for all their industriousness, remained alien to me, and who in the afternoon in the study room took their side of *Speck* out of a can and with their mouths full asked about some problem of Latin

---

2 "Flak" is an acronym for *Flugabwehrkanone* (or *Fliegerabwehrkanone*), or antiaircraft gun, literally "aerial defense cannon."

tenses. Because among those mobilized were not only the classes of Friedrich Gymnasium, but also the fourth and fifth years of Berthold Gymnasium and the class of the same age from nearby Emmendingen. This much more diverse composition opened doors, expanded the horizon, and made conversations more free. And of course everyone was so deeply caught up in the reflexes of the time that the barked orders of an NCO were accepted more unquestioningly than the admonitions of an anxiously nodding Monsignor.

The duty at Haslach Camp was as mindless as all military training drill. We had to march up and down the wide pebble paths between the sheds, throw ourselves onto the ground at a command, do rifle drill, put on footcloths, and, time after time, perform the salutes as prescribed in army regulations "with a straight back." Furthermore, we were instructed in gunnery and ballistics, cleaning latrines, putting locker contents "in order," and fetching coffee—which was brought from the kitchen in heavy pails and handed over to a distributor in front of the canteen. I can no longer remember whose idea it was that I shouted "Password!" whenever coffee arrived. My partner Franz Franken, at any rate, responded by singing a line from an aria. Over time, on the cry "Password," our opera texts became ever more crude parodies.

After about four weeks the basic training was over, but I was in Berlin for Christmas later than my brothers because at Wittenbrink's invitation I made a detour by way of Vienna. I stayed in Weyringer Gasse with a family who were friends of his, and every morning when

Wittenbrink and I walked into town past the Belvedere Palace, I saw Vienna spread out before me as if etched in silver. His friends said that unlike Paris, Berlin, or Washington, the city didn't swagger with imperial majesty; even Heldenplatz—Heroes' Square—had, for those who really looked, an attractive domesticity. Austrian charm admitted architectural irregularities and eccentricities right into the government districts, and the combination of the two created a metropolis which was both grand and human in scale. These reflections, discussed over breakfast, made such a strong impression on me because despite the obvious self-praise I found them new and convincing.

The more powerful experience, however, was the musical *rencontre* with the friends of the house who came around on one of the three evenings of my stay and tried to convince me that Vienna was the undisputed world capital of music, and that no one but Schubert was its supreme ruler, even before Mozart and Beethoven.[3] Until then I had known Schubert almost exclusively as a composer of lieder; now I heard, with growing astonishment, that his chamber music was of far greater stature, from the late quartets to the incomparable octet. Its inspiration almost amounted to an intoxication with death, exclaimed the youngest enthusiast among the guests, whom all addressed as Herr Privy Councillor, probably

---

3 Franz Schubert (1797–1828), beloved musical genius of the Romantic school, wrote symphonies, chamber music, church music, but above all lieder, which means simply "songs" in German but has become the universal technical term for musical settings of poems, as Schubert composed for his famous song cycles.

to avoid his almost unpronounceable Czech name. Even the frequently mocking scherzos seemed to be written solely to ridicule the very death conjured up only a few bars before, and yet at the same time displayed with every note how enslaved they were by it. A corpulent gentleman repeatedly ran on tiptoe to the piano to play a passage that had been mentioned, turned light-footedly around to add a motif from one of the songs, and begged us in each case to pay attention to "the panic-stricken ground note" which Schubert concealed behind all his musical charm. Everything he composed was "pure funereal music," someone else interjected, rushing to the grand piano to prove his assertion with the *Winterreise*, and underscoring it with sequences of notes from songs about "poor Peter" or "the fickle trout."

That is more or less how I remember the evening; of course, I've only mentioned two or three from a large number of themes and ideas. On the journey back to Berlin I went over everything again with Wittenbrink, and also posed the question whether the elevation of Schubert had something to do with the fact that he, unlike Mozart, never mind Beethoven, had been born in the city. Wittenbrink thought it possible. The Viennese were just very proud of their city and cultivated a certain Vienna vanity. But that was in no way to deny Schubert's uniqueness.

So the images expanded for me, became more complete, also more contradictory, like everything that I describe in these pages, which is the step-by-step appropriation of the world that my memory has preserved. Between Christmas and New Years—after hours of queuing from seven in the evening until the box office opened at nine in the morning—Wolfgang and I went to the Deutsches Theater. Embassy Councillor Aprea had, meanwhile, unfortunately been transferred to a more remote corner of the globe. Also I can no longer say whether this time we queued for *Faust* with Gustaf Gründgens and Paul Hartmann, for *Don Carlos* with Horst Caspar, or a treatment of the *Turandot* story, all of which we saw, without me being able to remember the order. With Aunt Dolly there was *The Magic Flute*, because she remembered that on the first occasion I had immediately wanted to see the performance again the following day.

In 1942 the usual Christmas spirit was absent. I, nevertheless, almost got it going when I expressed my thanks for the successful course of the day, but couldn't suppress the remark that the only thing I had missed was my father's usual outburst of anger—and thereby got it immediately. He accused me of taking an improper pleasure in discord, but I retorted that one bit of discord was always part of the Christmas holiday, in our home at least. As my smirking siblings evidently agreed with me, he angrily left the room. But he returned a little later and said, as he tucked the napkin he had thrown down back in the neck of his vest, "Forgotten! It's not worth getting upset about impertinences!"

The next day was clear, sunny, and cold. My father asked Wolfgang and me to walk to the Seepark with him. He talked about some political impressions of the recent past and then got around to Dr. Meyer, whom he had tried to call on in vain. He would go to the street behind Hallesches Tor again this week; if he failed to see Dr. Meyer this time, too, one would have to fear the worst. And "the worst" in this case literally meant the worst.[4]

After a few steps we left the park, because the paths were too icy. On the way back my father went on to say that he still had something to tell us which, to his horror, he had recently heard in a BBC broadcast and which he did not wish to repeat in the presence of our mother.[5] One of the commentators had reported at length on a House of Commons debate in which it had been asserted that the Jews removed from Germany were not, as was whispered furtively here and there, dumped in open country, which would have been bad enough, but were murdered by the tens of thousands. It was true that he believed Hitler and his accomplices capable of anything. But in this case he still believed it was one of those horror stories such as the unscrupulous English propaganda had already invented during the First World War. Consequently, he was looking for new, more precisely documented references. So far none of his friends had found them and the subject had not been mentioned again in any BBC broadcast, no matter how many hours he had spent in front of the radio.

---

4 Many Jews and opponents of the regime who could not flee in time despaired of their situation and committed suicide.

5 The Nazi propaganda ministry tightly controlled all the media of the time and listening to foreign broadcasts was difficult and illegal. Regular programs of the BBC and some Swiss stations were the only sources of outside information for many Germans.

He seemed very disquieted and we tried to talk him out of his fears. He prayed that what he had heard was not true, he said. The Nazis would not go that far, he concluded, as we turned into Hentigstrasse. Perhaps one should say more accurately: not for the time being. Because their backs weren't up against the wall. At that point it would be impossible to be sure of anything. Then the last fuses would blow. I thought of Dr. Meyer and Sally Jallowitz. Later, when I saw my father go to his study, I followed him and asked if he didn't, after all, know more. He replied that for all his inquiries he hadn't been able to find out anything certain. Perhaps everyone was afraid to reveal their knowledge. At the end of our conversation I made him promise to tell me when he did discover something.

A few days after our return to the boarding school, I, like the rest of the class, received my call-up papers. Our destination was Friedrichshafen on Lake Constance, which was surrounded by an extensive ring of antiaircraft batteries, not only because aircraft parts were produced there, but above all because of its cogwheel factory. "No war can be fought without cogwheels," Sergeant Grummel held forth before we moved off, to underline the importance of our deployment. He was a good-natured North German dockworker with an oddly crushed face, and he was responsible both for our appearance in public and for infantry training. As he explained his duties to us, he suddenly shouted "Into the field!" and "Take cover!" Then he led us to the uniform store, where we received the blue Luftwaffe uniform, fatigues, and the rest of our kit from service cap to boots. Steel helmet and mess tin as well, of course. We had hardly become acquainted with our lockers before we were summoned for roll call by Sergeant Major Knuppe, whom by the next day we were already calling "Knüppel" (club).

After that we were assigned to various functions. The greater part of the three classes that now found themselves together again had to carry out their duty on the 8.8 cm cannon, which were mounted in six-foot-high earth emplacements covered in planking. A smaller group was assigned to the U-Equipment, as it was called, which was housed in subterranean bunkers. The apparatus was used to determine the position of the aerial targets and the information was passed on to the gun crews. I was assigned to the U-Equipment.

The battery was situated amidst blossoming apple trees on a hill above the town of Friedrichshafen. Lake Constance glittered below, and over on the other side, in the middle of a jagged range of mountains, rose snow-covered Säntis. At twilight we saw the band of lights of the towns on the Swiss side and their flickering reflection in the water, while on our side, as far as Konstanz and Lindau, everything lay in silent darkness.

In the course of the first weeks several teachers had followed our class to continue teaching us the more important subjects. We went on learning Latin, history, and for a while also mathematics and one or two of the natural sciences. But the school lessons—entirely subordinated to the military timetable—were almost necessarily peripheral, until Dr. Kiefer turned up. He

appeared in front of the class in an unusual outfit, wearing a black cape and a red scarf loosely draped around
his neck.[6] He threw his slouch hat onto the lectern and
introduced himself with a brief address, which went
roughly like this: "I have a story to tell you of German
narrowness and provincialism. Also of the preeminence
of Italian and French culture, as well as of traveling players who were hardworking but hopelessly backward
and were still wandering around the country with their
cart when Paris already had several proud theaters and
Naples even had an opera house. Until Lessing, the first
German writer with a worldwide reputation, appeared.
In the hundred years that followed, his genius turned the
country into a center of influence of the arts and sciences
such as Europe had seen only once before: I'm now talking of Athens, or perhaps at a pinch of the Florence of
Lorenzo the Magnificent."

The artist's dress in which Kiefer made his entrance
evidently reflected the fact that he regarded the teaching profession merely as a temporary role with which to
earn money and basically saw himself as a painter. In the
hours when he was not teaching he would roam the terrain around the battery with easel, sketch pad, and fold-
ing chair. Sometimes one saw the man, his figure tending
to corpulence, among the apple trees, which were meanwhile bearing red-yellow fruit, searching for a suitable

---

6 This description as well as the later reference to Dr. Kiefer's corpulence may owe
as much to a famous poster as it does to reality. Everyone in Fest's generation had
seen or owned the likeness of Aristide Bruant as depicted by Toulouse-Lautrec in
precisely these colors and pose.

motif, climbing up a rise or down a slope; a few hours later he returned to camp, out of breath, but clearly full of inspiring impressions, with two or three pieces painted in the Expressionist style, and was happy to enter into conversations with us. Quite often he would then pick up the thread of the school topics of the morning.

He could talk without stopping about Goethe and Schiller, about Kleist, Georg Büchner, and also about the Shakespeare translations of Schlegel and Tieck, without once tormenting us with dull subject matter.[7] He retold Schiller's *Intrigue and Love* as a romantic tragedy involving Fred, the son of a senior civil servant, and the daughter of a caretaker who (as far as I remember) was called Irmgard Schönquell. As I wrote to my mother, Lady Milford seemed to have wound up with the name Pamela Grace in Kiefer's version; my mother thought her "someone who has been around too much for her own good." Without revealing the origin of the story, Kiefer also transposed *Prinz Friedrich von Homburg* to the present with minor modifications, especially toward the end, which might well have caused him some problems. He did the same with Goethe's *Faust*. Yet, in conclusion, Kiefer always explained that of course he hadn't

---

7 The Schlegel-Tieck translation (completed by Tieck's daughter Dorothea and Count Baudissin) of Shakespeare into German is so successful and faithful a rendition that it has made the English dramatist a virtual German author. August Wilhelm von Schlegel (1767–1845) and his brother Friedrich von Schlegel (1772–1829) were also the foremost theoreticians of German and European Romanticism; their writings have become the basis for most of modern literary criticism. Ludwig Tieck (1773–1853) was a major Romantic author with numerous novels, stories, and dramas to his credit; he was instrumental in preserving and editing early chapbooks and medieval texts virtually unknown until then.

himself experienced the events he related. Rather, he had wanted to convey to us in a relatively unconventional way one of the great works of classical literature. At the same time he had wanted to show that the widespread fear of the famous works of the poets was quite unfounded. Then he started on the literary interpretation of the text described. What he valued above all was doubt, which at a time of "prescribed faith" he had turned into a kind of idol. "In case of doubt, choose doubt! That should be your motto in life," he liked to say.

It was probably stories about Dr. Kiefer and some arrogant lines about the soldier's life that I included in a lengthy, somewhat formal letter to my grandfather in Berlin. At any rate, he replied immediately and informed me in a few words that on my next leave I should "present myself at Riastrasse for tea." A roommate, who saw the card lying on the top bunk bed, found the tone very funny and asked if I still used the formal Sie (you) with my grandfather. I merely responded, "No, no Sie and no formality. Simply big city manners!" He then spread it around that I was quarrelsome and ill-mannered.[8]

As we were cleaning artillery pieces in the barracks square, another roommate recommended the poet Josef Weinheber, of whom I had never heard. He also lent me a volume of poems, which I read with increasing

---

8 Like all European languages other than English, German has polite and familiar forms of address, which are used according to the degree of social familiarity or distance between the speaker and the person spoken to; the use of the formal mode indicates respect and was therefore used in the past not only for persons of higher social status but also for one's elders and parents, as it still is in France in some families.

interest. The title was *Adel und Untergang* (*Aristocracy and Ruin*). It was a noble tone (though I felt it was no match for Schiller) that I encountered in these pages, at times high-flown, heroic, again and again associating life and death, and full of the pathos of the time. He wrote of "holy wanderings," also of "universal fire," but already in the next line there were echoes of Expressionism with "soaring embers" and "ambrosian curls": all aristocracy and ruin, which then again shifted to a classicism that was always a little strained. I was also impressed by his play with rhyme and lines, above all in the lyric cycles. Wolfgang—to whom I gave one of Weinheber's volumes when we met in Frankfurt on the Oder, where he was doing his basic military training—had only ridicule for the "verbal clamor," as he called it, and parodied individual passages as a priestly *Dies irae*. I, however, who for a little while longer still considered Josef Weinheber's "blossom-garlanded brows" and "dream-curving mouths" to be notable poetry, became aware, thanks to this poet (and at a distance of several years), just how easily one can fall in with the spirit of the times, even when one was raised in opposition to it.[9]

At about the beginning of May 1943 a letter arrived from my father, which related some events in Karlshorst.

---

9   Josef Weinheber (1892–1945), Austrian novelist and poet who wrote traditional hymns, odes, and sonnets, but also tried to capture the cadences of common folk; seen as close to the Nazis and thus politically controversial, he appears to have committed suicide in 1945 (no one is quite sure—he died at the very end of the war, when many Nazi fellow travelers killed themselves). Aware of this undesirable legacy, Fest wants to distance himself from the man while maintaining his admiration for his work and its influence on him as a young reader.

He added that he had twice gone to Halle Gate, but had not been able to see our friend Dr. Müller; he had presumably been *assigned for duty*, and we could only hope that he would return home unharmed. Naturally, I had an awful premonition, and in my mind I again went over some poems and Dr. Meyer's remarks when we had parted and which had consolidated our relationship. In my reply to my father, however, I did not mention any of that. Instead, I concealed my disquiet behind some trivial matters and mentioned that I would probably get leave at the end of June, when I hoped to hear details from him. At the same time I confirmed the arrangement that I would bring two friends with me. We should leave everything else until then. And as a PS I had added: *What can we do?*

At the end of June I did indeed travel to Berlin with Helmut Weidner and Norbert Steinhardt. My parents were waiting for us at Anhalt Station. My father again appeared very dejected, and a little later, as I walked behind the others with my mother, she expressed the hope that our visit would cheer him up. We should do everything possible in that respect and avoid any political argument. She was worried, not without cause, and expected my support.

At the beginning our conversations did several times wander into politics, but my mother and I always managed to change the subject, and when Father Wittenbrink turned up in the garden in the morning I was able to say a few words of warning. My friends certainly shared our political views, I said, but no one could say how discreet they would be under pressure. Also I hadn't invited them to Berlin to have political discussions, but to show them Berlin with its palace, Unter den Linden, museums, and Alexanderplatz. We wanted nothing else but a holiday from our military duty, I said, to go to the theater and concerts, the bicycle races in the Sportpalast, and, as we deliberately and dismissively put it, to see the "colorful girls" on Friedrichstrasse. I felt something like an owner's pride as I took them around, most strongly when we went out to Potsdam—to Sanssouci Palace, the Marble Palace, and the Garrison Church—which I had loved since childhood and which was rather deserted these days.

The next morning, when we came down to the garden for breakfast, Wittenbrink was already walking up and down on his side of the fence saying the breviary. Hardly had we arrived when—in view of our prior warnings— he began a conversation about Mozart and how he had appeared in the world as a complete being. When he added that that was almost as amazing as the miracle of Cana, I took the liberty of warning him against the sin of heresy. Wittenbrink merely laughed and answered that luckily there was no Inquisition anymore.[10] But since my friends did not really respond to one musical subject or another, he changed to painting. His great preference was for the Italians and the Flemish and Dutch, he assured

---

10 Wittenbrink is using the typical code of the time—his reference to the Inquisition is intended to draw out the visitors to declare their political views; since they refuse to do so, he immediately changes the subject.

us, then he told us about the various schools of painting, of Siena, Florence, and Rome, and from there got to, as he said, "the great Caravaggio," whom he admired unreservedly, despite his liking for "all-too-naked flesh." It had always been his dream to own a picture by the great painter, but, given his short life—large parts of which were spent in bars, brothels, and prisons—he had left too little behind. His skill in using light as a kind of cold fire quite overwhelmed the senses; it warmed the viewer and at the same time made him shiver. We must on no account miss the opportunity to look at the works of "the great Caravaggio" in the Kaiser Friedrich Museum.[11]

We did then go to the gallery in the city center, but I think the few paintings which I remembered from earlier visits had already been removed by this time.[12] However, I showed my guests the Museum Island, we walked through the Nicolai Quarter and down Unter den Linden, as well as to my former Gymnasium and other supposedly important places, always avoiding my father's political conversations. Because all the time my friends were there I had a presentiment, possibly reinforced by my worried mother, that there would nevertheless be an outburst by my father. I asked once again as to the whereabouts of some friends, such as Walter Goderski, Bruno Block, and Dr. Meyer. But he had nothing specific to say.

---

11 Of the five Berlin Caravaggios, three appear to have been destroyed in a fire at the end of the Second World War.—Trans.

12 Because of the air raids most museums kept only a small number of works on display; the rest were safely stored off location, sometimes in abandoned mines, where they were found after 1945.

Thanks to my father's questions about the school classes, the conversation got around to Virgil, and Norbert, who was just reading a book about the state poet of Emperor Augustus, instantly presented himself as an expert. "Please, not a learned conversation!" begged Helmut. But once he had started Norbert wouldn't let himself be distracted and knew countless details, historical or legendary, which linked the rise of Rome to the fall of Troy. He related how Aeneas, as he discovers the terrifying picture of his native city, becomes certain that compassionate people must be living in Carthage, because the ability to feel the misfortune of others is what constitutes a decent world. At some point my father joined in by saying that in Germany Virgil had never enjoyed such renown as in the rest of Europe. It was no doubt telling that the *Odyssey* ends in married bliss, but the *Aeneid* with the foundation of a state.

On one of the following days I went to Riastrasse for tea, and for the first time in my life experienced my grandfather as a communicative, even elegant conversationalist. He did not just know, as we had always maintained, how to growl a few sentences about life and business, but was also able to talk knowledgeably about classic French literature from Montaigne to Chateaubriand. Surprisingly, he mentioned the "first small piece of literature" I had sent him with my letter and wanted to know more about Dr. Kiefer and the other teachers, which book had most impressed me recently, and how I reconciled my literary preferences with the mindlessness of military life. Also the attentions, which were usually our concern, now came from him: he poured tea for me, offered me biscuits, and from time to time asked what I would like. He also wanted to know my plans. I replied that what counted was to get through the war. Nothing else! He had heard about the letter in which I had declared I wanted to become a "private scholar," and he said, "Hold firmly onto that in these times! If some laugh, pay no attention! One always has difficulties doing the right thing!" My grandmother, who had sat down with us for half an hour, gave me an earthenware pot with her famous crème caramel.

Soon after that my grandfather said that we had to bring matters to a close. At the door, when I wanted to say goodbye, he shook his head and said, "Today I shall accompany you!" During the ten minutes to Hentigstrasse we talked about the landscape around Friedrichshafen and Lake Constance. I told him that during guard duty at the dark gun emplacement one of my comrades had called it "tender," but then, almost shocked, had immediately asked me to forget the word. When asked as to the reason, he said it didn't fit in with the soldiers' world and would only arouse laughter, which in turn amused my grandfather.

When we reached our house, I said that now it was my turn to accompany him back, that was only right and proper. Once again the old man said no. "Not today! Today I accompanied you home." And while I was still wondering why my sisters found my grandfather so intimidating, he said, almost admonishingly, "See that you get through it!" Then, he added, there are things one can do: "You know what I mean!" I had no idea, but pretended that I had understood. Finally, touching my shoulders, he suggested an accolade, turned on his heel, and left. When I told my mother about it, she said with a smile, "He just doesn't like any kind of sentimentality. That's who I get it from, after all!"

At the supper table the next evening my father's feared explosion of anger came. It began fairly harmlessly with his remark that in the face of an existence that was passing by, every person had a debt to pay—if the circumstances allowed it. Clumsily, I asked if by that qualifier he was trying to justify his own interrupted career, and from one moment to the next it burst out of him like resentment which had been too long bottled up. How dare I say that to him? he shouted, throwing down his cutlery in the presence of my schoolmates. For years he had suffered from his inactivity. For the sake of his family—so what? he interrupted himself. To damn the regime at the garden fence, to listen to the BBC and to pray for those in need: that was nothing at all! "Yes!" he went on. "I keep out of things. Like everyone else! And I've got good reason to do so! But I now know that under the present conditions there is no separation of good and evil. The air is poisoned. It infects us all!" And so on for a long time, more or less, and as far as we were able to reconstruct it later.

At this angry outburst, which was unlike any before, my mother stood up, but remained standing by the door. After a brief pause she went to his chair and put her hands on his shoulders. "I beg you, Hans!" she said quietly. "We have guests!" My friends sat there as if petrified, but my father was evidently not yet finished. "No one can acquit themselves," he began again, "not even the most justifiable hate grants us absolution! And what does that mean anyway? Hate is not enough. Just stop the talking! You only do it to get the guilt off your back!'

The scene only came to an end when my two sisters, startled by the noise, appeared at the door in their nightdresses, crying. With reassuring words my father took them back to their room and a little later returned to the table with an apologetic phrase. As he picked up his cutlery from the floor, he said that he stood by every one of his words. He apologized only for yelling, which was crazy of him to indulge in, and for his loss of self-control.

The three days which still remained I spent with my friends mostly in town, which was already marked by the air raids, and at the garden table. Dr. Hausdorf called once and in an unusually serious mood involved us in a conversation about skepticism, which he called the other truly human virtue besides faith. Where one of the two was missing, then human coexistence was made more difficult or even impossible; both together, on the other hand, guaranteed the little bit of tolerableness that human beings could achieve. The question as to how these opposites could be reconciled gave rise to a lengthy discussion in which we drove him into a corner. Yet once he had gone we said that he had been right. Life simply did consist of contradictions.

On the day before our departure we came downstairs just as Father Wittenbrink was doing a round of his garden, and when he saw us sitting down at the table he came toward us with quite impetuous strides. "I've got it at last!" he cried to us from a distance. "Forget the Scholastics and Thomas Aquinas! Forget Descartes and Leibniz! I have the definitive proof of the existence of God!" Wittenbrink seemed to be beside himself, and my mother, who was just bringing us tea, said later that his eyes had been damp. "The matter requires no compli-cated deductions," he went on, "but consists of one word, like all convincing insights. The most convincing proof of the existence of God is . . . Mozart! Every single page of his biography teaches us that he comes from another world and at the same time, despite all the tormenting conceal-ment, makes it visible. Why has no one seen it before?"

Wittenbrink continued in this vein almost entranced. "When has there ever been anything like it, that some-one doesn't need to work anything out, but simply writes down his inspirations, because he has always possessed them? Just compare Mozart's notation, on the whole, at any rate, with that of Beethoven! He struggles with everything which Mozart came into the world with, and so Beethoven always writes incantatory music!" Natu-rally, I've forgotten most of what Wittenbrink said. But I still remember the impetuousness of his outburst. Some of the ideas also, such as, for example, that someone can be as light as air and at the same time deep, serene, and sad, literally in the same note, great and never banal. That he can translate even the most glaring contradic-tions into complete harmony without taking away any-thing of their opposition. "Anyone who hears the *Ave verum,*" he said, "must realize that no human voice can express devotion in that way. And it's just the same with countless other emotions: for love the Rose aria from *The Marriage of Figaro* should be mentioned; for reverie the duet of Fiordiligi and Dorabella in *Così fan tutte*; for others, many movements from the piano concertos or passages from the string quartets." He continued talking in the same fashion. At best Wittenbrink interrupted himself by throwing in the phrase "proof of the existence of God" from time to time. My two friends understood almost nothing of what he meant. I, at least, had some kind of schooling behind me. The way he said it seemed all the more convincing, and that day I understood how content can sometimes take second place to tone.

Shortly before we left, when the suitcases were already half-packed, my father suggested a short walk. At the sandhills, when there was no one to be seen far and wide, he came back to when he lost his temper: he had been upset because he had dreadful news from the East. When I asked for details, he refused to reply, and said, "Not now! Perhaps another time. Because it would only put you in danger!" He simply mentioned it, he added, to make his irritability comprehensible. His behavior had been a faux pas. But I should know that there had been reasons for it.

Nevertheless, anyone who kept his eyes open and summoned up a degree of mistrust toward those in power soon came across more and more clues about mass murders in Russia, Poland, and elsewhere. Certainly, much sounded contradictory and was only passed on as rumor; but the accumulation turned what was reported into near certainty. I heard the first hints from Wigbert Gans on my next Berlin visit, and in Freiburg, too, there was whispering about indiscriminate shootings and mass graves. In spring 1944, and then again three months later, Wittenbrink, to the accompaniment of most earnest entreaties to keep silent, told me about hardly conceivable atrocities, which he had heard about from members of his congregation who had served on the Eastern Front and were at a loss what to do. He also said he had often discussed with my father—to the point where they were both in despair—what could be done about such crimes. Nevertheless, I should not say a word to my father about what I had learned, because Wittenbrink had promised he would tell us nothing. Besides which, each one of their conversations had ended with the two of them feeling even more oppressed by their powerlessness. In all the confidential pieces of information passed on to me, however, gas chambers were never mentioned. The frequently posed question was why the British broadcasting stations had not repeated and spread their knowledge of the extermination of large numbers of people, so causing outrage in the rest of the world. Yet London remained silent, said our religious studies teacher, whom I met as I left Freiburg Minster after one of the dissident, crowded Sunday sermons of Archbishop Gröber.

When, accompanied by my parents, I arrived at Anhalt Station with my two school friends, my father took us aside. As always, he walked down the platform to the end of the now partly damaged glass roof and a few steps beyond that, while my mother remained behind at the carriage door with the older of my two sisters. "I trust you," he said to my two friends, "and know that you won't repeat a word." When they nodded, he went on: "I expect to see the Russians at the Brandenburg Gate. Everyone accuses me of being pessimistic. I would like to be wrong, because in the long run knowing you were right is an empty triumph. I've already had too much of it." Back at the carriage door, he said, "Make sure, if there's anything you can do about it, that you stay in the West." Then, as we were already crowding at the window to wave goodbye: "I expect God to give a sign at the end. I don't dare say how that sign will turn out." As the train moved ponderously off we heard my father above the puffing sounds, as he ran alongside, shouting, "I hope we'll meet again!"

In Friedrichshafen we were back to the same routine as before with field duty, gun maintenance, empty hours in the afternoon, and thunderous snoring at night. During exercises Sergeant Grummel shouted all the time and tried to assume a grumpy facial expression. At irregular intervals, good-natured and potbellied Captain Kersting, who had a shop in Karlsruhe, inspected our drawn-up ranks and warned us to be even more vigilant. Because, since the fall of Mussolini and as the Allies slowly advanced, the air raids were becoming more frequent and now hardly a week passed in which we were not several times, by day as by night, called to man the guns.

The few teachers who had accompanied us to the camp were still there. At the blowing of a whistle we ran

with books and jotters in hand to the school hut. Dr.
Kiefer had meanwhile got to Georg Büchner's *Woyzeck*
and in the new year read Gerhart Hauptmann's *Before
Dusk* with us.[13] To the disappointment of the class he no
longer applied his trick of bringing the classics up to date,
but then, when no one was expecting it anymore, with
the help of an extended red-herring story, he took it up
again with Keller's *Green Henry*.

This time, too, in the face of the military situation,
he frequently talked about doubt as the citizen's first virtue, and I thought of Dr. Hausdorf, who said the same
thing in different words. Following a suggestion by Dr.
Kiefer, I started to read Nietzsche, as well as plays by
Oscar Wilde. Like many of my generation, I also studied
Spengler's *The Decline of the West*, as well as an anno-
tated edition of the Book of Revelation: all mixed up,
half-understood, gripped by an apocalyptic mood.[14]

The six or eight Russian prisoners of war, who
now also did duty at the guns, were a new item. They
dragged over the heavy 8.8 cm shells, kept the battery
emplacements and the huts clean, and carried out every

---

13 Both Büchner and Hauptmann were socially critical writers who attacked the
ills of their own time and often drew the ire of the establishment. Georg Büchner
(1813–37) published political pamphlets and wrote powerful dramas and a major
prose fragment; his works only came to be appreciated after 1918. One of the
most prestigious German literary prizes bears his name. Gerhart Hauptmann
(1862–1946) is Germany's main representative of Naturalism. His social criticism
was presented in both tragedy and comedy; although primarily a dramatist, he also
wrote novels and other narratives, receiving the Nobel Prize in 1912.

14 Oswald Spengler (1880–1936) was an exceptionally influential writer; his
philosophy of history essentially views the major cultures as organisms with
distinctive lifestyles which can best be captured by a world-historical morphology.

kind of work. They were without exception friendly and
ready to help, and sometimes there came from the small
Finnenzelten (Finnish tents) the "hummed singing" that
I remembered from Berlin. Over time we developed an
almost warm relationship with some of the Russians.
But a lance corporal, who was an unrelenting party man
and once saw me standing in conversation with Mikhail
and Lev, summoned me and warned me "not to frater-
nize with the Russian rabble." "That lot," he said, pointing in their direction, were "all revolutionaries. They
would like nothing better than to kill all of us. Every one
of them." Then, raising his finger, "If they could! And
you're encouraging them!"

We had to watch out for him, especially when we listened to foreign broadcasts late in the evening. Even the
station broadcast from the Balkans, which announced
itself with "Lili Marleen," aroused his suspicion.[15] When
I warned my classmates that listening to enemy stations
was strictly forbidden and was punishable by at least two
years' imprisonment, a majority decided that profit and
pleasure were too limited and the risk of "wireless crime"
too great. Despite that, about a dozen of us from now on
listened to the "enemy broadcasts" in an out-of-the-way
hut with heightened caution and attention.

The other innovation was the women headquarters
auxiliaries, who had arrived at the battery during the
Christmas vacation to "reinforce the clerical staff," as it
was put. They lived in a separate building a few hundred

---

15 A German army radio station based in Belgrade.—Trans.

yards away. Crafty comrades found out that in the "auxiliaries' billets" there were regular "auctions" at which
one of the girls would dance on the table to music from
the wireless; at some point the music would suddenly
be stopped and the "dancing girl" would freeze in mid-
movement. When the others standing around shouted,
"Take it off! Take it off! You don't need it anymore!" she
would begin to move again and, after some fumbling
around and with gestures that were as suggestive as possible, drop the next piece of clothing.

At Christmas 1943 I was in Berlin and it so happened
that during my stay Karlshorst was for the first time hit
by an air raid. The bombs didn't cause too much harm,
but the destruction and damage were impossible to miss.
Perhaps because of the greater proximity of the war the
days passed in a strangely depressed atmosphere. Winfried and I tried, somewhat clumsily, to lighten the mood,
and in particular to play the beau for our two sisters, who
had entered the poetic phase of adolescent girlhood. For
gentle Hannih we thought up more or less invented gos-
sipy stories about sentimental love, while Christa, who
was much more lighthearted and blessed with a down-
to-earth intelligence, preferred cheerful stories, even
more so if they were witty.

Things became more entertaining when Wolfgang
arrived in Karlshorst for a short leave of one and a half
days. On the way to a Christmas service he told me that
he had wanted to give our mother as a present a poem he
had written himself; one in Heine's style, but without the
ironic final couplet, which she so hated. But none of his

dozen attempts had been a success. The poem was supposed to include my mother's favorite phrase ("summer
wind"), her favorite activity ("piano"), and her main piece
of clothing at present ("black apron"), or at least contain a
play on these diverging terms. He had tinkered for a long
time, but he was "too dopey" to be a poet; he'd learned
that much at least. I retorted that he'd obviously tried to
scrawl the thing with his left hand. He laughed and said
he could make jokes about his lack of talent himself.

It befitted the mood of these days that shortly after
Christmas Eve I saw my mother sitting in front of her
keepsake casket, evidently deep in troubled thought. A
little before that she had lamented that every prediction
had turned out to be wrong: Wolfgang and I had become
soldiers after all; there was no end in sight to Hitlerism.
Now, one after the other, she was holding her beloved
trifles, which were kept in the little box along with some
letters and family documents: first locks of hair from her
children, notebooks in which she had kept a diary about
each one, three gold coins, which were presumably supposed to ensure everlasting prosperity, and so on. Also
some letters from Wolfgang and myself. She sat there
silently, staring at the wall in front of her, and jumped
as she suddenly saw me beside her. "You shouldn't do
that!" she said. "Imagine if I had been crying!" I sat
down beside her and asked if she often felt like crying,
and she replied, "I feel like it every day." Then she shut
the casket, put the key in her handbag, and said, like a
warning to herself, "But everyday feelings are not what
make up a life."

The antiaircraft auxiliary period ended in the middle of February 1944. Then we were informed that we would be drafted into the Reich Labor Service just two days after our discharge.[16] As one of the spokesmen of the unit, I negotiated with Captain Kersting an "interim leave" of two weeks before the start of our labor service deployment. Since my friend Helmut Weidner sympathized with my dislike of the boarding school, he invited me to spend the few free days in the guest room of his parents' home.

To my surprise, when I called at the boarding school in Freiburg—where I went on my second day back in the city—among three or four pieces of correspondence I found call-up papers ordering me to start labor service in two days' time. As I discovered, my schoolmates had received a letter that fixed the call-up for the end of February, as had been agreed with Captain Kersting and the army district command. After numerous discussions, which consumed the whole of the following day, I resolved to report for duty, but—with the help of a confusing story that was difficult to understand—I managed to get my leave after all.

So, when I arrived at the assembly point not far from the station at eight in the morning. I presented myself to a superior who was shouting orders and whose dirty brown uniform was trimmed with silver braid, and I

16 In peacetime this would have been the expected progress of the average young German male: Hitler Youth to Reich Labor Service to Armed Services, learning to operate in coordinated units with people of all walks of life. The Nazis, quite intentionally, did a lot to tear down social barriers.

once again laughed silently at the silly Robin Hood cap
of the labor service. When asked what I wanted, I muttered something about a clerical error, but as if I were no
more than an insignificant irritation for him, he barked
at me, "Do you have call-up papers?" and when I said yes
he gave me the order, "Well then! Step into the ranks!"

I pretended to fall in farther to the back, and then,
in a second attempt, made my way to the clerical hut.
The day before I had tried by telephone to get written
confirmation from Captain Kersting stating that I, too,
was entitled to two weeks' leave, but had only managed
to reach Staff Sergeant Knuppe, who had reprimanded
me: "You'll get no written confirmations here! You can
get a couple of foot cloths! But you'll have to pick them
up yourself!" After that I had drawn up a document
in which all the members of the 1926 age group of the
218th Flak Battery were granted special leave from the
twelfth to the twenty-sixth of February 1944 on conclusion of their duties, because of their exemplary service.
Dr. Hans Kersting's name was typewritten at the bottom
and it was signed by the eleven classmates I had managed
to reach the previous evening.

At the counter of the clerical office—after describing
my case—I held out the piece of paper to the officer on
duty. He looked at it helplessly and, after scratching his
head in irritation, asked for more details. When I presented the case as incoherently as possible and even contradicted myself, he interrupted me. "Come now, come
now!" he exclaimed. "I don't understand a word! Have
you been called up or not?" I responded in the forceful

tone of voice that everyone in the packed room adopted:
"Of course not! Here's the proof. It's a misunderstand-
ing!" As I kept on talking in order to make the matter
even more opaque, he cried out, "Man, what are you
pestering me for? I've got a thousand things to do! And
now I'm supposed to waste my time with idiots like you!
Away with you, out of here!" Despite my civilian clothes,
I gave a suggestion of clicking my heels and made myself
scarce.

For about half an hour I watched from a safe distance
as the conscripts climbed onto the trucks that drove up
and left shortly after. Two weeks later I was at the assembly point again, this time with the class, and reported to
the clerical hut. When no one could find my name, my
particulars were noted and I was sent away. For the next
two weeks I heard nothing from the Reich Labor Service.

It was during this time that I had an unusually fierce
argument with my father. Almost in passing I had mentioned in a letter that I had recently volunteered for the
Luftwaffe air force, and hardly had my letter arrived in
Berlin when my father was on the telephone. I could hear
his voice rising in anger. "Volunteered!" he shouted, trying to catch his breath. "For this war! Have you thought
of me? Of us?" When I said yes, he retorted: "That
I'll never understand!" I said that he must understand,
almost the whole class had volunteered, and from my
letters he knew something about their views. He denied
that as well, and at the end of the exchange, which got
little further than repeating what had already been said, I
let slip that reporting as a volunteer was the only way not

to be drafted into the SS, whose recruiting officers had recently been in the class. I no longer know what words I used to try to make my decision plausible to my father. Finally, after a long argument and even longer silence we hung up. In the letter which arrived a few days later he wrote with unbelievable lack of caution that one does not volunteer for "Hitler's criminal war," not even to avoid the SS. "This decision," he concluded, "you must leave to God or, if you prefer, to Fate. At any rate, it's not in your hands, even if that's what you assume."

No matter how often we talked about our difference of opinion or exchanged letters we still didn't manage to come to any agreement. Finally my father announced his intention to visit me specially in Freiburg and to lodge a complaint at the regional Luftwaffe headquarters in order to cancel my registration. I wrote to tell him that a withdrawal was not possible, and besides I might be expected to report for labor service any day. He said something and then, without waiting for an answer, slammed the phone down. Even years later we avoided the subject. Only once did we briefly come back to it and I have never forgotten my father's intelligently discriminating words. "In the only serious dispute we had during the Nazi years, you were not wrong. But I was the one who was right!"

After the departure of the class I had another fourteen days. Then, just before six in the morning, my hosts' doorbell rang. Two men in uniformlike coats with the brims of their hats turned down were at the front door. They asked for me and when they were told I was up in the guest room they ran upstairs without another word. When they got to the top they tore open the door of the neighboring room and woke me up just with the noise they made. "So you're the deserter!" they shouted. When I denied it and instead gave my name, they ordered: "Get yourself ready!" They waited outside the bathroom door, repeatedly urging me to hurry, and then led me out of the house. Downstairs, at the entrance, they explained, as if with one voice, that they didn't want any trouble and threatened me with arrest by the police. We were now going to the tram stop on Komturplatz, they added, and I had to stay ten steps in front. "Off you go! Now!"

The officer at Gestapo headquarters on Dreisamstrasse left me waiting for about an hour while he read through a bundle of files. When I plucked up my courage and asked him whether it wouldn't be better if I just left—especially as I hadn't had any breakfast—he looked up with a smile and said I would have much, much more time on my hands yet. "And breakfast? Well, if you want to call it that!" Half an hour later another officer came and discussed my case with his colleague, who leafed disinterestedly through a pile of papers. Then one of the two brought some tea and, a little later, the other, suddenly sitting up straight, began a kind of interrogation.

The examination lasted quite a long time; the questions concerned only the obvious. Nevertheless, the procedure was repeated several times, in the afternoon and the evening, as well as finally almost at night. Meanwhile, I had been put in a cell. On the second evening the officer who had kept me waiting so long at the beginning came and silently handed me a number of documents. One was the call-up for labor service; another my destination in the Stubaital in the Tyrol; a third my travel pass. "Tomorrow morning at 7:12 departure from Freiburg," he announced. "If you don't miss any connections you should be in Innsbruck at about six in the evening. From there you take the train up to the Stubaital" in the Tyrol.

Relieved, I made my way to Herdern, a suburb of Freiburg. During all the interrogations and in the breaks between them I had constantly thought of my parents and how worried they would be if they knew of my arrest by the Gestapo. The thought of my mother's sorrow had upset me more than my father's scruples. But he had just brought trouble on himself.

EIGHT

•

Of the Soldier's Life and of Dying

At the beginning of April 1944 my father received an official letter. It came from a party office and informed him that on the nineteenth of the month he had to present himself at the Karlshorst racetrack. He had been assigned to a unit building tank obstacles. He had promptly replied that it was no doubt known to the responsible department that in accordance with Paragraph 4 of the Law for the Restoration of the Professional Civil Service he had been dismissed on April 7, 1933. Consequently, in accordance with the graded catalogue of measures of the law, he was required to avoid every activity. As he knew that the administration attached great importance to the proper application of its decrees, his call-up must be an error. He awaited an appropriate notification "as soon as possible."

The letter was pure mockery. This time, however, even my mother was in agreement. Nevertheless, years later, whenever the conversation turned to these events, her mouth still began to tremble. But the demand to defend Hitler's Reich, which had brought her nothing but "troubles" to the lives of three members of her family, was going too far. And in taking this risk she had, as she later liked to say, "the luck of the bold." The protecting hand, which we suspected was being held over many of my father's rash and angry actions, spared him once more.

It was during these anxious days that I arrived in Neustift, more than three thousand feet up, at the end of the Stubaital Valley, with Innsbruck and the glittering Nordwand peak in the background. A camp with huts had been put up in a wood behind some farms. On the night before Easter one of the farms burned to the ground; at three in the morning when the firefighting, to which our unit had hurriedly been detailed, was over, I walked with my friend Franz Franken, whom I had met in the camp again, through the brightening dawn down the valley to Innsbruck. Perhaps it had something to do with the unique charm of the landscape that I soon hated everything to do with the labor service: the crumpled overalls we had to wear in which our so-called foremen drove us into the dirt right after the clothing issue; the army bread with the disgusting margarine; the "spade care," as it was called, in which we polished away at the shiny surfaces; and the ridiculous shouted commands of "Shoulder spade!," "Order spade!," or "Spade—present!"

Furthermore, at this late point in the war there was nothing useful to do anymore—no dike building, no draining of swamps, no road construction—so that the never-ending drill was as much a makeshift solution as the singing of the same old songs that hadn't changed for years about Geyer's black troop and the tents beyond the valley. One got the impression that the leaders and subordinate leaders of the Reichsarbeitsdienst were all failed career officers who suffered from a profound inferiority complex.[1]

After a few weeks the unit was transferred from the high valley near Innsbruck to Hohenems in Vorarlberg, and one of the commanders explained that we were now moving closer to the front that would soon no doubt open up in the West. What we actually saw at the end of April—across Lake Constance—was the destruction of Friedrichshafen, which had been spared in our time there, in a nighttime firestorm. We thought of our younger classmates, whom we had left behind in the town. With the first post I received a letter from my mother, which told me that my father had been called up to the army. Quite without the caution which she usually displayed, she added that with the help of the Wehrmacht someone had evidently wanted to save him from the clutches of a "higher authority." Because at almost sixty no one is ordered up to "active service," as

---

1 The Reichsarbeitsdienst (RAD) was a compulsory six-month public service required of all Germans, male and female, between the ages of sixteen and twenty-five.

it's called, but at most to the Volkssturm.[2] "But then, what applies to us?"

My mother had included with her lines a school report by Dr. Hermann or one of his underlings. "Father read it before he left," she wrote, "but he thought you should see it, too." It had been written by one of the officials at the boarding school in preparation for my departure from school. Like so many things it was lost in the confusion of the end of the war, so I can no longer recapture its tone of ecclesiastical bureaucracy. But the sentences struck me like blows, from which even the cutting marginal comments of my father could not protect me. This is more or less what was written there:

> Joachim F. shows no intellectual interest and only turns his attention to subjects he finds easy. He does not like to work hard. His religious attachment leaves something to be desired. He is hard to deal with. He shows a precocious liking for naked women, which he hides behind a taste for Italian painting. He displays a noticeable devotion to cheap popular literature; in the course of an inspection of his work desk shortly before he left, works by Beumelburg and Wiechert were found. That a volume of Schiller's plays was lying beside them does not make the find any better, since dramatic literature

2 The Nazis revived this old term for a local militia, which had not been used in centuries, to designate their final defense "force"; scraping the very bottom of their manpower barrel, it swept up all males between the ages of sixteen (sometimes even younger) and eighty (including older) to make a last stand against the Allied forces, who commanded vastly superior firepower.

demands much less effort than philosophical pieces. He is taciturn. All attempts by the rectorate to draw him into discussion were in vain. It is not impossible that J. will still find the right path. We wish it for him—and for you.

My father had put a note with the report. On it was written, in contrast to his usual strict manner: *So that you have something to laugh at in these serious times.* He had underlined the phrase about my lack of intellectual interest and written in the margin: *I don't understand. Dr. Hermann and the others in charge of the house seemed sensible people when I met them last year.* My mother, for her part, had noted: *Wolfgang got an outstanding report when he left. You're not so dissimilar! What does he do that's different?* I wrote back: *Here at the Reich Labor Service I'm constantly being reproached by my superiors, because I spend almost every free minute reading. A couple of days ago, after some clumsiness while putting up a tent, one called me "an educated idiot." What does one learn from that? School reports are* Seich *(rubbish)[3], as they say in Alemannic dialect.*

At the beginning of July 1944 my time with the labor service came to an end. I was drafted into an air force unit in Landau an der Isar. Chance had it that I made a friend on the first day. Reinhold Buck from Radolfzell was quite brilliant, with a temperament that swung between severity, delight, and the demonic. The hours he

---

3 *Seich* is literally "piss," meaning rubbish, nonsense when applied to speech.

spent over scores and notebooks were proof of the effort it cost him to come to rest. He wanted to be a conductor and was obsessed by music. So it was inevitable that even as we were making up our beds we got around to themes and composers who had for a long time been his passion as well as mine. A little later, as the whistles were blown for first roll call, we stood next to one another and missed one command or another, because we were talking about Beethoven's piano sonatas. The lieutenant who was inspecting the ranks and had picked up a couple of fragments of our conversation asked Reinhold in which major key Beethoven's Ninth Symphony was composed and received the answer: "In none. It was composed in D minor. And, if I may add, the opus number is 125." The officer was pleasantly surprised. "But *you* don't have a clue about anything?" he said, turning to me. "I do," I contradicted him in an unmilitary manner. "But more about literature." The lieutenant thought for a moment. "Then tell me off the top of your head the last line of 'The Erl-King.'" Without hesitation I answered, *"In seinen Armen das Kind war tot"* (In his arms the child was dead). From that day on he called us "the professors" when he ordered us to fetch coffee or clean the latrines.

After duty, which here, too, consisted of mindless infantry training, we became engrossed, evening after evening, in our passion for debate. We got excited about Mozart and his taste for *alla turca*, inspired by the Turkish Wars and the contemporary fashion for coffee-drinking in the late seventeenth century. I talked about the Viennese idolization of Schubert or about

Beethoven's dramatic sense of music and his simultane-
ous lack of interest in literature, which was so unlike the
stage genius of Mozart. At some point we came around
to Mozart's futile search for stage plays or librettists.
Yet Shakespeare had been translated since the 1770s,
and with a friend in Berlin I had imagined the spell of
a Mozart opera of *Romeo and Juliet*. A little later, as if
he wanted to defend Beethoven against Mozart, Buck (as
I soon called him) talked about the magnificent closing
bars of each of Beethoven's orchestral pieces, which, like
those of Brahms, seemed to strive toward a climax that
was also a catastrophe. I noted on a piece of paper: *The
craving for the abyss, there is something like it, says B.*

On our lengthy walks, however, we also talked about
literature. Once I told him about my Fontane reading,
my Schiller experiences, and my unsuccessful attempt at
Thomas Mann; also about Ernst Kiefer and his unusual
way of conveying literature. Buck, on the other hand,
returned almost obsessively to music, above all Romantic music. He called *Carmen* its highest point on the stage,
went from there to Wagner and on to Richard Strauss.
All in rather large leaps, I sometimes suggested, which
made making links so easy. But he laughed and said that
was the freedom that being half educated gave him.

However, the conversations we had—mostly in the
evening, walking outside the camp—also showed me
what gaps there were in my musical knowledge and that
in the unspoken rivalry which develops in every friendship such as that between Buck and me, it was only with
my literary knowledge that I could keep up at all. And

with the Renaissance. With Lorenzo the Magnificent, for example (of whom I had just read a biography), who was the rare example of a tyrant whom even lovers of freedom were, supposedly, happy to acknowledge as one of their own. The author had quoted one of the leading thinkers at Lorenzo's court saying that when Plato returned from Hades he would seek out not Athens but instead the Florence of the Medici princes. Astonished, Buck allowed me to tell him about the wonders and peculiarities of this epoch, its combination of intellectual boldness, splendor, and a sense of beauty. Sometimes, in the middle of the conversation, he forgot where he was, took a couple of steps to the side, and, in nervous haste, began to make notes.

On one of these far too short days we were woken earlier than usual and ordered out to the roll-call square. Three high-ranking officers stood in front of the assembled units. One of them read from a leaflet that an underhand and dishonorable assassination attempt—unworthy of a German officer—had been made on the Führer's life. The two other officers stood beside him, staring blankly into the distance. The deed, continued the reader, was all the more reprehensible as the Reich, since the invasion of Normandy, was also threatened from the west. Then several measures to improve our readiness for defense were read out.

Our superiors took the July 20 assassination attempt as an excuse to intensify the drilling, and several times fetched us out of bed in the middle of the night for an exercise. "If drill and increased imbecility are the only result," said one of our comrades, who until that point had hardly been conspicuous for his political remarks, then he regretted even more that the assassination had failed. Almost everyone found the abolition of military salutes, which was announced at issue of orders a few days later, and their replacement by the Hitler salute just as annoying. He felt like a monkey, Buck said in the circle of his comrades, and I added that I had recently seen a picture of a historical Berlin masquerade in which some of the masked were walking under a grotesque pig's or donkey's head. That's just how we must appear to others, interjected Buck, only they had done voluntarily what we were forced to do. He would have to think hard as to which of the two looked more ridiculous.

In retrospect the frankness with which this group of Gymnasium boys (which is what the majority of us were, thrown together from all over) declared their opposition to the given conditions is astonishing. No one, of course, wanted to make a show of courage. Everyone simply knew at a first or second glance whom he could trust and when caution was called for; and, without a word of conversation, anyone with even a bit of intelligence had a feeling for what could be said in front of whom and what it was better to remain silent about. Because at this late stage of the war there was hardly any doubt that even innocent-sounding remarks could be life-and-death matters.

So the days, which granted us an unexpected friendship, drifted by. But they didn't last long. In the second half of September the unit was lined up for roll call and after a few phrases, which were supposed to rouse us, we were divided into two groups. Then a clerk took the names, and as the trucks had already arrived at the barracks, the sergeant gave us half an hour for "regulation packing." To my dismay Buck and I found ourselves in different sections. Since this departure, too, took its course with the usual military waste of time, we were at least able to get a few moments to say goodbye to each other and some other comrades. I said something to Buck about the musical insights I had got from him, and that we should stay in touch. He replied that he must return the compliment, because only thanks to me had it become clear to him how much time he had frittered away in German and history classes. Now a couple of things had dawned on him, and on the whole he wanted to say that never in his life had he felt as free as in our conversations. "And that as a dumb-ass private! Who can make sense of the world?"

As we were taking our last steps a little way from the rest, Buck told me how, as a seven-year-old, he had dug up cobblestones in front of his parents' house on the marketplace of Radolfzell and put them aside. When a passerby asked what he was looking for, he had replied, "For the Devil, of course. Someone has to find him." And if he didn't exist, he wanted to discover what the secret was and what was hidden under the stones instead of the Devil. A little later he wrote to me in a letter that we had come a tiny bit closer to the market-square secret. When this "utterly stupid war" was over, we should start looking again as soon as possible. It was convenient that Freiburg was such a noted center of music.

Then we saw the trucks driving up, and out of the crowd of NCOs zealously hurrying around one shouted over to ask why we were walking so far away. An hour later the convoys moved off. A destination was not named, but we soon discovered that we were traveling north. In Aachen the two units separated, and about three days later, after numerous further interruptions and an interim halt in Tilburg, we reached a military camp near the Dutch town of Eindhoven. Even as we were getting down from the trucks the news spread that we were not going into action, because the British airborne troops that had landed a few days before had already been wiped out. At Arnhem and Nijmegen Montgomery had wanted to attack the Germans from the rear and capture the Rhine bridges, but the operation had failed. So there was once again time for practice in military mindlessness. At the arrival roll call the sergeant major addressed the column with the words: "Soldiers! My name is Neuber. I am the sergeant major. On duty I am—to the best of my ability—a bastard, but off-duty I'm a pleasant fellow. You will get to know both!" And then, suddenly bellowing with all his might: "All men, take cover!"

At the beginning of October 1944 our unit was transferred to a small town on the Lower Rhine. There we were trained in duties as sappers, in building pontoons and in moving bridges. A new friendship arose with our company commander, Lieutenant Walter Kühne, who summoned a few chosen comrades for an interview. After some words about my parental home and education, he asked me, almost without a transition, about Rilke and

I recited the first three or four sections of *Cornet Rilke* until he signaled it was enough. As I later found out, he asked others about Kleist, Fontane, or Stefan George and with the four or five boys who had satisfied his demands he formed a circle of lovers of literature. He was probably not much liked by his brother officers because of it. Any rate, I overheard two officers say, "Kühne's crazy! He should be kicking ass. Instead, he tries to make himself interesting by being highly educated."[4] One evening at this time I heard over the crystal set, though with a great deal of interference, *The Marriage of Figaro*. Once more I regretted that Reinhold Buck wasn't there with me. In the end, I thought, literature could hardly replace music.

As the month drew to a close, news of death came in from all sides. Once, on a single day, four comrades whom I had felt close to were reported killed in action, and I heaved a sigh of relief at every day that ended without terrible news about relatives or friends. Shortly after this I received a letter from Wittenbrink, which he had given to a parishioner who belonged to a signals unit. Wolfgang was not well, it said. Lieutenant Kühne moved heaven and earth to find out more. In mid-October he told me that Wolfgang was seriously ill and had been taken to a hospital in Beuthen in Silesia. My mother had rushed there from Berlin when she heard the news, and was with him day and night. My father, too, was trying

4 This is an example of an important distinction still in existence, even in the officer corps; those with a broad liberal education or *Bildung* set themselves apart from the others, the less educated. They also have more in common with those who have and show *Bildung* than with other members of their own social class.

to get special leave. Both were terribly afraid and my mother, in particular, was in despair—that was the message Lieutenant Kühne had got from a medical orderly, who had scribbled it down on a piece of paper. Blinded by tears and with nothing to hold on to, she often lost her way in the unfamiliar surroundings, Kühne read to me. "She admitted that to a stranger?" I asked. I couldn't believe it. "You're right," he said, "here on the piece of paper it says only that she couldn't get her bearings at all in the town, and prayed to God to spare her son. Then it says that because she was weeping all the time she found it hard to carry out the simplest tasks. And at the end it also says that it is very important to her that Wolfgang's brother is told everything."

The news struck me like a thunderbolt. Probably, I thought later, because it was utterly unexpected and it made my worst fears come true. Of the friends I had made and lost in the course of the years, it was Wolfgang to whom I was closest. Not only had I always been able to talk to him, but we had discussed many things of lasting importance. Even when we had arguments or differences of opinion, there always remained an indissoluble bond. Free from the usual jealousy of younger siblings, I admired his wit, his independence, and his pride. Almost ten years before, when the second supper had been inaugurated, he had told me (giving my chest a nudge) that now it was we two against the world, and at the time that high-flown phrase had been quite incomprehensible to me. When it became clear what he had meant, I realized why our arguments, which might have destroyed other friendships, resulted in no lasting offense between us. In a way I thought him invulnerable. Only now did I begin to have a presentiment that the world was stronger than we could ever be.

An endless week—in the course of which I again and again tried to find out more news, and several times applied in vain for short leave—passed without further details. I often went for a walk in the evening, and to distract myself asked one of the comrades from the Kühne circle to accompany me. We stumbled over the uneven terrain. I avoided all reminiscences. Instead, we talked about books, films, or actors, as well as the discovery of those years, Georg Trakl, and also Stefan George.[5] At times I suspected that my companions—no matter what the subject—wanted to talk me into having a confidence, which I myself could no longer summon up.

On a bright November day, as I've never forgotten, there came certainty. Wolfgang had already died in the middle of October 1944 in the hospital in Upper Silesia, exactly one week after his twentieth birthday. Slowly, thanks to communications from my mother, which often reached me by surprising routes, I found out more details. In the course of a military operation near Riga, on the Baltic front, he had contracted a lung infection; summoning up all of his strength, he had been helped to battalion headquarters by two comrades. There his

---

5 Georg Trakl (1887–1914), a major lyrical talent, was drafted as a military pharmacist in the First World War. He is presumed to have committed suicide after seeing the effects of the war on the battlefield and in a military hospital.

commander had first of all shouted at him for being a "malingerer," then driven him back to the front line with his drawn revolver. Two hours after arriving at the make-shift dugout, he had collapsed, lost consciousness, and been taken to a hospital. A few days later a train carrying the wounded had brought him to Beuthen.

When my mother got there, Wolfgang had passed the night with a high temperature and had difficulty breathing. On October 13, his birthday, he said to her, "Today death was with me. We came to an agreement. He granted me another postponement." After two earlier operations he had to endure an operation on each of the following seven days. "They don't have any anesthetic and painkillers here anymore," he groaned after the fourth operation. "I can't bear it much longer." On October 19, after overcoming endless difficulties, my father got to the sickbed while Wolfgang still had moments of clarity. Ten hours later profuse perspiration set in and Wolfgang's face was covered in glassy beads of sweat. Abruptly recovering consciousness, he begged our parents, "Please don't write 'In deep sorrow.'" Then he lost consciousness again, and minutes later, with a last move-ment of his hand, he died. According to my mother, he had replied to the devout consolation that she uttered, "Don't worry! The little bit of life I had didn't leave me any time to get up to much mischief." And after a pause in which he fought for breath: "I liked it."

Wolfgang's death was an unspeakable misfortune for our family. My mother had always said as long as we were all alive she would not complain. Now that pillar of stability had broken down. In the almost twenty-five years that remained to her, whenever Wolfgang's name or an episode involving him was mentioned, she rose from her seat and left the room. I was there on some occasions and followed her. Each time I found her in one of the other rooms, where, her head in her hands, she tried to compose herself. Once in the mid-1960s, when I inadvertently talked about Wolfgang, she simply looked at me and with an imploring "Please!" left the room. Later, she said that after everything else, Hitler had also taken her son and she hoped, quite without Christian magnanimity, that he would never be granted forgiveness for it.

At the news of Wolfgang's death all the lordly manner of my supposedly unapproachable grandfather collapsed. His villa not far from the Seepark had already been destroyed in an air raid, and with my grandmother he had moved into my parents' apartment, half-empty now, since my sisters, to avoid evacuation, were at a girls' Gymnasium in the Neumark east of Berlin. He had locked himself in his room for two days, not let anyone in, and answered all pleas with a dismissive blow on the door. My two sisters, who liked to call him "hard-hearted," later related that when he silently returned to the family table his eyes were red from weeping.

For me, too, the death of my brother was a profound break. I had once said to Reinhold Buck that in his life each person has four fundamental experiences: first, being overwhelmed by a perfect musical work; then, reading a great book; then, first love; and then, the first irreplaceable loss.

Wolfgang Fest just before his call-up to the army in 1943

Among the viler Nazis in our unit was a Medical Corporal Schneider, a man of about forty, a male nurse by profession, who (as he often boasted) had joined the party in 1933. Some of us suspected that he had been assigned to our company of mainly middle-class school-leavers as an informer. At any rate, we called him "the Ear," because he was constantly eavesdropping and treated everyone he met with the mistrust of the born spy. Someone had evidently told him that I had spoken with disgust of the death of my brother, and in particular of the battalion commander who had forced him back to the front line. Without hesitation, Schneider formally reported the "incident," and, together with the overzealous Sergeant Major Mahlmann, tried to submit it directly to the court-martial to whose sphere of responsibility the regiment belonged. Lieutenant Kühne, however, asserted his superior rank as company commander and—feigning outrage, he stated in the presence of the sergeant major—he had come to a provisional decision. I was given a "final warning," but given the difficult military situation I was declared indispensable for the time being. After the foreseeable final victory, however, which I also impatiently anticipated thanks to my trust in the Führer, continued Kühne, I would certainly be placed before a court-martial and, should the accusations made against me prove well founded, be punished by the full force of the law.

The next day I had to come to the orderly room and Mahlmann immediately brought up what had taken place. He bellowed angrily, "I can see through it all!

Always Kühne, Kühne, Kühne! That's going to stop! Otherwise, I'll be the one who is up at regimental headquarters in full dress uniform!" When I described the incident to him, Lieutenant Kühne remarked, "Once Mahlmann would have been someone to fear. In the present situation I don't worry too much about him. I feel more unease at your behavior. Of course, I understand you. But don't do anything else stupid! Even someone who has the better arguments doesn't let the Mahlmanns and Schneiders of this world notice it." And, patting my shoulder, "Not least because we despise them."

In November 1944 our unit was moved to the army training camp at Cologne-Wahn. We had hardly arrived before preparations for Christmas began. Fir twigs were nailed up everywhere, hung with tinsel or apples, and sometimes even a candle found somewhere was attached. As always the celebrations began with an hour of contemplation, which opened with an address boldly cobbled together by the commanding officer about salvation, sacrifice, and final victory; then there followed a drawn-out "O Tannenbaum." Franz Franken—the opera enthusiast I had got to know during our time on the antiaircraft battery, and who was in one of the battalions at this camp—had managed, within a short space of time, to form a chamber orchestra, which performed Mozart's "Eine kleine Nachtmusik" and Handel's *Music for the Royal Fireworks*. The three hundred or so participants returned once again to Christmas with a tearful "Stille Nacht"; then it was time for the jolly part of the festivities. Without a pause, the tables became boisterous

Lieutenant Walter Kühne, who saved the author from a court-martial, in front of his house in Stelle, near Lüneburg, in the early 1950s

and whoever had been sitting at them seemed, as if at a signal, to romp back into the forests from which his ancestors had emerged in primeval times.

As soon as circumstances allowed, I fled to my books. On the second day of Christmas my father was unexpectedly on the phone. He hinted he was awaiting the Russian attack somewhere on the edge of West Prussia. We talked about family things and about Wolfgang's death, and I had the feeling that he hid his need to avoid any kind of sentimentality behind somewhat worn phrases. He mentioned my mother's dreadful state, the wretched farewell when he himself had to leave for the front again, and that he didn't have much more to say. "It's all been said, and even this call can only tell you what you already know. And as for Mother," he added, "you have known of her sorrow and the reasons for it for a long time."

Then he asked me about my books and I said that I had taken some from Berlin or Freiburg, and had exchanged some for cigarettes or other things. One day I had come by an officer's map case and since then had kept my "library" in it. It contained nothing but the obvious: Goethe's *Poems*, selected ballads by Schiller, a volume of Hölderlin, and a couple of thin paperbacks with quotes from Jean Paul, Schopenhauer, and Nietzsche. Also the copy of Ernst Jünger's *On the Marble Cliffs* that he had given me, and I even had Josef Weinheber's *Selbstbildnis (Self-Portrait)*. "But no Thomas Mann," I added as a weak joke. Altogether, apart from a map of the country between Cologne and Düsseldorf, there were thirteen books in the leather bag which was attached to my belt. Then the conversation suddenly broke off.

The next day I unexpectedly bumped into Reinhold Buck outside the canteen, and I was so surprised that with a quite uncustomary gesture I embraced him. From then on we were, as far as conditions allowed, inseparable and spent whole evenings together in some empty hut or other. We told each other what had happened in the past weeks, and realized that without us knowing it our units had the whole time been quite close. I talked about the radio broadcast of *The Marriage of Figaro*, he about Mozart's highly developed psychological understanding. When I related Wittenbrink's "proof of the existence of God," he said that, for once in history all the conditions of the ideal moment had indeed come together, which made the great work of art possible, and the pious might say, God had revealed Himself. For fifty years. At Mozart's death this moment had already almost passed. Beethoven and Schubert, with extraordinary efforts, had extended it for a while. That made their contribution all the greater. With Wagner it was finally over. In him one heard too much loud panting, he said. "You must be thinking of the beginning of *Das Rheingold*," I interjected ironically, but he replied that *Rheingold* was one of the exceptions; there, even he (for whom the Nazis had spoiled the pleasure in Wagner) could, without any effort, hear the "breath of the universe."

Whenever the canteen was empty we could even listen to the wireless and, whenever possible, in the time that followed, we scoured the stations. We also talked about literature, about which we agreed much less often than music, and I remember only that Buck regarded the poets "of the second rank," such as Eichendorff, Geibel, and Kerner, as "mere text providers" for Schubert and Schumann, and called Rilke a "word cobbler" who had turned my head. At some point I told him about Wolfgang's death. Buck said that after the war the battalion commander who forced my brother back to the front line should be put on trial. Then we talked about the first dead we had seen, and I told him about the NCO who had been sprawled across a shattered tree near Düren, while he remembered six or seven Englishmen who had lost their lives when their plane came down close to Groningen.

On several evenings Buck spoke repeatedly about death. "Don't have any illusions," he said, "there's no escaping it." He only hoped, he added, during a walk across the barracks, whose buildings were like tenement blocks, that death trod loudly when it came. When I asked what he meant, he replied that he didn't want to be surprised by his going. Not like a thief in the night, he added, ending with a wild giggling. One must be fully aware of the end! "But of course, without suffering." He hinted at making the sign of the cross and went on, in his way of pushing everything to an extreme: "I don't want to die wretchedly—not like one of those stinking lumps of humanity I saw lying in the field hospital, groaning away." He made me promise to stand by him in death, one way or another.

But the following day we were unexpectedly separated once again, and Buck said, as we parted, that he

Joachim Fest's friend, Reinhold Buck

hoped to get through the war, despite everything. With a smile he said, "That goes for you, too. No wretched dying!" Already ten steps away from me, he stopped and shouted half to the side, "One so rarely finds a friend!" Afterward I tried for a couple of days to find out through Lieutenant Kühne where he had been deployed, but without success.

My company was sent to Euskirchen near Bonn to lay glass mines on a half-finished military airfield. The newly developed explosive devices looked like preserving jars, and when they exploded burst into countless tiny splinters that caused terrible wounds. Day after day, as we worked out in the open, American Lightning fighter-bombers would appear and use us for target practice as we lay exposed amidst the glass jars gleaming in the sun-light. That was the next set of dead I saw. After night-fall we fetched them from the field and laid them out in a hall; finally, together with the corpse in the tree, I got to twenty dead. Then I stopped counting.

Back in Cologne-Wahn we spent the days, and occa-sionally the nights, practicing pontoon-building, often standing up to our knees in water in the icy River Sieg, and a couple of times we even tried it in the fast-flowing Rhine. After about two weeks we were informed a room at a time that the next day we were starting out for Mett-mann near Cologne. The reason given was that Mont-gomery, although with some delay, was moving toward the Rhine. The approaching end of the war began to make itself felt in the muddle with which we were sent back and forth. Even before we took up position in

Mettmann, the deployment was broken off and we were
ordered back to our starting point.

That day we stood shivering for several hours in a
forest of thin, awkward trees. Without warning we heard
a whistling sound and at the same moment two shadows,
which we took to be a new type of American plane, flit-
ted over us, no more than one or two hundred feet above
our heads, so that we threw ourselves to the ground looking for shelter. Later, we found out that they were Mess-
erschmitt Me 262 fighter-bombers, which, powered by
jet engines that had recently gone into mass production,
flew faster than the speed of sound. Immediately, there
was talk again of "miracle weapons" that would change
the course of the war. Even as we were still talking about
them we had to assemble again and received the order to
get onto trucks which had just driven up.

That, however, was not yet the end of the confused
deployment situation. About thirty miles farther south
we were just as abruptly given the order to get out and
march. At Leverkusen we passed a military hospital
where we took a short rest, surrounded by staff cars and
military ambulances. Pitiable sounds came from the
buildings near us; doctors and male nurses were running
around shouting; in the corridors we found long rows
of bandaged figures, looking like shrunken larvae, and
between them tubs full of sawn-off limbs.

Around midnight we crossed the railway bridge near
Cologne's cathedral, where a cold smell of burning wafted
toward us from the riverbank. The streets along which
we marched consisted of buildings "blown through" by

the wind, as the popular phrase had it; in between them we made our way over blackened mountains of rubble and hills of ash. Whole facades covered by missing relatives' or friends' messages stood ghostlike in the emptiness: HANNES, WHERE ARE YOU? GISELA.[6] When a gust of wind blew over the fields of ruins we felt grit crunching between our teeth. Sometimes someone opened a hatch or removed the cardboard from a cellar hole to see who was coming along the street; in other places white faces appeared in a square hole in brickwork. Pointlessly, some sirens suddenly howled. The pathetically swelling sound involuntarily reminded me of Liszt's *Les préludes*, which had accompanied the victory announcements of the Russian campaign on German radio and had not been heard for a long time. Instead, the talk now was constantly of a "straightening of the front," the camouflage term which the propagandists of the regime had invented for "retreat."

On the night of March 8, 1945, after crossing the Rhine again, we reached the town of Unkel, which was on the right bank of the river opposite Remagen.[7] Exhausted by the marching and our impressions on the way, we were granted "an hour's rest." Then we each received twenty rounds of ammunition, after which we

---

6 Since all civilian means of communication had ceased to exist, these search messages were the only way to find out whether someone was still alive after the bombing raids and evacuations.

7 This is the famous bridge at Remagen which was the only major structure across the Rhine still standing at this point and thus hotly contested by the warring parties; it had the highest strategic value, especially for the Allies.

crawled up a wooded slope as far as the meadow which bordered it. At the other end of the meadow, about two hundred yards away, was an isolated farmhouse which lay in darkness. At the edge of the woods we got the order to dig one- and two-man foxholes at intervals of ten yards. Now we were also told that the American Ninth Tank Division had captured the undamaged Ludendorff Bridge only hours before and an armored advance guard had already crossed. Several attempts by the Germans to blow up the bridge or to smash the American units had failed.

When all the orders had been issued, Mahlmann called me over and instructed me to dig a two-man hole in an advanced position about seventy yards from the farmhouse. Surprisingly, he ordered the hole to be excavated a couple of yards this side of the edge of the woods in the open meadow and personally led me there in the shelter of the trees. When I asked why the foxhole was not to be dug in the woods like all the others, he simply retorted that it was not for me to ask questions here. After all, since Lieutenant Kühne had maintained with such conviction that I was so uncommonly eager for final victory, I should surely obey every order without hesitation. Then he ordered me, while standing at the edge of the wood, farther out into the open field. "Go on! Start now!" He went back into the trees to (as he said) check the work of the others. As I dug up the soil, we came under fire; the ground was plowed up without me being able to tell where the shooting was coming from. Once someone started to scream, which turned to whimpering, but there, too, I couldn't tell whether it was an American or one of ours. Now and then a machine gun tap-tap-tapped through the black, empty night.

At about six in the morning Mahlmann came back and only now did I realize that he wanted to use the two-man foxhole with me. He let his stocky body down beside me, grumbled about this and that, and finally ordered me to be lookout, because he wanted "to have the pleasure of a brief nap." A fine drizzle started again and I covered us with the tarpaulin. When he woke up in the first light of dawn, he asked whether anything had happened and whether I had observed any movement in the farmhouse. When I replied in the negative, doing so in quite unmilitary fashion with my mouth full (because after eating my "iron ration" I was chewing a heel of bread I had saved up), he demanded that I should look again. When I replied that after two days without food I wanted to eat this piece of bread first, he shouted at me abruptly and quite incautiously that I was constantly contradicting him. "And that with a trial awaiting you! It's going to stop!" he bellowed. "Once and for all! It's an order!" When I went on chewing at my crust, he shook his head and grumbled, a bit more quietly, that he had to do everything himself.

Calming down, he asked in an almost resigned voice, "What's happened to discipline?" He scrambled around for a moment and stood up, put on his helmet, and raised his head above the top of the foxhole. "Well, is there anything?" I asked. "Perhaps Corporal Fest could take the trouble to get up here himself," he barked again. As I, forcing down the last piece of bread, made ready to do so,

I saw his knees suddenly go limp. "Sergeant Major, what is it?" I shouted and grabbed him by the shoulder. When there was no answer, I repeated my question. Suddenly Mahlmann sagged down with his face against the wet side of the foxhole. I carefully turned him over and saw a small sharp-edged bullet hole in the middle of his helmet. When I pushed his gas mask behind his neck and raised his head, several rivulets of blood coursed in short spasms down the lifeless face soiled by the damp earth.

Sergeant Major Mahlmann was dead. But his demise didn't move me. How easy it would have been for him, I told myself, to dispense with the court-martial against me or to say one comradely word. But he had never been capable of that. At no time have I ever forgotten what went through my head as I saw him lying beside me, motionless, his mouth open, the darkening trails of blood on his face: sometimes, I thought, even if only rarely, the right man gets hit. I should feel a little pity for him, I reproached myself beside the dead man in the hole. But I could muster nothing of the sort.

Minutes passed. As the noise of battle which had intermittently intensified died down I jumped out of the hole in one bound, was at the edge of the woods in five steps and, as bullets struck the trees around me, ran without stopping to a nearby tree-lined depression which led to the farmhouse. About fifty paces from the building the inhabitants had put up a shelter, which was now deserted. Exhausted as I was, I lay down, but was unable to sleep. Instead, I ate the iron ration I had taken from Sergeant Major Mahlmann before leaving the foxhole.

"At least you've done me *one* good turn!" I thought. I did not know that I would not eat again for the next six days.

After that, crouching low, I crawled over to the farmhouse, whose four wings enclosed a large yard. The room behind the small window, which I came on just before the nearest corner, had been emptied. Yet a few steps farther, when I came to the end of the wall and carefully looked around it, I almost bumped into an American GI, who was holding his submachine gun at the ready and instantly started shouting, "Hands up! Come on! Hands up, boy!" He took the rifle and all my equipment from me, including the map case. "What's that?" he asked, and when I replied that it was just books, he said, "We'll check that!" Then, with a great deal of hysterical shouting, he led me across the yard. The tiled room, whose door he pushed open, had evidently served the owners as a parlor. The GI pushed back his helmet and ordered, "Sit down! And don't move!" Without taking his eyes off me, he opened all three doors, behind which I made out about twenty American soldiers, and shouted something incomprehensible into each room.

The lieutenant who entered shortly after that spoke perfect German, with a slight Palatinate intonation, so I asked him whether he came from the Mannheim area. But he hardly looked up from my paybook and retorted that he hadn't made the journey from Milwaukee to the Rhine to make conversation with a Nazi. He inspected the map case, looked thoughtfully at the Goethe and Hölderlin poems, at the collections of quotations, and whatever else had been found on me. After glancing briefly at a few pages he threw the books onto the nearby pile of rubbish, where bits of wall plaster, scraps of fruit, empty meat cans, and other junk was heaped up. "All over!" he said. And when I wanted to know what exactly, he barked, "Everything!" and "No conversation, my boy!" Finally, the map case flew onto the refuse.

Before the lieutenant started the interrogation that was evidently coming, I plucked up all my courage to ask whether I could keep some of the books. "They'll just rot here," I remonstrated. He looked at me in annoyance, but hesitated. Then he said with unexpected harshness, "You Nazi louts will have to get used to the fact that you'll have no say about anything now. Or even better: that you're not even allowed to ask for anything anymore." For a moment I wanted to answer back that I wasn't a Nazi lout, perhaps he had noticed that there hadn't been a single Nazi book in my map case. But then I refrained from making the objection. He's like Mahlmann, I said to myself. Typical military blockhead! But as if he had guessed my thoughts, the lieutenant went over to the pile of rubbish and picked out three of the thrown-away books: Goethe's poems, Ernst Jünger's *On the Marble Cliffs*, and Josef Weinheber's *Self-Portrait*. A curious selection, I thought, as he threw the books down in front of me. I asked him why he had left all the others. He replied, this time somewhat more civilly, "None of that German greed again. The other books stay where they are."

He ordered me to follow him into a neighboring room. At a small table sat a youthful captain holding an illustrated magazine, apparently unaffected by all the turbulence of battle, and for the first time I saw a person of rank with his feet on the table. He asked who was being brought to him. The lieutenant briefly stated what he had found out about me, my unit, and the names of the officers. The two exchanged several more sentences in what seemed to me more like Double Dutch than English, and the captain threw his magazine aside to ask me a couple of questions himself. What was the operative officer on the German side called? What did I know about a Major Scheller and about the National Socialist political officer? And more questions like that. At the end he told me to pull up the sleeve on my right arm, and merely said the conversation was over. As I went out, he picked up the magazine again, put his feet on the table, and shouted, "By the way, we're going to leave your hometown Berlin to the Russians. That's what you deserve, after all."

In the more distant room to which I was then led I encountered three more prisoners, none of whom, however, had belonged to my unit. We had hardly exchanged a few words when a sergeant came in and ordered us to follow him. Escorted by two GIs with submachine guns, and repeatedly forced to take cover by shell fire, we ran across a big field toward Unkel. On the deserted street right by the first houses lay dead soldiers, most in contorted postures, some also stretched out on their backs, their sightless eyes turned to the sky. The colors of death everywhere, I thought, as we ran down the street alongside a house front. There was also a woman among the dead, her apron covered in blood, and a few yards from her lay a dead soldier who had evidently been flattened by the tracks of a Sherman tank into a board, dark red at the edges. "Like in a cartoon," said the German NCO running beside me, but I thought what he said was out of place and retorted, "Shut up! No jokes about the dead!"

We spent the evening on the cellar steps of one of the houses by the roadside. Over the hours more and more groups of prisoners arrived. Soon there were about twenty of us; there was a rough shoving and pushing on the steep, narrow stairs. After darkness fell there was suddenly shouting and movement; we were led out of the town and through the Erpel Tunnel to the Rhine crossing. One of the guards, who spoke German, warned us to be extremely careful, because the bridge had been badly damaged by attempts to blow it up, and indeed we passed by a number of large holes, through which we could see the Rhine flowing black and bubbling far below. On the approach road, on the other bank, there was a jam of vehicles with silent soldiers sitting on them or waiting in the tank hatches. Occasional shells landed from the German side. Some GIs had a radio working, from which came unfamiliar music; others were standing around with mugs of coffee; others again smoked in front of their officers, and everything looked altogether relaxed and unsoldierly. Our group was led past the vehicles and into Remagen. We stopped in front of a building like a school in whose yard about a hundred prisoners were already waiting. Then five rows were formed and our escort, their helmets pushed back on their heads, distributed us over the five floors to the accompaniment of constant shouts of "Let's go!" and "Come on!" I was assigned a place in the attic.

There was a terrible crush under the beams and in the corners. Everyone tried to secure a sleeping space for himself, although later, as I discovered to my surprise, no one lay down to sleep; instead everyone began to exchange experiences with everyone else, about dramatic events, trouble with superiors, small skirmishing successes which in a moment grew into great battles, or the deaths of comrades. An American sergeant appeared several times and roared "Shut up!" or a barely audible "Quiet!," but the conversations continued without interruption.

Then suddenly, at about midnight, a bright flash and deafening blast stopped everything. For a fraction of a second (so it seemed to me later) there was an eerie silence after the hellish boom. Immediately after that everyone realized that a shell had struck the attic, and instantly an indescribable tumult broke out. The room was filled with shouts, cries for help, and chunks of masonry flying about, by the rattle of bits of roof falling down, and other sounds one couldn't place. At the same time shoes were hurled through the air, plaster, pieces of uniform, the contents of pockets. Something damp struck me in the face. Later I discovered that it had been a torn-off shoulder strap and had smeared my head with blood. Smoke and a dreadful stench filled the air. Whoever could, picked himself up and tried to reach the stairs. The lance corporal who had lain beside me behind the roof prop and talked incessantly about his family for the last two hours stretched out his arm and said that he wasn't going to make it away from here. I should remember him to his wife, and to Mouse and Hansi. To my question—almost unintelligible in all the noise—regarding his name and address he simply furrowed his brow, tried to find a word, and then said nothing more.

I pushed into the throng at the top of the stairs and even managed to get a few steps down, then everything came to a standstill. An American waving a submachine gun forced his way up and shouted, this time in an unmistakable Berlin accent: "Everyone stay where he is. The gate below is locked. Otherwise I'll shoot!" And then, again and again: "Last warning. My gun is loaded! Attention! I'll shoot!" But finally he had to give way, because the pressure on the stairs was simply too great.

Meanwhile, a senior American officer had appeared. A German captain had assured him "on his word of honor as an officer" that the prisoners could be left in the yard even in complete darkness; no one would escape. He had chosen "reliable people" as overseers; they had vouched for themselves with rank and name. Then the care of the wounded was discussed and a mutually acceptable solution found. At a signal the two hundred or more prisoners came out of the doors and windows into the yard and spent the night in the open in the freezing damp. The intermittent shelling had ceased. In the early hours of the morning, impatiently expected, the trucks rolled up.

As we climbed onto the vehicles, a good-natured black American answered the question as to where we were going: France, of course. "To Paris!" he added. "But not to a brothel!" He burst out laughing. He couldn't stop, and even a little later, as we passed the place where he was posted, he pointed at us, laughing, "No girls! No fun!"

I felt a shock when, just before the border, we abruptly turned toward Euskirchen and from there headed toward that airfield on which a few weeks before we had laid the glass mines. After about an hour of wearying waiting around we had to get down from the trucks, and at every moment I expected the order to clear mines.

Quite lost in thought, I suddenly heard my name called. In front of me stood Medical Corporal Schneider, who had until recently tried to have me court-martialed, but who now showed something like warmth and expressed his pleasure at our unexpected reunion. "When did we last see each other?" he asked, and protested how much he had always liked me and my fearlessness "in front of the epaulets." Had he ever even suspected how mendacious and inhuman the Nazis were, he would have been my most loyal friend, but, thank God, he wasn't aware of any wrong he had done me.

One could have easily suspected and even known what had remained unknown to him, I retorted, particularly if one had joined the party before 1933. But Schneider acted as if he hadn't heard my objection, and told me that about ten thousand Americans had already crossed the Rhine on the Ludendorff Bridge. Hitler, he said, as informed sources already knew, had convened a drumhead court-martial to condemn to death the six or seven officers responsible for Remagen. I acted as if his confidences didn't interest me, and simply said, "Just stop it, Schneider! Times have changed, as you know!" He looked at me in astonishment, and I'll never forget his dumbfounded, foolish expression as I simply left him standing there. After two hours we were ordered onto the trucks again, and the convoy continued its journey.

Our destination was not, in fact, Paris, but a small place not far from the French capital called Attichy, which at this late stage of the war had acquired some notoriety as an assembly camp for what would soon be hundreds of thousands of German prisoners of war. As we climbed down from the trucks in front of the camp, French civilians pushed toward us from all sides. They spat at us or cheered the women who struck us with their fists, while the American guards formed a cordon to stop the attacks. That was the beginning of the "heroic Resistance," said one of my neighbors, who, after we had passed through the camp gate, introduced himself as a French teacher from Hanover.

What stays in my mind from Attichy, more than anything else, is Schubert's Unfinished Symphony, which at our arrival thundered from all the loudspeakers, and was still doing so nine days later when we left: day and night without stopping and with an annoying click after the sixty-fourth bar. The music was interrupted for every announcement, after which the gramophone needle was dropped onto the scratchy record again by a half-deaf GI. There was also talk in the camp of an organized squad of "Irreconcilables," as they called themselves, who quite unceremoniously killed any prisoner who made a disparaging remark about Hitler or the war. The squad would throw him into the huge, open cesspool and push him back into it every time he bobbed up.

Eight days later, shortly before we were moved from Attichy, I got into conversation with a prisoner who had caught my attention, because I thought I knew him. Indeed, it turned out he had belonged to the group from which I had been separated in Landau. I told him about my capture, the deployments from Arnhem to Remagen, and asked whether he knew Reinhold Buck. He said they had not been friends, but that he had admired Buck from a distance. "He was a genius," he said. "I heard him play furiously and masterfully on the violin." I asked him why he was using the past tense. "Oh, Buck," he said, "he's dead! And if I'm right he was only about two hundred yards away from you when he was dying, a bit to the east of the farmhouse where you were taken prisoner." When he saw my shock, he went on to say that Buck had bled to death in a two-man foxhole. That's what was said, anyway. He had been shot through the thigh, no one knew how, and had evidently not known how to apply a tourniquet to the wound. In a leather bag in his trouser pocket they had found a little Beethoven badge.

I was stunned and couldn't speak, so he tried to say something comforting. "You can be reassured," he said encouragingly, "I saw it with my own eyes. Buck lay there very peacefully."

I still remember my reply. "I didn't want to hear that!" I said. "Buck didn't want to die. And I didn't want to hear about his death being peaceful—not someone like him. I'd rather hear how he struggled to tie up his leg to his very last breath." Until we were moved on, if I found myself anywhere near that prisoner, I avoided him as best I could.

NINE

·

The Escape

At midnight, after a three-hour drive, the convoy of trucks came to a halt with a squealing of brakes. Glancing out, we saw sheds and warehouses on one side, on the other a large field picked out by gleaming searchlights. About two hundred soldiers, their guns at the ready, were running around in front of the convoy and shouting the already familiar "Come on!," "Let's go!," or "Hurry up!"

We had hardly jumped down when we saw, about thirty yards away, a two-winged gate, the entrance to a broad field surrounded by a high barbed-wire fence. Working under searchlights, a unit of pioneers was engaged in erecting watchtowers at intervals of 150 yards. Then the highest-ranking prisoner, a lieutenant colonel, was summoned to a group of American officers who had arrived shortly before and ordered to lead the almost ten thousand prisoners into the camp. "Where are the barracks?" asked the staff officer. "Or do you at least have tarpaulins and blankets?" At that a young, wiry American officer pushed to the front and called out in a caustic voice, "This isn't a hotel!" He waved his submachine gun in the air as he spoke. "But we have the key to lock the gate. Warn your people against trying to escape! Our soldiers have orders to shoot without warning! Do you understand?" The lieutenant colonel raised his hand to his cap and ordered us to march to the barbed-wire gate. The helmeted American soldiers cocked their guns as loudly as they could and stood shoulder to shoulder on both sides.

We stood on the fenced-in piece of land for about six hours until it began to grow light. Thick banks of fog surrounded us and, when they cleared, a flat-topped hill became visible to the west, dominated by a cathedral with three towers. Hardly had the picture taken shape, however, when it disappeared again in the sleet that set in. As far as I remember, it fell on us for almost three days. During this time, hungry and freezing, we measured out the course of the camp streets and dug ditches for the future pipes. We were also divided into companies. Anyone who was recognized as a member of the SS was taken away to a quickly laid-out special camp; there, as if at a command, the arrivals squatted down and stared straight ahead with an expression of defiant sacrifice. Sleet and snow kept falling and at the morning wake-up call the field was strewn with many humped white mounds, which began to move in the dawn light and gradually began to take on human shape.

On the third day a column of trucks drove through the camp gates and at regular intervals bedsteads, blankets, washbowls, and other necessaries were thrown off their backs. Already, by the following day, the shelters for the prisoners had largely been put up and the watchtowers around the camp erected. At the same time we were divided into work parties of varying sizes, each of which had its sphere of activities within the depot. I was assigned to the hall for office supplies, with its tall scaffolds of shelves that carried all kinds of blackboards, typewriters, adding machines, writing implements—more than three thousand different items. In other halls were stored uniforms, vehicle parts, leather gear, and everything needed by an army, with the exception of arms.

On the afternoon of the first day under canvas there was a camp assembly. On the broad middle street between the rows of tents stood the commandant, Captain John F. Donaldson, escorted by the wiry officer with the cutting voice, who introduced himself as Lieutenant Bernard P. Dillon, and a second lieutenant, Charles W. Powers. At a little distance from them First Sergeant Don D. Driffel, First Sergeant John S. Walker, and Sergeant Paul F. Geary, as well as other NCOs and privates, had taken up position. After a short address broadcast over the camp loudspeakers—in which he spoke mainly about work, discipline, and obeying orders—Captain Donaldson inspected some of the ranks. Every twenty yards or so he stopped and addressed a prisoner, with a corporal in his entourage taking notes. As chance had it, the captain also stopped in front of my group and asked

me my age, rank, and where I had been taken prisoner.
Before he went on, he instructed his clerk to note everything down.

The next day I was called to the headquarters hut
outside the camp gate. On my arrival I found three prisoners who had likewise been summoned by Captain
Donaldson. He asked me basically the same questions
as during the assembly, only he took much more time
and also inquired about my family, my education, and
my father's profession. In the middle of the conversation
he interrupted himself and called over an interpreter,
because after only one and a half years of school lessons
my English was not sufficient for more complicated conversations. When he dismissed me, he advised me to
improve my English, because he would like to have me
as an assistant at his headquarters. He added something
like "Don't worry, it will all turn out for the best."

The captain was a tall, elegant man. He was bald and
his face was dominated by a twirled mustache to which
cream was evidently applied and whose ends came to
needle points, giving his appearance an eccentric touch.
He clearly attached great importance to measured movements, and his speech, too, sounded altogether refined.
At the same time his deep bass testified to a great—
almost civilian—warmth. Never, at any rate, did he take
advantage of his rank by using a peremptory tone, and
there was nothing strained about his authority. He soon
displayed a noticeable liking for me and once, after I got
into a quite nonsensical argument with him about the
admiration of both the Germans and many foreigners

for Hitler, the always anxiously muttering First Sergeant Driffel admonished me not to forget the "paternal affection" that Captain Donaldson felt for me: otherwise, my privileges could come to a rapid end.

As far as personal matters were concerned, Donaldson was altogether discreet, so that in the almost two years in which he was my superior I never found out where he lived or anything about his family or what he did in civilian life or how he would have answered those questions which he put to me. He seemed to prefer topics of culture and politics in the wide sense over all other subjects. Once he discovered my love of music, he quizzed me about it in long evening conversations. It was the same with my literary preferences and how I had come to the history of ancient Rome or the Florence of the Renaissance, although it was evident that he found incomprehensible a mind that developed such abstruse tastes. He was surprised that I knew nothing about Dreiser, Faulkner, or Hemingway—names I heard from him for the first time—and concluded from that how shockingly removed from the civilized nations Germany had become under the Nazis. When we knew each other better, he wanted to know details about my family, about my brother who had died in the war, my other siblings and friends. I remained silent, however, about my parents' difficulties, because I felt that to describe them would be to make myself appear self-important. Instead, I told him about friends who had fled Germany, about harassment in our neighborhood at home, and about the pressures of living in a dictatorship.

I enjoyed my duties with Captain Donaldson and—taking to heart his advice about learning English—got hold of a volume of the Army Pocket Books series called *The Loom of Language*. At first, because a reasonable probationary period had been agreed at headquarters, I had enough time, particularly during night duty, to work my way through it, page by page. Sometimes the captain looked over my shoulder and explained unusual expressions with a few words on the origin of an idiom or metaphor.

On May 11, 1945, when I went to the camp gate, I saw agitated prisoners crowding around the noticeboard where the orders of the commander and occasionally important news items were posted. The reports that aroused such an unusual degree of interest were taken from various newspapers and stated that, after capitulation to the Western powers in nearby Rheims, the Wehrmacht had now laid down its arms to all the victorious powers in Karlshorst.[1] Already from a distance one could see there was a fierce debate taking place; as I came up one of the prisoners was just saying to a group standing there: "Well, it's over at last! It was high time!" The majority of them looked at him without saying a word.

A few yards away stood a German sergeant, who had repeatedly behaved in such an overbearing way that it was clear he thought the time for ordering people around was not yet over. He shouted at the soldier, "What does

---

1 The German armed forces surrendered in Rheims on May 7, 1945, and in Karlshorst, Berlin, where the Russians were headquartered, on May 9.—Trans.

'at last' mean? That we've lost the war? Is that what you wanted?" He glanced around, looking for approval. The man he had addressed, who was already walking away, turned around, went right up to the sergeant, and replied, straight to his face in a soft but unintimidated voice, "No! But that the damned war is over!" A corporal joined in and bellowed over the heads of the others, "It was an idiotic war anyway! From the start! Who believed in victory?" Another shouted into the growing confusion, "The Führer's genius! Dear Lord!" And soon everyone was shouting at everyone else, some men even came to blows, and again and again the words "idiotic war" and "the Führer's greatness" were repeated. It showed how sensitive the subject still was.

At any rate, one could read from the men's faces that in many cases the acquired reflexes continued to work. In not a few there was reflected a disbelieving shock at the openness with which some expressed themselves about the Hitler years. Then the corporal who had first used the phrase "idiotic war" walked off, shaking with laughter. The overbearing sergeant shouted after him: "Traitor! Crook!" As neither word had any effect, there followed "Deserter!" But the corporal, a man of about fifty, didn't turn around. He simply raised his arms in the air and waved them from side to side, and repeated, laughing contemptuously, "Yeah, yeah! The Führer's genius!'

The following day when I encountered this corporal on the camp street, we talked about the incident. He proved to be altogether entertaining and ended up inviting me to his one-man tent. As a painter and sketcher, he said, he was by profession, so to speak, always "a couple of steps" out of the world. But the madness of this war was something he could never have thought up. It was sometimes said of the Germans that they had no relation to reality: he thought it was a fairly stupid cliché, but Hitler had made it true. And the stupidity, as well. Against the whole world: he would never understand what had got into the Germans. And the Germans themselves hadn't understood it either, as the previous day's row had made clear.

His views were food for a good many more conversations. Since he was incessantly painting or drawing our American guards—or their wives, children, and sweethearts from photographs—he benefited from numerous privileges. In between, he painted camp views, landscapes, or flowers on small plywood panels. He came from the Bergisch Land, the hilly region south of the Ruhr, and his name was Alfred Sternmann. Among his privileges, apart from his own tent, were a proper cupboard instead of a metal military locker, two easy chairs, and a kettle and a water container to make tea. He also had a divided-off studio. So whenever my duties permitted I spent the afternoons with him, drinking tea.

To improve my linguistic skills I got a GI at headquarters to procure more books from the Pocket Library for me.[2] I read the adventures of Tom and Huck for the second time and, apart from that, got some other titles

2 This library of small-format paperbacks made available to GIs and, later, interested Germans, literary works that had been unavailable in Nazi Germany.

from Lieutenant Dillon—who had some knowledge of literature, but only came out with it reluctantly—among them Joseph Conrad's *Heart of Darkness*. A little later a corporal on the headquarters staff introduced me to the author whose works then accompanied me for the longest time during my imprisonment: W. Somerset Maugham. Perhaps influenced by my father's prejudice against novels, I was rather skeptical when I began to read *The Razor's Edge*, the tale of a restlessly driven man. But as soon as I finished it I immediately began *Of Human Bondage*, the story of an inexorable decline; and was finally able, with some difficulty, to get hold of *The Moon and Sixpence*. It was impossible to obtain more works by the writer, except for a volume of novellas, which mostly contained sharply observed love stories coming to a dramatic crisis.

The city of Laon, seen from the POW camp in which the author spent almost two years (oil painting on wood by Alfred Sternmann)

Astonishingly, no one recommended Steinbeck to me or Dos Passos, who had already been famous for a long time by then.

In the course of the months in which I was studying Somerset Maugham, I never came across a single awkward or even boring line. My reading, together with that first conversation with Captain Donaldson, also brought home to me that my knowledge of literature had so far been too much dominated by classic German works, that I knew neither Musil nor Heinrich Mann nor Thomas Mann, nor Balzac, Flaubert, Dickens, or the great Russians: all of them names that frequently came up, but which meant very little to me. Beyond that, I got to know, through the periodical *Die Brücke (The Bridge)*, which was produced especially for the American POW camps, the names of contemporary German authors like Friedrich Reck-Malleczewen, Reinhold Schneider, and Romano Guardini; I was particularly impressed by the poems of Erich Fried.[3]

The relaxed behavior of the American soldiers toward each other continued to surprise me. Between the higher and lower ranks there was no "Attention!"; only

---

3 Friedrich Reck-Malleczewen, a German writer who, among other things, analyzed the effects of mass hysteria in his writings, was born in East Prussia in 1884 and died in Dachau concentration camp on February 17, 1945, shortly before the camp was liberated by the Allies.

Reinhold Schneider (1903–58) dealt extensively with issues of power and religious belief and the conflict between earthly power and divine providence in numerous essays, dramas, and narratives.

Romano Guardini (1885–1968) was a most influential Catholic theologian and youth leader after 1945; the Nazis had forced him into early retirement in 1939, but he returned to teach at Munich University.

when orders were being issued was there any standing
at attention with the arm stiffly angled to the edge of the
cap. Even senior officers were friendly to privates in an
unaffected way and during discussions one often saw
both squatting down together. The security measures
were quite relaxed as well. The work parties leaving and
entering the camp were merely counted; as a result, it
became customary that on some evenings four or five
prisoners stayed in Laon and in their place the same
number of prostitutes came into the camp disguised
in work clothes. Then in the morning the two groups
changed places. First Sergeant Driffel once told me that
he had long ago seen through our trick: "You Germans
think you're damned smart. But we've known for a long
time that you're hanging around in the brothels in town."
He would, nevertheless, take no action. Because in the
same situation they would have done exactly the same.
As long as no one goes missing.

As my relationship with Captain Donaldson became
closer I was able—with the support of some fellow prisoners—to earn a few privileges. So we expanded the
handball and soccer tournaments, which had been at
first only camp championships, to other nearby camps
in Rheims, Soissons, and Saint-Quentin. We also proposed that a group of those interested be given classes
in politics, in particular on the rudiments of democracy.
Captain Donaldson was indeed able to get hold of a kind
of educational officer, whose possibly all-too-high-flown
expositions the majority of the participants met with
their own hard-boiled irony. Nevertheless, the classes

of the "Commanding Professor," as Captain Grey was mockingly called, were not without their effect. The biggest surprise was that he not only put up with objections from his listeners, but encouraged them, and a first lieutenant from Hamburg, with whom I soon had quite a few conversations, said after one of these debating sessions, "The good man is very convincing. But the Americans are just guileless people. A man like that doesn't know that freedom always goes wrong in the end."

But above all, working with some other prisoners it was possible to get surplus food supplies into the French camp in the fortress of Laon. The Americans regularly drove all foodstuffs that had not been used to a nearby rubbish dump and left them in a moldy heap to be fed on by rats, mice, and other creatures. In the French camp, however, about four thousand German prisoners were incarcerated in wretched conditions. One of them whispered to me during a visit that they would dearly love to have the stacks of loaves, the sacks of milk powder, the dried eggs, and the corned beef that were left over every day in our camp. It didn't take many words to convince Captain Donaldson of the absurdity of this situation. Nevertheless, military bureaucracy took a couple of weeks to comply with the request.

When I passed through the fortress gate on the hill, riding on one of the first trucks, emaciated figures silently began to unload the sacks and boxes. We were strictly forbidden to speak to the fortress prisoners, but one or two of us managed to exchange a few words with them, and we heard about hunger, dirt, and atrocious sanitary

The handball team of Laon Camp: the author and fellow escapee
Wolfgang Münkel are fifth and sixth from the left, respectively

conditions. The deliveries were then repeated and a few of us were slipped the message that the French guards passed on only a small part of the provisions to the prisoners, while the larger part of the consignment ended up on the black market.

In autumn 1945 Hubertus zu Löwenstein—my father's friend who had emigrated to the United States— tried to get me released with the help of his influential contacts. But his efforts were just as unsuccessful as the calls made by the academic Emil Lengyel, another of my father's friends, who had visited us several times during the Hitler years. However, they could at least inform me about the fate of the rest of my family. They let me know that my mother and my two sisters had survived somewhere in Berlin. About Winfried I was told, somewhat mysteriously, that he had "escaped the bloodhounds at the last moment," while all trace of my father had been lost somewhere in East Prussia. At the end of a letter Löwenstein wrote that he would have liked to send me food but, after making inquiries, found out that it was not allowed. Lengyel wrote me the same thing.

It was now that I began to keep a diary. A world, I thought, in which nothing happens, must be made more exciting through ideas committed to paper. I noted my conversations with Captain Donaldson, no matter how little there was to them, or the problems with Lieutenant Dillon, who evidently believed that a certain amount of bad temper went with putting on a uniform. But I also wrote down the arguments of the lower ranks with each other or with the Polish detachment that had recently arrived, as well as conversations with a slowly growing circle of friends.

The figure at its center was Erich Kahnt, a tall Saarlander, proud of his chubbiness, who liked to busy himself as cook, poet, and conversationalist; also part of the group were Wolfgang Münkel, who was devoted and sensible, and Klaus-Jürgen Meise from Hamburg, who, as one of the Swing Youth, had been imprisoned by the Nazis and covered every inch of his tent corner with colored pinups. And, of course, the close relation with Alfred Sternmann continued. There was almost nothing in my notebooks about Berlin; because of the censorship, the three or four letters I received from home reported only the inconsequential: *Thank goodness, you're still alive! We survived, too. How are you? Do you get enough to eat?* . . . and so on. Longer and more substantial entries were given over to the Commanding Professor, who, as ever, always came back to the habeas corpus acts and the Bill of Rights. When one of the participants in the course complained about Grey's eternal repetitions, our teacher was ready with a disarming explanation: these two documents were not only of fundamental importance, but he had simply loved them ever since he was young. "Yes!" he insisted, "'Love' is the right word." And for the sake of our country, that should be exactly our attitude, too.

I also wrote down what I thought worth recording about the camp handball team, of which I was soon a member, and the tournament trips, as well as my impressions on the way. It was not long before this had developed into a penchant for describing landscapes as precisely as possible, but also for capturing each human figure mentioned in a vivid portrait recognizable to the reader by at least the third sentence. Several years before, when I described the two sides of Hans Hausdorf—the serious and the punning—my father had accused me of a lack of respect, and to my response that I was merely describing reality, he had objected, "Then don't look so carefully! One can draw people more gently, more understandingly, if you'll permit the word!" Now, however, it was a matter of looking carefully. When I read Sternmann the three pages in which I had tried to portray him, he picked up his drawing block and began, even as I was still reading my text, to put down the first strokes of a drawing of me.

At about the same time I resolved to write down what I had learned about the Renaissance over the years. I did not know the exact dates of the persons and events, but I had committed to memory many episodes in the lives of Lorenzo the Magnificent, Verrocchio, and Alexander VI, Pico della Mirandola, Michelangelo, and Julius II, Guicciardini, Botticelli, and the unforgotten "great Caravaggio." Driffel got hold of a bloodthirsty, inventive potboiler about Lucrezia Borgia for me. It was called *Love, Power and Daggers: All Red as Blood* and the name of its author has disappeared from the world, as it has from my memory. Finally, with the help of this muddled and colorful material, which I spread out on my desk at headquarters when I was on night duty, I tried to write an essay.

Although I was aware of the gaps in my knowledge, I got so much pleasure from a subject that was in every sense human and splendid that I soon began to write a biographical sketch about the Luccan condottiere Castruccio Castracani. For weeks I had searched for biographical data about this contemporary of Machiavelli's but given our conditions at the time, I had been able to gather only a few haphazard references. As a result, I did not know much more about him than his origin as a foundling, which, possibly for propaganda reasons, was surrounded by mystery, as well as the notable connections which, with astonishing farsightedness, he had already made as a young man.

Nevertheless, I did find out something about Castracani's intentions: above all, that in his early twenties he had wanted to conquer Tuscany and after that to subjugate province after province until all Italy was in his hands. His senator's toga bore the inscription: *He is the one whom God wants.* Beyond that (according to my sources at the time), he dreamed the dream of every powerful man of the period: an alliance with the papacy or (should that fail) its subjection. As, in his unbounded ambition, he was setting out to do just that, he died a pitiful death from influenza. My piece was eventually forty pages long, and I sometimes thought it was probably this "banal" end, after so many mighty projects—the Thomas Mann punch line, so to speak—that had attracted me. More or less the only thing I still have of this first effort as a writer is the title: "The Hour of Castruccio." When Werner Schreiber, who dropped by from time to time for English conversation, objected, "Not a title! Too weak!," I retorted that it was better for a provisional title to be too weak than to announce itself with a "roll of thunder."

In spring 1946 we were alarmed by rumors that very soon the Laon camp was to be transferred to French control. We also heard about a formal agreement with Washington, concluded shortly before the end of the war, to provide the French with a million prisoners for forced labor. This talk, particularly as it grew more dismaying by the day, gave rise to increasing disquiet. Many prisoners thought that the French, as the great losers among the Allies, wanted a bigger piece of the victory bonus than was due to them, and in the camp some radical groups, which also existed, even discussed the possibility of a violent uprising. The prisoners who worked at headquarters were almost every day bombarded with demands to use their influence with Captain Donaldson to prevent these plans from happening. But when I, too, pestered him, the camp commandant merely shook his head—"Sorry!"—and said that such decisions did not fall within his area of responsibility. "I would like to help you. But it's impossible." A few days later I resolved to escape.

The number of breakout attempts had already increased after the first rumors of a handover to the French. Technically, it was comparatively easy to contrive an escape, because the guards were rather negligent and every week at least one goods train went from Laon to the American Zone of occupation in Germany.[4] Those in charge of the camp were therefore forced to tighten control. Lieutenant Dillon, together with the command staff in Rheims, urged greater restrictions, while Captain Donaldson said the prisoners should not be treated with undue harshness. They had already had more than enough of that. He saw it rather as his task to make their lives easier, he once remarked to me with his amused, gentleman's smile. But he was powerless in the face of the order that shortly before departure each train should be searched by a special unit from Rheims.

---

4 After Germany's military defeat in 1945, its territory—except for those parts permanently detached and given to other states like Poland or the Soviet Union, for example—was occupied by the Allied forces and initially divided into four occupation zones: American, British, Soviet, and French. Different laws, rules, and regulations pertained in all four and travel and commerce were severely limited, hampering the reconstruction effort. These zones only ceased to exist in 1949 with the formation of the two German states, the Federal Republic of Germany in the West (i.e., the three zones occupied by the United States, Great Britain, and France) and the German Democratic Republic in the East (the former Soviet Zone). But all foreign powers retained a military presence well into the 1990s, and the United States does so to this day.

It had become usual for prisoners to make escape attempts in pairs to be better prepared to meet the unforeseeable, so I first of all turned to Walter Heuser, who was supposed to have a taste for adventure and to be both daring and helpful. Surprisingly, he turned me down on the grounds that he didn't know where he should escape to. His whole family had died in the air raids. "Well, away from the barbed wire," I objected, "away from the French! Is that not enough?" But I couldn't change Walter's mind. It seemed to me that despite his reputation, he considered the risk of a breakout to be too great. After that I asked Wolfgang Münkel, who appeared both determined and levelheaded. He came from Mannheim, which was in the American Zone, and not only agreed without hesitation but immediately began to give thought to what one had to take into account in an escape, so as not to fail pitifully like most of the previous undertakings, particularly the recent ones.

First of all we drew up a list of things we would need. It began with a box of provisions, which would contain eight cans of corned beef and four cans of meat and beans for each of us, a few packets of Zwieback, three cans of beer, and a carton of cigarettes each. In addition, two canisters of drinking water, two woolen blankets, and, thanks to contact with a friendly but discreet French officer up in the fortress, authentic discharge papers made out in our names. We assembled these objects in the space of three weeks. And, of course, I stowed away my diary and the two Renaissance texts in my little leather bag, which so far I had got through all checks. At the end of April the rumors in the camp suggested that July 1 was planned as the day of the handover, so time was running out. A few days later we got hold of one of the confidential timetables, according to which a goods train was heading for the Stuttgart area on May 16. The description of the load listed uniform parts and rubber tires, and included the information that the eight rear wagons would be carrying asbestos pipe casing, which would be packed in long wooden containers. We decided on one of these asbestos wagons, because they seemed to us to offer the best shelter.

As camouflage, we ordered a container made of the same wood from the camp joiner's shop, but the box made for us, since it had to provide space for two people, was necessarily about twenty-five inches longer and almost twelve and a half inches wider than the ones for the asbestos. At the last moment we learned from an unwitting remark by First Sergeant Driffel that from mid-May departing trains would not only be searched but that tear gas would be used to flush out any escapees. After a few days we even managed to track down a gas mask, although such pieces of equipment were not part of the depot stocks. Unfortunately, we could get hold of only one.

When everything had been brought together and packed away in as space-saving a way as possible, we told the loaders in which wagon they should put the escape box. Then we informed the two crane operators that we wanted to get into the box in Warehouse 7 and be brought to the crane outside at the tracks by a forklift truck; there we were to be the first item to be put on the wagon bed: TOP and BOTTOM, LEFT and RIGHT were marked on the box. After that the asbestos containers were to be placed around us and finally on top of us, until there was nothing to be seen of our hiding place. A twenty-five-inch-wide escape path had to remain open, however, in case of emergencies. The crane operators promised to arrange everything as we wanted it.

At three o'clock in the afternoon we crawled into the coffinlike case, and the packer Loisl handed us the lid with which we could close and open the box from inside. We were driven to the crane, heard commands, and felt ourselves being lifted up and to the side until, with a jolt which shook the whole box, we were set down on a flat surface. A little later we heard steps and muffled voices. "Is there anything else?" asked one, and immediately after that we heard another: "We're loading the asbestos now. That's the end of any communication." After we had thanked them, we heard several "Safe journeys!" and "Say hello to home from me!" Then the boxes rumbled up and our container trembled as they were put down in the wagon.

The waiting began. As long as the work details were busy around the railway tracks and the daytime bustle dominated we could move about with a degree of freedom. But at some point we became increasingly aware of our arms, legs, and their suddenly numerous extremities; we were all the time knocking into each other. Hour after hour passed. We tried to while away the time, but repeatedly got in each other's way and struggled with our numbed limbs in the confined space. In stories which were as drawn-out as possible we talked in stifled voices about childhood experiences, remembered our parents, teachers, and friends, and I got on to my admiration for Rapid Vienna and Admira Vienna with Sindelar, Pesser, and Hahnemann. Once I even tried to recount Karl May's *Treasure of Silver Lake* and *The Shadow of the Padishah* (*Durch die Wueste*) and to recite Wilhelm Busch's verses, while Münkel again and again came back to the beautiful Archivolde, whom he had got to know as a soldier in Holland and who had become his great love, the bitter opposition of her family only increasing the mutual attraction. Once we tried to make as many words as possible out of the word *Sardellenbüchse* (anchovy can), but didn't get far. There was no end to the pushing around in our wooden box. Nor to the pain in our limbs.

All that ended in the evening and at night. In the weeks before we had repeatedly inspected the railway yard after nightfall and noticed the loud echo produced by the concrete surface. This observation forced us to be as quiet as possible during the nighttime silence, and we could only permit ourselves a few words; now and then we cleared our throats or shifted our bodies from our left side to our right every forty minutes or so when a passenger train thundered by. Only when the daytime sounds began did we feel halfway safe again. Then the train was usually shunted onto another track. That was the best opportunity to freshen up, which consisted of a few drops of water on a towel with which we wiped face, neck, and hands.

Until then every goods train had left the depot on the third day after taking on a load, but this time some trouble seemed to be holding it up. At any rate, we began to worry about our stock of provisions. If even on the next day we noticed no preparations for departure, I said, surprising even myself, I would go over to the camp to get hold of at least a couple of cans of corned beef. With the food that was left we would arrive hungry in Germany, although we needed as much strength as possible for the subsequent part of the flight, wherever it took us.

Münkel thought my plan was pure madness and raised countless, mostly sound objections. But I argued that a pinch of "madness" was something like the salt in the soup of life. Several times we became so agitated that each begged the other to limit his outbursts to those moments when a train passed. Then again, we sometimes laughed out loud, and as I warned him to be quiet, he said merely, "Another joke! What's wrong?" "There is a crisis," I replied, "in every risky undertaking." The following evening, without saying another word, I undid the catches of the box lid, forced myself through the escape path, and, after a careful glance around the brightly lit railway yard, let myself down to the ground.

I got past the camp gate without any problem. The sentry was one of the Polish soldiers who had recently arrived. He sat frowning in his sentry box, effortfully spelling out the words of a comic strip. Most of the prisoners also walked casually past me; evidently word of our escape had not got around. The biggest risk was presented by the first tent on the left by the gate, in which I myself

had been accommodated with seven comrades. Looking up Erich Kahnt in the next tent was also dangerous,
since one of the occupants would inevitably recognize me
and could betray me without realizing. Consequently, I
took a longer route to Sternmann, established that he was
alone, and made myself known to him with a few whispered words. Naturally, he already knew of my disappearance, especially as in the days when my decision had
taken firmer shape I had hinted at it in our conversations.

The planned handover to the French had also shocked
him, but he had concluded, when we talked about it, that
he would then just paint French women and instead of
the empty beauties of Kansas the livelier expressions of
Paris or Nice. He loved lived-in faces more than regular ones, he said, and had always found the portraits of
Goya more fascinating than those of Ingres. Then he
gave me his store of cans of meat and some sweet biscuits
wrapped in cellophane. As I left we promised to resume
our friendship once we had returned to Germany.

As I still had my special pass, the Polish sentry let
me through with a brief wave and when I returned to our
box at about midnight Münkel was infinitely relieved.
He admitted that he had already thought of breaking off
the whole undertaking. Yet now he was so glad at the successful excursion and the size of our improved food supplies that—after he had heard how easy it had been—he
wanted to go into the camp the following evening. "But
it probably won't happen," he said, "because the train is
sure to start tomorrow! At any rate we've got a few cans
of meat left over for Germany and two cartons of the

most valuable currency there."[5] This reminded me of my grandfather's story about the blood sausages. But I decided to keep it to myself so as not to discourage Münkel. Then came the night again and the confinement.

The train, of course, didn't leave that day, either. The wagons were several times shunted around, but in the end we always heard the familiar voices: the orders of Sergeant Stracker, the instructions of Corporal Weiland with his unmistakable piping voice, the bellowing of Corporal Bauer. In the late afternoon the engine was moved up and, as far as was possible, we slapped each other on the back with joy. "Now we're off!" we said, as a couple of shrill whistles sounded. We heard the rapidly approaching dry rhythm of the locomotive rumbling over the sleepers, before the engine withdrew again. We had no explanation for these occurrences. We heard the working parties going off again, then the orders of Corporal Bauer echoing in the distance for the last time. Finally, there was silence.

When darkness fell, Münkel went into the camp. Since, before the escape, he had performed sexton's duties for the camp's Catholic chaplain, he slipped between the tents to the priest's accommodation, then to the kitchen and from there brought a bag full of food to our hiding place. On his return he had considerable problems

---

5 Cigarettes were the most sought-after fungible commodity after 1945. Since the old Reichsmark was completely devalued, a black market featuring direct exchanges of commodities took the place of the monetary economy, and cigarettes, especially American brands, became the new money. This situation was ended by the introduction of a new currency, the Deutschmark, in 1948.

getting past the Polish sentries, who had just started their guard duty. But now we were glad of his additional contribution to our provisions. With this store we could hold out for another five days, he said, but, after some thought, we decided finally to break off the attempt if the train didn't set off tomorrow.

The hours passed in desperate waiting. Our nerves were raw. Toward evening, when we wanted to check whether we could leave our hiding place without risk, the guards moved up. Until then the three double sentries had always taken up positions at the front, the end, and the middle of the train, and our wagon had always been about fifty yards from the rear sentries. That evening, however, the two guards came to a halt in front of the very wagon where our box was. All night we heard them talking unintelligibly right beside us—their jokes, their suppressed laughter—and heard them puffing on their cigarettes. We were forced to be completely silent and denied ourselves any cough, the least movement, even a couple of whispered words. At most we could use the brief minute when at intervals of just under an hour the passenger train went past; but these trains stopped just after midnight. Even the sleep into which we fell from time to time was only possible by turns.

Unnerved by the strain of the night, our limbs almost paralyzed, we deliberated in the morning how and when we should give up our plan. We had now spent six days in the wooden box and there was no end in sight to the adventure. Finally, as the shunting of the wagons began again, we agreed to give it one more day. And then, for the first time, the train didn't go just the annoying eighty yards before coming to a stop again, as on previous days. Instead, this time it went about three hundred yards. After it came to a halt with a loud clatter, we were able to tell from the echoing sound that we were in one of the roofed depots at the end of the loading area.

We remained there for about an hour, during which orders sounded and sliding doors banged. After a lengthy pause, steps came closer. Suddenly, there were American voices above us. Several men were busy with some kind of equipment. One of them complained that the wagons were not sealed, while another said that as a result the gas would only have half the effect and make escape easier for the "German bastards."

We gathered from the remarks of the two soldiers that our departure was imminent: from previous information, we knew that the gas was released at the last control point. Minutes later we heard a repeated clicking noise gradually coming closer and closer, which was each time followed by a hiss; it obviously came from the gas cartridges which had been thrown in among the cases of each wagon. After about four minutes the sounds stopped, and we spent another hour motionless in our box. Then, talking loudly, members of the special unit came up and evidently listened at the sides of the trucks with special instruments whether any coughing or suppressed groaning could be heard. Münkel had put on the gas mask. I pressed a damp cloth to my nose and mouth. Finally, we heard the members of the squad called together and, squealing, the almost ten-yards-wide sliding doors of the depot were pushed apart. Hardly was that noise over when one of the officers shouted a command. There was the sound of hurried steps and a little later the train left the depot.

We can only have got as far as the loading area outside the depot, when to our dismay it once again came to a halt. We heard another locomotive being coupled up; after that, however, as the half-mile-long train got up steam, we knew that the period of painful waiting was at an end. Overjoyed, we nudged each other and realized that we were talking at normal volume once again. It was freedom at last, we said simultaneously, no matter where we got to now. We had a bottle of cognac or something similar with us; we now drank a toast to each other.

At that very moment our box was thrown high, fell down, bounced again and yet again, before giving way to a crashing rumble. The thick boards of our case cracked open, the piercing whistle of the locomotive sounded nearby, and as our box began to break up under the pressure of the asbestos boxes, the wagon tilted to the side, stumbled over a couple of sleepers, and toppled down the a gentle slope. In our box everything turned topsy-turvy. The heavy water canister fell on my right knee and as I was still rubbing at the painful spot, complete silence fell.

It must have been about ten minutes before we recovered from our dazed state. My first thought was to get rid of the illegally obtained discharge papers, since their discovery could have the most unpleasant consequences not only for ourselves, but also for the helpful Frenchman who had obtained them for us. After a brief discussion we tore up the documents, which were printed on stiff, heavy paper, into small pieces, in order to swallow down the scraps with the help of water.

We had just begun the difficult business of swallowing the paper when, with a lot of commotion, helpers and onlookers came up and began to pull at our box. No more than six hundred yards from the camp entrance the train had come off the rails because of spilled ballast. We choked down the paper and were just chewing on the last shreds as the box was opened with a crowbar. As we raised ourselves up we saw right in front of us the powerful figure of First Sergeant Driffel, who rubbed his fists and with fat cheeks shouted that he had rarely been so pleased to see someone again. Then he held out his hands in an inviting gesture and when we reached out for him, still in a daze, he punched us with great force and said, "No kidding, boys! Off to the cage!" After that he handed us over to the guards.

The "cage" was a space of about thirty square yards fenced in on all sides with heavy wire. It was situated outside the camp close to the gate. When we were put in it we were greeted by two prisoners who had already been incarcerated for a long time for theft; a little later, two more escapees were brought in; they had been picked up on the same train. As darkness began to fall, Lieutenant Dillon came by and explained that we would be tried by court-martial in Rheims. To my question whether, according to the Hague Convention, a prisoner was not allowed to try to escape, he looked at me ill-temperedly, responded with a curt "No!" and turned on his heel.

In the morning we were led to the Barber's Room. The corporal on duty asked us whether we wanted to keep our hair long or—as was usual in the army—wanted it clipped back to one centimeter. When I decided to keep it long, he remarked with false friendliness, "Aye aye, sir!," but in accordance with regulations, he said, he would have to trim a narrow strip through my hair. I shrugged my shoulders and said, "Fine. Go ahead!" So he picked up the electric clippers from the shelf and cut an approximately one-and-a-half-inch-wide, ridiculous-looking path across my head. So as not to give him any chance to gloat, when he asked if it was okay like that, I replied, "It's fine." But the following day, when another barber was on duty, I had the one-centimeter crew cut. My fellow prisoners, including Münkel, did the same.

The barber led us to the camp of the Polish guards and each of us was assigned two guards, who had orders to keep us busy. They were tirelessly inventive in thinking up new ways to harass us. I was ordered to dig a hole two by two yards, and when the work was done an "inspection" was conducted with a ruler. One demanded the perimeter be straightened at points, and finally said, "Not good! German and bad! But good for me!" Then he threw one of the stubbed-out cigarettes lying on the ground beside him into the hole and ordered, "Bury it. But faster!" and added that he had at least ten cigarette butts to bury. "Camp should be clean. Captain Donaldson always says so!"

So it went day after day. The temperature at that time of the year was tolerable; what was harder for us to bear with the open-grated roof was the rain. Sometimes a storm or gusting wind drove us all together, wet and freezing, into one corner. Even more unpleasant was the harassment by the guards. I had no idea until then how much humiliation can be inflicted with a wheelbarrow, a couple of buckets of water, and a spade. Nevertheless, when we returned to the cage in the evening, we assured each other that we would not make any laments, never mind complain.

On one of the first days of imprisonment Captain Donaldson had appeared at the wire fence and had addressed me reproachfully: "Why did you do it?" For a moment I thought of holding out my bloody—in places suppurating—hands with the reply, "And why do you do this?" Instead, I merely replied that he knew my reasons. We had often talked about them. He was not allowed to hand us over to the French, besides which it was the attested right of every prisoner of war to try to escape. At that the captain blankly twisted one of his mustache ends and walked off with stiff strides.

The accusation in my words evidently bothered him. At any rate, the next day First Sergeant Driffel turned up and let me know from the captain that according to international agreements prisoners of war did, indeed, have the right to escape attempts. However, the charge against us was not simply escape, but "conspiracy to escape," because there had been two of us. Furthermore, we would be accused of theft—after all, we were wearing American army jackets. He himself, said Driffel, would add that the sentence would certainly not be imposed for the escape, but because we had let ourselves be caught. When I asked the sergeant whether the captain had really come up with that nonsense about a "conspiracy," he barked that he always told the truth. I retorted that he should, then, on his word of honor, assure me that he had my manuscripts, which had no doubt been found in the box, in safekeeping. They were in the hands of the court for examination, came the answer, and would be returned to me at the end of my period of imprisonment. "Possibly!" added Driffel.

Almost six weeks passed with the same unpleasantness every day. One evening a Polish NCO came toward the cage, arguing with a prisoner, whom he repeatedly kicked and then knocked to the ground. Then the prisoner, who did not dare defend himself, was further beaten with a rifle butt. We shouted at the NCO to stop mistreating the defenseless man. Instead of stopping, almost blind with rage, he struck the man on the ground even harder. The prisoner's attempts to protect himself grew weaker and his body became no more than a limp heap. Just then, Captain Grey happened to pass. He instantly put a stop to the beating and sent the NCO back to his quarters. The very next day he had the cage opened and sent both us and the other prisoners back to the camp.

The court-martial in Rheims—about which there had been so much talk—never took place. After Captain Grey's intervention and the emptying of the cage, I was detailed to duty in the quartermaster's office of the Polish camp. When I met Captain Donaldson on one of the camp streets he greeted me sternly. Yet with a hint of a smile, I couldn't help but say to him, while displaying the palms of my hands on which scars had scarcely formed, "You punished us without a formal sentence. That's still unfinished business between us."

Donaldson appeared stunned at the accusation in my words and evidently had no answer. As I remained standing there, he responded something like this: At the beginning, back then on the camp street, he had taken me for a young German of a familiar type—romantic, open, earnest. He had perhaps put this picture together himself. There were crazy ideas about the Germans in circulation; he had taken them for propaganda. Now he knew he had been mistaken. I, too, was just a German like all the rest. He had already told me how deep his disappointment was. Then he added, somewhat contradictorily, "Sorry not to have you at headquarters anymore!" Now I did not know how to reply, and for a long time afterward asked myself what I should have said. Then, after staring into midair for a little while, he forestalled me by saying, "Take care of yourself, Joachim!" It was the first time he had addressed me by my first name. Shaking his head, he left me standing.

One September day in 1946 First Sergeant Walker, who, during my time at headquarters, had often liked to drop by for a chat, came to see me in the quartermaster's office. He had been posted elsewhere for several months and I greeted him by remarking lightly that if he had been preparing the charge against me in Rheims, then I could understand why the trial had not taken place. He merely laughed and said he thought that there really had been a problem. Then he added that he had had nothing to do with my case and had been busy most of the time with duties in Le Havre, and was now glad that he would soon be returning home to Chicago. I said that I envied him, especially as I had recently heard of my father's return from a Russian prisoner of war camp, in one piece but in very poor health.

"Perhaps you'll see your father again soon," said Walker. When I asked in a slightly irritated tone of voice what he had done to make that happen, he replied, "I'm doing just that, my friend." In the last few days he had been able to look at official correspondence marked TOP SECRET. He was letting me know now and announced, as if he were talking about the most obvious thing in the world, "The matter is decided. You guys, at least, won't be handed over to the French. You're going home." When I looked at him with some astonishment, he added: "And another bit of confidential information. I'm very pleased about that!" And then, "most confidential of all," he said finally, "not a word to the others!"

Nevertheless, it was five months before the train to Germany arrived in the marshaling yard of the depot. We had no idea where it was taking us. It seemed likely that it would be a place in the American Zone. I had given Freiburg as my hometown, because I had friends there and Berlin seemed unsafe to me, and, in fact, after two days the train taking us to Germany stopped in a camp at Heilbronn, near Stuttgart. In a moment the good-humored atmosphere and the singing about all the

Rosemaries, Erikas, and Heidis[6] evaporated, because everyone assumed that our camp had simply been transferred from Laon to Heilbronn. But then word quickly got around that Heilbronn was a transit camp for release.

I stood in line for more than two hours before it was my turn. A paunchy sergeant wearing spectacles asked me to stand at attention while he checked my papers, and in high spirits at imminent freedom I asked him in German: *Strammstehen?* (Stand at attention?) In a few words rasped in a strong Hamburg accent, he reprimanded me. So at the end of my time as a prisoner here is yet another former German, I said to myself, while he went through my belongings. Luckily, he left me the three books I had managed to hold on to through all the perils of captivity. Scratching his head, he looked carefully at my diaries, laughed at a few passages in my text about the Renaissance, and asked about the Castruccio story, "What's the point of that?" I tried to give a short explanation, but the fat man waved his hand dismissively, "Forget It!" Then he threw everything handwritten onto the pile of rubbish behind him and said, "You don't need that anymore!" I tried to make him change his mind with a couple of friendly remarks, but he grew irritated and cut me short: "That's it! Here are your papers! Now get out!"

At first I was unable to think of a retort. I simply stood there, motionless, while the sergeant waved me away.

---

6 These girls' names are all titles of and central to popular soldiers' marching songs known to all.

Finally, I made what seemed to me to be a quick-witted response: "In ten minutes I'll be going through the camp gate over there. From then on I'll be very happy that people like you will have to address me courteously again!"

He stopped short. Then he angrily threw the leather-bound volume with my favorite poems at me. I held the book tight and paid no attention to his shouting. My first taste of freedom was to act as if I couldn't hear him. The last time I glanced back, he was still looking at me, open-mouthed, even as he waved the next prisoner over. For a moment I thought that I had opened his eyes. Not until some time later did it occur to me that he had not understood at all what I wanted to tell him.

In another ten minutes I was out of the gate.

TEN

•

Not Home Yet

From Heilbronn I traveled to Freiburg. In my kitbag there was some underwear, my toilet things, the three books I had been left with in Unkel, and the leather-bound poems, which I had in part written down from memory, in part taken from books available to me in the camp. Leafing through the pages I once again read the verses of poets unfamiliar to me until recently, such as Blake and Keats, also Mallarmé and Baudelaire and one or two favorite poems like Auden's "If I Could Tell You," which begins "Time will say nothing," and Shelley's "Ozymandias." I had copied them out on evenings at headquarters when I had nothing to do, and then given them as a loose-leaf collection to the bookbinder Franz Scheuer. He had bound the pages so magnificently in leather cut from baseball gloves and the best officers' boots that even the fat sergeant at the release camp had been taken by the volume.

When I got off the train in Freiburg I was glad— after all the destroyed towns of the European landscape of ruins through which I had passed in the last three years—to see a city that was only a little damaged. The one heavy air raid had not had too serious an impact, apart from a trail of rubble between the cathedral and the main railway station. At any rate, one encountered nowhere here the dirty colors which dominated the devastated cities all the way to Berlin; the aquatint tones of the town, the gentle sandstone red and unobtrusive grays, behind them the green of the castle hill, seemed almost like home. In a letter to my parents, in which for the first time in years I could express myself more or less openly, and, above all, explain why I had not applied for release to Berlin, I wrote: *All in all I was out of the world. Now I'm back. Not yet home. But in Freiburg at least, which has almost become in a small way my home. Who would have thought it!*

The mother of my friend Helmut put me up in her house in Herdern. Her husband had died in the air raid on the town; her son was buried in France. But her attractive daughter was still there, as was my brother Winfried. After a few hours of exuberant conversation I went for a long walk with my brother—as we also did on the days that followed—across Sonnhalde Hill or up the Castle Hill. He told me about our parents and our two sisters, who, in 1944, after a third warning, had joined the BDM—the League of German Girls—but had concealed their membership from my father. Then he reported on the expulsion from Karlshorst,[1] the small flat in the Berlin district of Neukölln that the family had been allocated, the fate of my grandparents, and my Gymnasium class in Freiburg. In the last days of the war, according to Winfried, almost half of my former classmates had been shot not far away on a hillside in Alsace by a unit of General Lattre de Tassigny's forces that did not want to take prisoners.[2]

Winfried asked me how I had got through war and captivity, and I told him about the six days without food, the lieutenant from Heidelberg in Unkel, Captain Donaldson, and the escape attempt. During our walk I had the idea that instead of a book about the Italian Renaissance I would make the great cataclysms of history my subject in the coming years, because historical catastrophes were not only a matter of the epoch just passed but of life in general. Winfried merely laughed and said I should come down to earth again as soon as possible. First of all I had to earn my school-leaving certificate or *Abitur* and study something useful. "The plums are for the middle of life," he added. "Besides which the topic is not at all as interesting to others as you assume." People

---

1 A large part of the district of Karlshorst—relatively undamaged in air raids and fighting—was taken over for use by the Soviet military authorities and until German reunification remained an area to which German civilians had only limited access.—Trans.

2 General (posthumously Marshal) Jean de Lattre de Tassigny (1889–1952), an early adherent of Charles de Gaulle, commanded the French troops occupying Germany in 1945; in 1950–52 he commanded the French Expeditionary Forces in Indochina (Vietnam).

only wanted to hear about the misfortune they had suffered once they were over the worst; but they were a long
way from that now. Not even he was there yet.

Our conversation was a clash of two temperaments.
Winfried had a greater sense of reality then, and he had
wit. On our second or third walk he answered my question about his experiences in his modest way: "Oh, nothing special." When I then asked what was special that
he wanted to conceal behind the "nothing special," he
said simply, "Well, a small escape." I had to insist before
he came out with the story and related how the war had
ended for him. In the last days of March 1945, the French
troops had reached the other side of the Rhine at Brei-
sach. When Winfried then received his call-up papers,
he decided to spend "the next few hours," as he supposed, in a hiding place on the outskirts of Freiburg. Out
of consideration for the Weidners, he let them believe he
was obeying the conscription order. In fact, however, he
had agreed with the baker Welle, who lived at the end of
the street, that he would wait for the arrival of the French
in the family's allotment hut.[3]

But then the waiting went on and on. The French
troops let days pass without making any preparations for
a crossing of the Rhine. After Winfried had spent almost
two weeks behind piles of coal, potatoes, and refuse, he
went for a brief walk "to stretch his legs," but after only

---

3 Many German cities are still ringed by small allotment gardens called *Schre-
bergärten* (Schreber gardens), named after Daniel Gottlob Moritz Schreber (1808–
61), who wanted the industrial worker to retain some connection to the soil. Many
of these gardens contain a small building.

a few steps ran into a Gestapo patrol. He was taken to
the same police station in which I had been interrogated
months before. Winfried took care not to mention where
he had been staying or who had helped him. On the third
day he was brought to the local barracks. He was put in
a cell with eleven others who had either deserted or, like
himself, not obeyed the call-up; no one could say for
sure what was going to happen to them. Some thought
they would all be shot; others objected that even now
there were no executions without formal proceedings; a
few claimed to have information that they would all be
released within forty-eight hours. The Führer, after all,
was "no monster."

After another few days the twelve prisoners were led
to the barracks yard. There a lieutenant with a small staff
and four older, very worn-out-looking soldiers were waiting for them. A sergeant announced that they would now
march to the nearby town of St. Peter, because the Wehrmacht command considered it too great a risk to have so
many "unreliable elements" in the ranks for the forth-
coming battle with the French; after all, it was a question
of final victory. After some disciplinary instructions the
order to march was given.

That afternoon, escorted by the sergeant and the
four soldiers, they marched up the Dreisamtal Valley.
Winfried assured me that he had never had the slightest doubt that in St. Peter they would be put in front of
a firing squad. Halfway there, they took a forest path in
order to avoid attracting attention, and after a mile or two
stopped for a short rest. He decided, acting on the spur

of the moment, to do something "extremely crazy," as he later said. Without warning, he threw himself to the side and leaped down the slope at a point where there were only a few shrubs growing.

After a moment of astonished silence, he heard agitated commands and shouts behind him.

Shots were fired. But they struck the trees around him and ricocheted and whistled around his head. As he crouched in a hollow, he could hear the voices of two searchers about twenty yards behind him. Then they were ordered back by the sergeant, who, worried about further escape attempts, had remained up on the path with the prisoners. Winfried waited until the sounds of the group had faded away and then made his way back to Herdern. Close to Friedrich Gymnasium he spotted a military police patrol coming up the street, but was able to disappear, unseen, into a house entrance. "That would really have been the end," he thought as he heard the two men come past the door talking loudly. At the baker's house they were dismayed, but did not hesitate to let him use the hiding place again.

This time he was more cautious. He spent almost all of the following days underneath a woodpile; he left no trace of his presence when he went out for some fresh air for a quarter of an hour at night and on his return carefully arranged the wood above himself as a decorative chaos. A few times he heard voices very close by. After more than two weeks, the French at last moved into Freiburg on April 20. "I was not free," Winfried concluded his report. "But I could at least move my limbs.

That was quite a lot. It was days before I could walk normally again." Later it was said that his fellow prisoners had all been shot in St. Peter, but he did not know whether the information was more than a rumor. It was probably true, but he had not checked it. He had never wanted to make a big thing of his escape.

A few days after my return, just before Christmas 1946, I called on the headmaster of my school. Dr. Breithaupt had been my homeroom teacher and thanks to the vicissitudes of the time had now become rector of the Friedrich Gymnasium. Already on entering his office I realized that he had remained the strict, stiff man who had introduced us to Greek and taught us to read the *Odyssey*. Since he had enlisted my help privately on a number of occasions, I expected a certain amount of understanding on his part. Instead, he remained surprisingly cool and listened condescendingly to the account of my experiences, which I summed up in a few sentences, before curtly responding to the not unimportant question of which class was to be recommended: "You can enter the top form (senior class), which will give you a bare six months until the examination. Or the class below—there you lose more than a year, seventeen and a half months to be precise. But then you have better prospects for obtaining your certificate. The choice is yours. As rector of the Friedrich Gymnasium it only remains for me to say: there will be no special considerations!" Dr. Breithaupt seemed somewhat taken aback when I merely muttered a disappointed "Thank you," turned on my heel, and left. That same day I decided that, to lose no time and to get school over with as quickly as possible, I would enter the senior class.

At Christmas my mother came to Freiburg and was likewise put up at the Weidners. She had already been trying since late summer to get the necessary permit from the American occupation authorities, before she was finally allowed to make the journey to the French Zone. We were dismayed by the emaciated, scraggly picture that she presented, and how empty her eyes were. Now we heard for the first time details of the evacuation of Karlshorst in early May 1945, which it was better not to mention in correspondence, since letters were still monitored. Each person was allowed just one suitcase, into which, given the haste that was demanded, my mother had stuffed only what was most necessary: some underwear, bread, a suit and a jacket for my father, some laundry soap, and a few documents quickly snatched up. She had had to abandon her beloved "casket," buried in the garden.

To list the numerous acts of violence—in particular against the female relatives on my father's side—would take up an entire chapter. At the beginning, Uncle Berthold on the Walken Farm had borne the barbarities of the Russian conquerors with impotent anger, but when the brutalities against his wife and daughters had gone beyond all measure, he had begged one of the soldiers to show some human consideration. Instead of even listening to him, the soldier had drawn his revolver and shot my uncle in the head. Even more shattering was the fate of my "other" aunt, Franziska, who was crippled by polio: pulled out of her wheelchair and repeatedly raped, she was flung back into her chair and thrown down the cellar stairs, where she died after moaning for more than two hours. It was a long sequence of atrocities, which my mother revealed unwillingly and only after some persuasion.

In those days almost every story ended with acts of violence of some kind. As the Red Army approached, my sisters had left their Gymnasium in the Neumark, east of Berlin, and returned to Berlin; they now learned that their classmates—all aged between twelve and fifteen—had been raped, before being abducted and disappearing in the expanses of Russia. The war— so presumptuously begun and so often accompanied by whipped-up fantasies of final victory—had come back to Germany in the most terrible way.

It was not until some time after her arrival that my mother mentioned the death of her parents, and Winfried agreed with me that she really didn't want to talk about it at all. She said, however, that my grandmother had died in spring 1945, around the time I was taken prisoner. After the destruction of her house in an air raid and the death of her crippled daughter, she had shown ever less interest in life. That had still been noticeably different on my 1944 visit to Riastrasse, and when I embraced her on taking my leave she had said with a shy smile, "Now you have to grow up! At your age a lad has better things to embrace! Not his grandmother!" Then she embraced me. Later, she had complained that for thirty years she had only been there for her family. But now? What could she do with a life that had no meaning?

At the end she had spent many hours in the church and had visibly wasted away. One of the last things she said was that she had served God and her poor daughter "all her life with heart and hand." That was why she was not worried about the end. The next day the doctors confirmed her death. The certificate noted an advanced immune deficiency. But one of the doctors said drily that she had simply died of life.

My grandfather followed her about a year later. The chaos of the evacuation meant that Karlshorst Hospital, which my grandfather had cofounded, had to be moved to a former hotel in the district of Friedrichshagen, which was where he was taken. Like my grandmother, he too asked every day into the emptiness what was the point of it all. He had always been surrounded by deference; now, after weeks of being moved from one place to another, he found himself in a hospital ward with sixty beds on which groaning patients awaited their end. Several times he asked my mother what else life still held in store for him and when she, at a loss, replied, "Well, no plans, no duties anymore! Just live!" he spoke of being the victim of a fraud. He had always believed that in almost eighty years he would get a couple of clues as to what one was really in this world for. But now he knew that life just made a fool of one.

When he had taken refuge in the hospital he had possessed nothing anymore. In the course of the evacuation, Russian soldiers had first taken his briefcase and his pocket watch, then his jacket and vest, so that he—always the *chevalier à la mode*—had appeared before the nuns in shirt and suspenders. And the few things of value left to him, including his wallet, had one day been stolen from under his pillow, and a little later, his remaining clothes had also been taken, so that he literally owned nothing anymore except the nightshirt on his back. When he was asked how he felt, he said that he was ashamed of his poverty; after that the nuns placed a screen around his bed, so that he had more privacy. "Yes, it's better to be alone, when one's dying!" he said. To the sisters' admonition not to talk so blasphemously, he merely said that his words were utterly serious. For years everyone had said that his wife had followed him as submissively as a maid. Now he was following her. Without her he no longer knew why he was here. He was leaving life "as quickly as possible."

Then he asked what the date was. When he heard it was the fourteenth of July, he said that he had nothing more to do, nothing more to say, and nothing at all to celebrate.[4] Cause of death should be given as: no interest anymore. He thanked everyone, extended his folded hands toward the nuns standing around his bed, and commended himself to God. It was sinfully desired death, he admitted finally. But God would show understanding; He loved the sinners who stood by their sin. The doctors established typhus as cause of death. Two days later he was taken to the cemetery in a wooden box and put in the earth in a paper bag.

---

4 July 14 is, of course, Bastille Day, when good German democrats celebrated the ideals and ideas of the French Revolution—before it descended into the Terror.

We heard further details about events in Berlin at the end of the war—about the courage of Hannih and Christa and the tragedies in the neighborhood—on our almost daily walks with Mother. She loved the benches on the Castle Hill, but often we also walked over the hills above Herdern to the Sonnenhalde, then on to the "professors' huts" on Rötebuckweg, where Martin Heidegger lived.[5] About our father she said that after his release from Russian captivity in autumn 1945 he had suddenly stood at the door like a shadow, and after a few stumbling steps, supporting himself against the wall with one hand, he had collapsed. Then, over many weeks, he had been "brought back to life" by a nurse. He had regained half of the more than one hundred pounds he had lost and so was now "halfway there" again. Hardly was he able to stand on his feet again when he was already going to political meetings and sitting at Christian Democratic Union committee tables in one of the two—far too big—suits that had been saved.[6]

---

5 Martin Heidegger (1889–1976) was the most influential philosopher of the twentieth century, whose reach extended far beyond academic philosophy; while banned from his university post after 1945 because of perceived connections to National Socialism, he would still occasionally descend from the mountain to give extremely popular lectures.

6 In the West, German democratic parties, outlawed and persecuted under Hitler, had to be either re- or newly established, like the two major parties of the left and the right, the SPD and the newly formed CDU, based on the former Zentrum membership but now expanded to include Protestants as well. The Free Democratic Party (FDP) initially represented the old Liberals of the German Southwest and would join coalition governments with either the CDU or the SPD. A number of other parties, one representing the millions of refugees, would eventually dissolve, leaving mainly the three parties described here. In the East, the old SPD and the Communist Party (KPD) were merged into the ruling Sozialistische Einheits Partei Deutschlands (SED).

From the summer of 1946 he spoke in public again, weak but composed. He talked about the subjects that had determined his life: the gradual collapse of the Weimar Republic, the Reichsbanner and the indecisiveness of the republican forces, the "debasement of the law" during the Nazi seizure of power, and the duty to take on political responsibility. Each of his speeches in mostly smoke-filled taverns ended with the sentences with which most of his letters to us also concluded: What had just happened to our country must not happen again. Once was shameful enough.

In early 1947 I found myself sitting behind a school desk again in Freiburg. The rooms were the same, the teachers were the same, the subjects and the names were the same as they had been before: Cicero and Homer and Lessing and Goethe. And although even the faces of my one-year-younger classmates appeared curiously familiar, I felt myself to be in an alien world. I was still crouching in a foxhole, as it were, of which the others hadn't even heard. It was as if their problems, what they argued about or agreed on, and even their jokes came from very far away. I was not yet, as I had written in my first letter home, back in the world again.

In April Roger Reveille announced he would be coming to Freiburg.[7] He had business in nearby Colmar in Alsace and was (as I remembered him from Berlin)

---

7 Freiburg im Breisgau belonged to the French Zone of occupation, like most of the Black Forest area at the time. French plans to annex these parts of Germany were foiled by the other Allies.

Johannes Fest, in a passport-size photo taken about
six months after his return from Russian captivity

loud, charming, and imaginative. He was embarrassed
when, because of a chance remark, the subject of the
behavior of the French occupiers arose; to the one example of the aggressive arrogance of his fellow countrymen
that had been mentioned he could add a dozen more. At
lunchtime he invited me to a mess that was reserved for
high-ranking French officers before accompanying me
back to my apartment for coffee. There I showed him the
leather-bound volume with the handwritten poems that
I had brought back from captivity. Roger remarked that
he would like to have it, but I said that, understandably,
there was only one copy. That didn't bother him, replied
Roger, but I demurred. "There's nothing to be done! It's
my most important memento!"

As he was leaving he put the volume in his pocket
as if it were a matter of course. "Hey! Hey, Roger!" I
exclaimed. "You can't do that!" We had just been talking about civilized forms of behavior. He shouldn't act
like an officer in the occupation forces. I could not give
away the book, because my heart and my memories were
attached to it. But he acted as if he didn't hear me and
went out to his car. "Roger!" I repeated loudly. "Please,
leave me the book! It's also a trophy! I can explain it to
you!" But Roger was now someone with business to do.
"I'm sorry!" he said at the car door and patted his pocket
with the palm of his hand. "I wanted to have it from the
start! And still do! Don't let it bother you! A small repa-
ration!" I angrily went back into the house even before
he had started the engine. Soon after, Roger wrote me a
letter of thanks for my welcome, the friendliness of which

he would not forget. I never replied to it—nor to a further letter which followed a couple of weeks later.

Soon I found time again for the things I liked and which I had long done without. In the first concert for which I obtained a ticket, Wilhelm Backhaus played Beethoven's Fifth Piano Concerto, and I got into conversation with another member of the audience, who found the composer's pathos profoundly French. I replied that Beethoven's metaphysics, on the other hand, were incorrigibly German. My neighbor said one didn't talk in such "national" terms anymore; that would be impossible for a generation or more. After that a longer discussion developed in which my acquaintance revealed himself to be a lecturer from Tübingen. The exchange ended with my question: Was it still acceptable to say that Beethoven was German? He said the statement was indisputable, but it was better to refrain from making it. "Our country," he concluded, "is not à la mode at the moment." He wondered if I had noticed this fact.

A longer-lasting friendship developed with Fritz Werner, the manager of the University Bookshop am Augustinermuseum. His quiet, bespectacled appearance did not at all betray his passionate love of literature. He looked like a character from Thomas Mann's gallery of eccentrics, even if another friend later remarked he was more like a figure from the paintings of Carl Spitzweg.[8] He

---

8 To Germans, Carl Spitzweg (1808–85) was a beloved painter of humorous portraits and scenes from the everyday life of his time—comparable for Americans to Norman Rockwell and his paintings.

was slight and he carefully combed streaks of hair across his bald head, which was framed by a circle of unruly curls. His great love was the poet Gottfried Benn, and already by my third or fourth visit he invited me into his office at the back of the shop, where between tall stacks of books he introduced me to poems such as "Negerbraut" and "Jena," and attuned me to the unmistakably "Berlin tone" of the poet. Gottfried Benn introduced me to a swagger in verse form such as I had never encountered before. From him I also learned phrases like "jostling blood," "burning gorse," "honied lands," and "waves of white violets." It was a completely new lyrical realm that opened up before me, and once he realized how much I was affected by Benn, Werner even cleared a corner of the shop for me to read the problematic essays of the poet, in which he is all too often carried away by his own brilliance. But Werner did not lend me anything too valuable, he informed me; for him Benn belonged on the top shelf, because anywhere else he risked losing him.

Instead he offered me some titles from his "secret chest." I should be familiar with Werner Bergengruen's *A Matter of Conscience,* as with everything by Stefan Andres, he said.[9] He also fished out something by Knut Hamsun, who only four years before was being cele-brated, as he noted with a scornful laugh, but was now forbidden. But he would think of me, he added, and of

---

9 Werner Bergengruen (1892–1964) converted to Catholicism and was a friend of Reinhold Schneider's; he is best known for his novels and novellas. Stefan Andres (1906–70) attempted to wed the traditions of classical antiquity with modern Christianity in his novels and stories.

Ernst Rowohlt's first cheap paperbacks; I got Hemingway's *A Farewell to Arms* and, as a special favor, Tuchol-
sky's *Castle Gripsholm*.[10] "No one gets more than one
paperback," he said. I was the exception. Nevertheless,
as he reproached me years later, after that I was constantly pestering him for some large, cloth-bound American or French volume. Sighing, Werner took note but
first introduced me to a circle of young poets founded
by Claus Bremer and Rainer Maria Gerhardt that met
once a month at the department store on the Cathedral
Square. Once I even read two poems I had written to the
few people who gathered for the department-store evenings. I lost them afterward.

At about the same time I received my school-leaving
certificate and—thanks to my old Berlin school where
things were drummed into one—I had good marks in
Latin and Greek, as well as German and history, so that
I easily achieved the grade average required at that time
for university admission.[11] Ten days later, provided with
an American special permit for those persecuted by the
Nazis for their political views, which also covered close
family members, Winfried and I set out for Berlin.[12]

---

10 Ernst Rowohlt (1887–1960) and his publishing ventures are synonymous in
Germany with literary paperbacks; he made both world literature and modern
German literature available to a very wide audience.

11 At the end of the *Abitur*, or qualifying exam for university admission, the grades
attained in the various subjects were averaged out to a composite grade, which had to
be at a specific level for entry into university and thus graduate studies.

12 Despite the author's protestations that his family did not want any special
considerations for their antifascism, it is clear that they were granted special
privileges by the occupying authorities, as indicated by the special permit for travel
issued to them, which apparently entitled them to fly into Berlin on an American

I interrupted the journey in Mannheim to see my fellow escapee Wolfgang Münkel again, while Winfried went on to Frankfurt. It was long after midnight in the ruined city and we were still exchanging memories when we suddenly heard someone throwing pebbles at the window and shouting something. It was a woman's voice, speaking German with a guttural accent: "Open up! It's me!" Then came an unintelligible name. Puzzled, Wolfgang looked at me. "Should we open up?" he wondered. "At night?" I said there were two of us and we had hardly anything to fear. He went cautiously down the stairs; I followed at a distance. Then I heard a scream, followed by silence. When I—not without some anxiety—went farther downstairs, there was a couple passionately kissing at the door. A little later Wolfgang introduced me to Archivolde, the young Dutch woman about whom he had talked incessantly in our escape box. It was the first time they had seen each other after almost two years, and, Wolfgang said, he interpreted as a good sign the coincidence that the day on which we had met again had also reunited him with his great love. Now all obstacles would be overcome.

In Frankfurt I met up again with Winfried. We boarded a transport plane in which some seats had been installed and for the first time the picture of which I had taken in only scattered elements in captivity took on

---

cargo plane. Back then nobody but armed forces and highly privileged individuals flew in airplanes of any sort. And they are met in Berlin by people arriving in cars; in the 1940s very few civilian cars were on the road and none without special connections and permits.

firmer contours. A new world of unblemished appearances presented itself to us. The stewards who accompanied us to the plane displayed the perfectly creased
elegance of American soldiers, and the immaculately
made-up stewardesses who showed us to our seats and
served drinks provided evidence that it was not just courtesy that could be acquired, but that every detail from
permed blond hair to the most winning smile was a matter of skill.

A royal reception awaited us at Tempelhof Air-
port. The whole family had turned up and the greet-
ings were exuberant, with many "Hallos!," embraces,
and tears. There were about ten friends standing beside
my parents and sisters: Hausdorf and the Ernst family,
Wigbert Gans and his mother, Paul Mielitz, and some
of Winfried's friends as well, but also Aunt Dolly wearing clothes of a somewhat faded splendor. I proposed
going to an Aschinger's establishment nearby. I would,
I said, so much like to eat a welcome sausage, if there
were enough meat ration coupons to go around. Two in
the reception party had come by car; Wigbert Gans, his
mother, and Winfried's friends had come by bike. Even
years later, whenever I remembered the cheerful bustle
in Aschinger's, I had to think of the story that Fritz Kortner told at Walther Hirsch's house.[13] How a taxi driver at
Tempelhof had recognized him on his first visit to Berlin

---

13 Fritz Kortner (1892–1970), German stage and film actor and director, emigrated
to Hollywood in 1933 and returned in 1949 to a triumphant career in postwar
Germany.

after the war, and had greeted him by name and tugged the peak of his cap. Asked how things had been in the years that had passed, the driver had replied, gesturing at the expanse of ruins all around, "You know, Mr. Kortner, you actually didn't miss much!" Kortner added that this one sentence, imaginable only in Berlin, had for a moment allowed him to forget the revolting Nazi period and made return easier for him.

Berlin took your breath away. I had passed through Frankfurt, Cologne, Düsseldorf, and several cities in the Ruhr, but none was like Berlin.[14] Even as the plane banked over the city toward Tempelhof there was nothing to be seen but a gray-brown desert of ruins, stretching to the horizon. The central east–west axis with the Tiergarten park, which I could make out, was an extended wasteland. I recognized the district around Nollendorfplatz and the quarters of the city center, but everywhere rubble was heaped up behind eerily empty facades. Later, I saw a district that I had once recognized by its churches, shops, or public buildings; it was identified now only by a few surviving street signs. Often one strayed for minutes at a time before hills of rubble as tall as a house and asked oneself how people could be living in these ruins. Yet there was a bustle of activity, people were all going somewhere on urgent business, most of them with their clothes hanging loosely on their bodies, and, curiously,

---

14 In fact, statistically speaking, the scale of damage was rather less in Berlin than in the cities Fest mentions; but he was shocked on returning to Berlin after a long absence and it was his hometown.—Trans.

Aunt Dolly with the author in the 1950s

these passersby gaunt with hunger often seemed to me to be smeared with soot, their faces to display a kind of dirty, ghostly pallor.

Among the curiosities of my first impressions was also the unfamiliar music which could be heard in so many places: boogie-woogie, Glenn Miller, drawn-out howling clarinet notes in between. On Hasenheide, on Schlossstrasse near Innsbrucker Platz, and in numerous other places there were dance bars from which the music of popular American bands boomed out onto the street. "Don't Fence Me In," "Sentimental Journey," and "I'm Beginning to See the Light": these were tunes I soon could not get out of my head. The American Forces Network and the German radio stations also broadcast this ever more popular music, which was constantly being whistled on buses and trams.[15] Every pub had jukeboxes, Coca-Cola, Nescafé, and Hershey chocolate bars. It was the impact of a very young, casual, engaging world, a culture of baby faces and crew cuts. A greater contrast to Freiburg was hardly conceivable; sometimes in this Berlin, which was still my home, I felt as if I were on another planet.

Once our friends had taken their leave we went up to the apartment on the third floor of a tenement house in Neukölln. My mother was proud of how far the rooms had already been furnished. However, I was shocked.

---

15 AFN broadcasts, especially the musical programs, became the primary source for up-to-date information and then contemporary music, including jazz and swing and big band, for all those who identified with the new order; it also led to a rapid spread and acceptance of American English at the expense of previously dominant British English. The young, above all, listened to and identified with this radio network.

Because what stood there was a faded settee, a badly damaged sideboard, a table, and six different chairs acquired on the black market. In addition there was a double bed. The kitchen was shabby, but my mother had halfway restored its sparkle, and in the next room I saw two iron bedsteads for my sisters. "Old Katlewski had better furniture," I said, and my father replied, "In workers' homes everything is always neat and tidy. But look at Berlin Southeast or Lichtenberg today. Nothing but a pile of rubble."

Then everybody was talking at once. We were finally free of the need to be careful about what was said, which for years had weighed on everyone. My sisters talked about the capture of Karlshorst, the girls' hiding place in the church tower and their subsequent expulsion; Hannih related how her younger sister Christa, then only thirteen, had not for a moment hesitated, even if with tears in her eyes, to butcher the two surviving chickens and her pampered favorite pet rabbit, "Pious hips," before the approaching Russians arrived.

Probably to distract attention from herself, Christa reported the spiteful details of the expulsion, but also added that in the one and a half years of my father's absence our sensitive mother had proved to be a robust person and had completely shed her Liebenthal gentility. Without much ceremony she had taken charge of the building, issued instructions to the occupants, conducted tough negotiations on the black market, and had traveled into the countryside on the roofs of the suburban trains to get hold of a handful of potatoes, a cabbage, or a paper bag of wrinkled winter apples. Christa once called her "the strong woman from the Bible," but my mother indignantly rejected that; the description did not suit her. "Above all, please, not in my presence," she said, adding a little later, "I would still rather—awkward as I now am at my age—sit down in front of the piano."

Shortly afterward, when, unavoidably, the name of my elder brother was mentioned, her mouth began to twitch. While we were still trying to hit on an innocuous subject, after moving restlessly back and forth on her chair, she left the room without saying a word. Later she returned with the casual question whether, after having gone to Aschinger's, we wanted to indulge in a second meal.

My father's condition was much more worrisome. He was hardly recognizable: a man abruptly grown smaller, slighter, gray-haired. Most of the time he simply sat there, his eyes sunken, where previously he had always set the tone. After repeated questions, he talked—as if he had to dredge his memory—of the shellfire that had poured down onto Königsberg in the final days before its surrender; of the flamethrowers; of the terrible stench of corpses in the ruins, which continued to spoil his sense of smell. On April 8 or 9, 1945, shortly before the fighting in the city ended, his small group of defenders was approached by some civilians with white flags and bits of weaponry they had gathered. The civilians tried to persuade them to give up. But joining those wanting to capitulate was as risky as continuing the battle with the Russians. After some urging, the people with the white flags recognized this and finally they crawled into a hiding place. "Well, and then came captivity," my father concluded and fell back into his silence.

When the evening had drawn to an end and my father had retired, we asked ourselves whether the conclusions which he had once been able to draw so convincingly had really been so feeble tonight or whether it had only been the strangely expressionless voice—which, as if displaced, seemed to come from behind the backrest of the chair—that gave the impression of an empty recital. Once, during the course of the evening, he had lamented the loss of his library: the Goethe edition, above all, which he had bought with his first earnings, the Shakespeare and some other volumes, such as those by the historian Hintze, the Kugler with its unforgettable drawings by Menzel, the massive edition of Görres's works. These losses, he said, preoccupied him more than the home they had been forced to give up, along with everything in it, the garden and the old friends scattered here and there. But even this lament was uttered in a detached voice. My mother explained that my father still had a third of his weight and his strength to get back; we had to be patient.

In the next few days a number of things came up which had been forgotten in the lively conversation of the reunion. Now and then my father even displayed something of his former temperament and sometimes also his caustic wit. "They've taken away our Karlshorst home," he said at one point, "although we had no skeletons in the closet." After a short pause he added, "They're now

being manufactured by the Russians and put on our bill."
Changing the subject, he said that suddenly the country
was full of people who had always been "against them."
He didn't want any part of it. With a wife and five children, courage didn't go very far. At any rate, apart from
helping out in a small way a few times, he hadn't been
able to do anything; his main concern had been to keep
the totalitarian infection from affecting his family and
one or two friends. It was not so different from certain
illnesses, he continued, by which one is destroyed if one
gives way to them. When it came to the Nazis, as he had
often observed, even the passing thought of giving in had
been enough and a person was already lost.

On another occasion he spoke of the main error that
he and his friends had fallen victim to, because they had
believed all too unreservedly in reason, in Goethe, Kant,
Mozart, and the whole tradition which came from that.[16]
Until 1932 he had always trusted that this tradition was
proof enough, that a primitive gangster like Hitler could
never achieve power in Germany. But he hadn't had a
clue. One of the most shocking things for him had been
to realize that it was completely unpredictable how a
neighbor, colleague, or even a friend might behave when

---

16 This is a commonplace of all literature on German and Jewish reactions to Hitler
and the Nazis: their belief in the power of German high culture— represented by
names like Goethe, Kant, Mozart, et al.—and the strength of Enlightenment traditions led them to assume—erroneously, as it turned out—that vulgarians and obviously unenlightened primitives like the Nazis could never succeed in the long run in
that cradle of modern European civilization which Germany was to them.
    Immanuel Kant (1724–1804), the basis of much of modern philosophy, was re-
garded as the quintessential embodiment of all that is good in Prussian and German
thought and behavior.

it came to moral decisions. To this day he still had no explanation for that.

He was also a member of a denazification court, from whose proceedings he returned in low spirits every time.[17] Soon he was dismissing the work of the court as mere "phrase-mongering"; the "tribunalization" of the Hitler years appeared to him to be extremely dubious, no matter that he regarded the Nürnberg war crimes trials as justified a thousand times over. And the first, still somewhat flat jokes we heard from him were about the 131 questions on the American questionnaire for those requesting clearance from a denazification court. Consequently, he didn't feel that he had the right—as one of the cases of recent days demanded—to pass sentence on a father of three, who at the end of the thirties had been appointed head of a local Nazi Party branch, as "incriminated."[18] "Horrible!" he said. When Winfried objected that my father hadn't compromised, even though he had five children, he retorted, "Still horrible!" Of the lengthy discussion, the details of which I have forgotten, only the sentence that life has reasons

---

17 These courts were set up to weed out old Nazis from the administrative and other services of the emerging postwar German states, an undertaking that was so complex that British and French authorities never really pursued it, while the American efforts petered out more slowly. Only the Soviets carried out a ruthless campaign of eliminating all known or suspected Nazis from positions of public power. Poor information, denunciations, and the settling of unrelated old scores made this undertaking highly problematic.

18 An Ortsgruppenleiter would, for example, have an office, but was unpaid. Being classified as "incriminated" would at this time limit employment possibilities. —Trans.

which no court in the world can understand has stayed in my mind.[19]

I urged my father to write down some episodes of his experiences, but he rejected the suggestion with almost indignant firmness. He didn't belong on the pedestal on which the authors of memoirs displayed themselves. But what he had to report deserved to be heard, I insisted; even his family had been told only fragments at best, and most people were keeping their mouths shut; no doubt they had their reasons. "If you don't speak," Winfried supported me, "too much will remain in the dark."

After my father had thought for a while, he finally said, "We all remain silent. Out of shame, fear, and apprehensiveness. I remain silent, too. It's indecent to talk!" When he heard others talking about the times and what they had experienced, he often thought that the Nazis had got rid of any sense of shame along with everything else. "Perhaps it will take time to grasp that," he added. At any rate, in the elevated position in which he would inevitably be placed by writing an account of his life, he would feel out of place. "I don't belong there. You can say what you like!"

And so on, always in the same vein. Haltingly, with pauses, but without the least doubt. Toward the end of my stay, after several futile attempts, I asked him about his terrible outburst of rage when my schoolmates from Freiburg were visiting; at around that time, on a walk

19 Precisely this conflict between legal and moral responsibility for one's action is central to the novel by Bernhard Schlink, *The Reader* (New York: Vintage, 1997).

through the Wuhlheide Park, he had hinted at atrocities, knowledge of which would have put me at unneces-
sary risk. I asked him when he had learned for the first
time of the mass crimes in the east, of which, earlier, he
would not have thought even Hitler and his accomplices
capable. I didn't say that I had learned about them from
Wittenbrink and others in spring 1944. My father stared
silently into space for a while. "Not for the first time!"
he said then. "There were rumors, and a BBC broadcast.
Alarmed by these hints I spent almost three months at
the beginning of 1943 looking for irrefutable evidence.
Then I was sure: they were murdering as if possessed!"
And then, after another pause, "I did not want to talk
about it then and I don't want to talk about it now! It
reminds me that there was absolutely nothing I could do
with my knowledge. Not even talk about it! You understand that." And finally, "In the house of whole battalions of hangmen it is better to remain silent! One doesn't
talk in front of mass graves!"

On the day before Winfried and I departed, he said
into a moment of silence that he never again wanted to
be asked about the Nazi years or what had happened.
Nor about his memories. Because, for better or worse,
one only appeared self-important by doing so. That was
not his way. In the end, with his sometimes blunt manner, Winfried defused the rising tension with the words
that in such a position one unavoidably appeared "either
a hero or an asshole." In an effort to play down his actions
and behavior, my father added that he had often thought
during the Hitler years that in his own life he was merely

recapitulating the basic situation of Prussia: isolated, surrounded by enemies, with no ally far and wide. That's the
way he had seen the world from quite an early age, and
one didn't abandon a perspective like that, just because
such conditions really had intervened.

Occasionally, Herr Gravenholt from next door would
burst into our largely low-key conversations. He—like his
no less massive figure of a wife—radiated an indestruc-
tible vitality. He would throw himself uninvited into an
easy chair and boom, "Well, still going on about the end
of the world?!" The ruins of yesterday did not especially
weigh him down. "We're all of us born lucky!" he tried
to encourage us. "And we're on the brink of a fairy-tale
ascent. The ruins are our finest promise. We've got no
alternative except to get out of the dirt by every means we
can!" I thought of Reinhold Buck, Helmut Weidner, and
the many others. We had only become Sunday's children
by getting through the war. But Gravenholt thought that
nothing could stop people who had survived such times;
from now on the good spirits were on our side. He leaned
back in the easy chair with a sigh, wiped his face with his
handkerchief, and burst out with "It's unbelievable! But
the black market takes it out of me!" He took a salami out
of his briefcase and asked for knife and beer glass. "Not
refined," he himself admitted. "Refinement has to wait
until the day after tomorrow! But I'm already on my way!
Cheers!"

During my Berlin stay, in a street near Tempel-
hofer Damm, my father bumped into Fengler, the block
warden who in Hentigstrasse had played the "hot-pot

inspector" and cost my mother (as she put it at the time) two deadly sins. My father drew the man, who couldn't avoid him on the deserted pavement, into conversation and asked him if it was he who had warned him about the Gestapo visits and made sure his outburst at the "Hitler Youth rascals" was not taken seriously. Also, had he redirected my father's refusal to work on building tank barriers to the regional army command, because everyone knew that the party would give short shrift to an "objector"? My father said he wanted to thank him.

Fengler denied everything. He was no "traitor." He had sworn an oath of loyalty to the Führer. An honest man like him didn't simply forget such a thing. Anyone with eyes in his head could see that the country built up by the Führer and respected by the whole world was now only a heap of ruins, but Fengler continued to deny any involvement in contributing to this collapse: "Not a bit of it!"

My father had seen through Fengler's intention of dragging him into a political argument, but he refused to be sidetracked. He didn't want to get into a debate that would lead nowhere, he told Fengler, but was merely looking for an answer to a simple question, which, after all, reflected very well on him. After a lengthy exchange, Fengler admitted that he had been the caller, and when my father inquired why he had been ready to do so, the response was: "Perhaps because it was the decent thing to do." Asked why he found this admission so terribly difficult, Fengler replied that he was no scoundrel. And to my father's remark that he had not just been concerned with a cause, but apparently with people as well, Fengler said that possibly this was what had made him weak. But he still found his behavior unforgivable: breaking his oath to Hitler would weigh on him for years to come. "At least he didn't proclaim himself an opponent of Hitler," concluded my father, "or ask me for an exoneration certificate."

My Berlin memories of this period include an encounter with Jean-Paul Sartre, who, when he introduced himself, was as pleased as a schoolboy at having arrived in the city without attracting any fuss. He spoke to a small circle of about thirty people in a Charlottenburg apartment. A French teacher had invited me and said the writer had come to investigate the conditions for a visit planned the following year, when his play *Les Mouches* (*The Flies*) would be performed. Sartre had been one of the first to take up a position on the German question: the starting point of his talk was the problem of the responsibility of nations and the fate of children when both stand naked, so to speak, before the powerful. But the "Grand Vizier," as I called him at the time, also talked about Germany, France, Europe, and the dawn of freedom. Everything that he said seemed to me to be notably well informed and yet disordered, in part also muddled, but always touching on our sense of the times. Everyone was impressed.

If I sum up my responses, I learned through Sartre that a degree of muddleheadedness can be quite fascinating; a view I later corrected when I began to see him as at once more serious and more dependent on the

current mood. I had already begun to think that during his polemical dispute with Camus, and hence long
before he visited Andreas Baader in Stammheim Prison.[20]
Afterward, he had remarked to those accompanying
him, "What an asshole!" But then, in public, he burst
out with the usual deliberately misleading lament about
prison conditions. On the Charlottenburg evening, when
one of the guests asked a question about the future of
freedom, Sartre talked about the play of new art forms,
about the American novel, Dos Passos, jazz, and contemporary cinema. One of those invited summed up our
impression in these words: the writer seemed to him like
a South American peasant working his way forward with
a machete through the thicket of confusing contemporary phenomena. But what is cut down, I put in, is quite
fortuitous. Oh yes, said the other, and the parrots as they
fly away display the most beautiful wing colors. "Only
Sartre," added a third person, "does not see himself as a
parrot, but as a prophet."

It was during this time that Aunt Dolly visited us.
After all these years her elegance had faded and her
mood was not much better. When I suggested going
to the opera as we used to do, she said, "If you can find
anything!" and complained about the deterioration of

---

20 Andreas Baader (1943–77), a student, and Ulrike Meinhof (1934–76), a journalist, were the leaders of a radical leftist group, the Baader-Meinhof Group or the
Red Army Fraction (RAF). They were imprisoned in Stammheim Prison, a political
prison since the eighteenth century, for carrying out terrorist acts against the Bonn
Republic in an attempt to overturn the neocapitalist system, which Bonn represented to them; they are alleged to have committed suicide, but many observers
doubt that official version of their end.

Berlin's opera houses. I concluded that she was no longer really interested in opera, clothes, or anything else.
Rather, she had not got over the great disappointment
of her life. Later Hannih and Christa told me that Aunt
Dolly had grown quite bitter and had recently remarked,
in passing, that she could never ever forgive life for what
it had done to her.

Aunt Dolly was sipping listlessly at her teacup when
there was a knock at the door. A man we didn't know
introduced himself and, after a long-winded introduction, handed my mother a skimpily wrapped package.
"It's for you, madame," he said, "or rather for your husband, who I believe is still alive." The visitor explained
that he had discovered these things on a mountain of
rubbish on Wuhlheide Heath, and, since the books bore
their owner's name, he had through various connections
traced our address. When my mother invited him to sit
down and opened up the package in front of us all, the
first thing she found was the index volume of the big
Goethe edition, then a volume by Jean Paul, as well as
one by Emil Julius Gumbel about right-wing assassina
tions in the early years of the Weimar Republic, and there
was a smaller-format memoir of an Italian trip with the
never-forgotten title *Arcadia Lies by the Arno: A Journey
to Florence*.

But the pleasure of this initial moment of recognition
was also marred by profound disappointment. Every volume was soaked through and the spines had come apart, so
that whole sheets were missing. Even the better-preserved
parts were damaged by wind and weather, the pages stuck

together and largely illegible. My father, who had meanwhile joined us, had tears in his eyes, as we later realized, almost with a shock. The next day he visited the
area on Wuhlheide where the books had been found,
but there was nothing but a mass of papery pulp. At
some point the four books that had been brought back
also disappeared. My father remarked that he would
not search for them again, because they reminded
him of too much that had gone missing because of the
damned Hitler years. We suspected he had disposed of
the books himself.

One afternoon Paul Mielitz dropped by for tea, as
he often did. He had proved himself a staunch friend for
many years, ever since he and my father had been in the
Reichsbanner together. We were just talking about the
rather plain Italy book found among the volumes saved,
and my father expressed his regret that he had been to
Italy only three times. He had been hindered, of course,
by constant money problems, he said; but also, perhaps,
because his affection for "the land where the lemons
bloom" had always had something to do with "escape
and playfulness," not with anything serious like England, where the philosophical and practical grounds of
democracy would shortly be explained to him at Wilton
Park.[21] Italy had seemed to him no more than a caprice,
the most charming caprice in the world, but for the Prus-

---

21 Wilton Park was an estate in England that was used as a POW camp. In 1946
it became one of the postwar conference locations where the democratic renewal of
Germany was discussed.

sian that he was, like every caprice it bordered on the impermissible; sometimes more than that. "A beautiful spell," he turned to his guest, "but what does an old trade unionist know about all that? I don't even know if in Italy today, after Mussolini, they have trade unions again."

One could tell that Mielitz had borne with impatience the five minutes my father spent on his Italian caprice. Then he let it out: "Great news! Fantastic! You won't believe it!" And more such exclamations. "A sensation! I've been allocated a house in Lichterfelde. A house! No, a whole villa for the little house I lost! Just imagine: a villa in posh Lichterfelde. Even though my mum always said, 'Paul? He'll never get anywhere!' As a socialist— don't make me laugh! Now she hasn't lived to see it!"

My father shook his friend's hand and said something like "Good luck! Here comes the social climber!" We all joined in. The rest of the visit passed with a few sentences about the previous occupant, who had ascended to high rank as an official in the Nazi Party with a notable lack of scruples. But more time was spent on the plans for the housewarming, the guest list, the most suitable date, the furniture, the drinks, and the fact that, inappropriately, only "shabby Berlin pretzels and rolls" could be handed around. Then Mielitz left to go back to his cramped Kreuzberg flat.

He was hardly out the door when the debate began. We talked about legitimate compensation, about justice, and already imagined whole suites of rooms and the garden we would soon have again. "But please, without fruit bushes. They tear your clothes and scratch your arms!"

Hannih said excitedly. Christa thought that in Lichterfelde only ornamental gardens were allowed anyway, and
apart from that she would prefer a swimming pool. During this animated babble of voices—in which my mother,
with a sense of foreboding, did not join—my father sat
there with a withdrawn expression and didn't say a word.
When there was a brief pause I saw deep furrows of irritation on his forehead.

"Am I surrounded by lunatics?" he exclaimed. "Are
you all in your right minds? Do you really want me to
be paid for my political decisions? Then I might just as
well have joined the Nazi Party and made a career for
myself. A villa in 'posh Lichterfelde,' says Paul. But there
are much posher ones in Zehlendorf and in Grunewald
anyway. But that's not where a class-conscious worker
goes. And guest lists with rolls! Dear Lord! And no
fruit bushes! A minute ago I asked myself if I was surrounded by lunatics. Now I know: they're everywhere!"
He cleared his throat a couple of times, while, in embarrassment, we said nothing. "So not another word about
it—at least not when I'm around." He pushed his chair
aside and left the room.

We sat there not knowing what to say. I thought that
there was much that was true about his objection, but
it was Winfried, always level-headed, who spoke first.
"He's completely right!" he said. "We were trying to take
away his life. Everything we said must have sounded like
an insult to him. We behaved like crooks. And it won't
be long before others follow us and make a profit out of
the Hitler years. I can already see them coming . . ." And

he went on talking so convincingly that everyone agreed with him. The final word was left to my mother: "After this performance you now know that he still has his spirit. The depressions will come again, I'm sure of that. But his spirit, too! We just have to wait!" There was never again talk of a villa in Lichterfelde or anywhere else.

From my mother I learned that my father—after he had already been appointed a superintendent of schools in 1946—was agonizing over whether he should accept a seat on the Berlin city council, as he was on all sides being urged to do. In the end he decided on a "test run," as he liked to say, on the Neukölln borough council, and, if his health held up, to stand for the city parliament the following year. At the same time he took on the position of chairman of the Society for Christian-Jewish Cooperation—"in remembrance of my good friends Dr. Meyer, Dr. Goldschmidt, and the Rosenthals," he once said, adding, "but not forgetting poor Sally Jallowitz." On his last visit to Karlshorst in early 1943, Jallowitz had rejected my father's suggestion that he go into hiding: "I'm not so easily killed, dear friend!" Later, with pleasure and great sadness, my father found his name on a memorial plaque in Israel.

The list of characters I came across by chance in the few weeks of my Berlin stay could be extended indefinitely. One person who should not be absent from it is Peter Schulz, who had started as a law student at the Humboldt University and was a subtenant on the floor above us. He was sharp-witted, cool in a lawyer's way, and at the same time cynical. When, for obvious reasons under the circumstances, we yet again drew comparisons between the two political systems, he spoke openly of his readiness to "go to the East."[22]

Peter Schulz had great hopes for Communism and held that nothing more than a pretty illusion was being presented of the capitalist West. "They've got their experts for that!" he often repeated. The future, at any rate, belonged to the East: "That's where the sun rises!" In six or eight years at the latest, socialism would be ahead in all respects. "And freedom?" I asked. "That comes after," he said. Freedom was only a consequence of affluence, not its precondition. Freedom first was "one of the lavatory wall slogans of capitalism."

We often spent whole evenings on such questions, and with Peter Schulz I for the first time discovered that stubborn, conventional people frequently utter nothing but commonplaces with respect to everyday life, but as soon as the conversation turns to political questions, they not infrequently express fantastically foolish ideas. In the West, too, it was the dreariest philistines who could be won over by almost any eccentric craziness.

When I asked him what he would do if things did not turn out the way he anticipated, he made a dismissive gesture. Very simple, he responded. If he remained in West Berlin and the Russians took over the city, they would

---

22 "Going to the East" after 1945, and even more after 1949, when the two new German states were founded, meant going to the Soviet-occupied zone or the German Democratic Republic. Many German leftist intellectuals chose this state as the better chance for a truly new Germany, free from fascism and capitalism. Among the most prominent were Bertolt Brecht, Stefan Heym, Wolf Biermann, and many others. Western media preferred to report only defections from the East to the West.

send him to the mines. "Finished. Lights out!" But if he
went over to the East and it was taken over by the West,
then at most he would have to attend a "reeducation
course," perhaps two. Then he would come out again as
a model democrat. And, after brief reflection, he added,
"I'm not indulging in any dirty tricks there. Although I
learned them in the Hitler Youth. Understand?"

"Well," he asked me shortly afterward when I made
my farewell visit, "have I learned my lesson for idiots, in
your opinion?" I shook my head. "Only the wrong one!"
I retorted. No doubt Peter Schulz successfully worked
his way up. But despite some efforts, no one in the family or any friend ever heard of him again after the end of
1948, when he moved to the Soviet Occupation Zone.

Someone else who belongs in this gallery of brief
Berlin acquaintances is Otto Zarek, who had returned to
his "once-loved Berlin"—"just to take a look around."[23]
He had been a well-known author in the 1920s and now
wanted to get to know a young German. He was introduced to me through the good offices of a committee
member of the Christian-Jewish society. We met in the
restaurant of a French officers' club, which was reputed
to have a kitchen of an international standard. Zarek had
brought a promising author with him called William
Golding, who would later have a worldwide success with

---

23 Otto Zarek (1898–1958) was a Jewish homosexual writer and thus had two
strikes against him in Nazi Germany, which he left in time to go to Hungary and
England, only returning to Berlin after the war. An early Expressionist, he wrote
novels and was active in the theater and as a journalist.

Lord of the Flies and was awarded the Nobel Prize in Literature.

Both were amusing, intelligent, and tireless in their English malice about colleagues, whether they were talking about George Bernard Shaw, T. S. Eliot, or Christopher Fry. But more extravagant was Otto Zarek, who evidently took English eccentricity all too literally. He interrupted even the slyest anecdotes with long-winded digressions on the best restaurants in the world, which is, of course, one of the dullest conversational topics in existence. After flight and terror, explained Zarek repeatedly, he now only patronized "select establishments," and without exception drank renowned Italian white wines or a classic Bordeaux.

Nevertheless, in the course of the evening I couldn't get rid of the impression that neither the dishes nor the vintage Bordeaux meant anything to Otto Zarek. To my astonishment he hastily shoveled down each course on the menu as it came and, after a ritual connoisseur's glance, poured glass after glass of wine down his throat. I thought during this display of gluttony, which William Golding also observed with surprise, that Zarek was unable to enjoy anything anymore. Instead, he only wanted to prove that the years of terror were over. Later on, after he had become Boleslaw Barlog's dramaturge at the Schiller Theater in Berlin, we became close friends.

At the end of my weeks in Berlin, when I had already packed my suitcases, Walter Kühne turned up from his seclusion near Lüneburg. He had prevented court-martial proceedings against me thanks to a fairly

transparent dodge and wanted to meet my parents,
from whom he had received a report about my brother
Wolfgang's death, which he had passed on to me. Now
he brought me Thomas Mann's novella *Death in Ven-
ice* and remarked, glancing at my father and appealing
for understanding, "You've probably got over and forgiven Thomas Mann by this time!" My father replied
with a somewhat forced smile, "Got over, yes; forgiven,
no." For all its limits, the book opened up for me further
doors to the literature of the first half of the century. In
the years that followed, I found my way to Gide, Rudolf
Borchardt, Henry James, and even Oswald Spengler.[24]
The latter's tone irritated me, however; always a little
too much enamored of doom and seeming to address
the reader from the parapets of the universe. As in those
infinitely remote prewar days, we then went out to Potsdam, encountered further restricted areas, talked, drank
watery lemonade (more for the sake of memory than anything else), and walked back past Kleist's grave to Wann-
see Station. That was the first time that life seemed to be
gradually returning to its familiar pattern.

Arriving at the station in Freiburg, I came upon Dr.
Kiefer, who had taught me when I was stationed with the
antiaircraft battery in Friedrichshafen, consulting the
departures board. He was still corpulent, engaging, and

---

24 André Gide (1869–1951), prolific French writer of prose and dramatic works,
was influential also as a founder and editor of the *Nouvelle Revue Française*. Rudolf
Borchardt (1877–1945) was a German-Jewish writer who survived the war in Italy;
nationalist and conservative in his essays, he is best known for his translations of
Pindar and Dante.

exuberant. Every Wednesday, he said, he had a *jour fixe* for particular friends in his apartment in Jacobistrasse, and since I had been one of his favorite pupils he would be very pleased to invite me. I could get all the details from Willibald Knecht, the publisher's son, who had also been invited. "Willibald Knecht was killed in action," I interrupted Dr. Kiefer, but there was no stopping him, and he talked about the professors, journalists, and writers who would be there, even some artists. "Well, you get the idea! So, till Wednesday!" Furthermore, he shouted over from the station doors in a voice loud enough to be heard by everyone, he had recently invited the great actor Martin Held, who would shortly be appearing in Freiburg in a lead role. *The Devil's General.* Had I heard of it?[25]

So I was again drawn into contact with Dr. Kiefer, who had indeed assembled a notable circle. We talked with unusually objective and personal frankness: about the largely undiminished reputation of Freiburg University; the musical life of the city; the affectations of the French occupation authorities; and whatever was happening at the time. But the unmatched attraction of the evenings was Dr. Kiefer's daughter Juliane, whom the junior academics and even more so the older professors crowded around. She looked as if she had just stepped out of a painting by Raphael and I have forgotten neither

---

25 This play by the dramatist Carl Zuckmayer (1896–1977), first produced in 1946, was one of the few works of literature at that time dealing with the immediate past. The author had emigrated to Vermont in 1938 and returned to Switzerland after the war. He was well established through his popular comedies before the war, best known for their earthy characters and blunt language.

the envious nor the reproving glances when the beautiful Juliane, as happened from time to time, invited me to sit beside her.

These evenings, too, confirmed the impression of normality. Basically, I had spent the past twenty years outside the sphere of normal life: whether under the pressure that had constantly borne down on my parents, or at school, or the boarding school, or in the army, or as a prisoner of war. We children never complained about the difficulties the Hitler years had imposed on us; in fact, protected by our parents, we experienced them, rather, as a happy and never-threatening adventure. But was that life?

I was inclined to study law, possibly to balance my amateur's preference for the Renaissance. At least, so it sometimes seemed to me, the Berlin visit and the conversations with my father had brought me closer to reality. "The Weimar Republic foundered not least because of dreamers who were running away from the world," he once said. "Stick to Italy! That way you'll learn to understand the present. But don't forget Berlin." And later on: "The closer you get to political reality, the more you have to leave behind. Unfortunately, you also will lose what Wolfgang once called—I've never forgotten it—your romantic quirk. Reality will never make you entirely happy! But there's no choice if we want to avoid another shipwreck."

When I asked why the two could not be combined, the Renaissance with the political here and now, he said carefully that he did not believe I had a vocation for politics in the narrower sense; he would set aside the self-evident responsibilities of all citizens. I was intellectually too curious and too interested in new things. Democracy, on the other hand, if one approached it responsibly, was rather boring. The great designs had already been formulated; there was no opportunity for anyone to be original anymore. One had to be destined for it. Or one should rather let it be. Then, he concluded, "You can leave a door open for yourself. That would mean that you don't study medieval history but law. If you study that, then everything remains possible."

So—on my father's advice and halfway seeing sense—I began to study law. Friends encouraged me in this decision. During the many intervals between law classes I attended lectures by Gerhard Ritter on modern history, by Gerd Tellenbach on medieval history, by Hugo Friedrich on Montaigne, and the Germanist Walther Rehm's quite unique lectures on images of modern European man from Don Quixote by way of Hamlet and Faust to Don Giovanni. He was indisputably the most admirable university teacher I encountered.[26] Overall, the university was something of an Arcadia. In addition, there were new contacts, visits to the theater and to concerts, as well as dates with Marcienne, an enchanting exchange student from Paris, and bicycle tours in the Black Forest.

---

26 This is a partial listing of the star professors at Freiburg in the 1950s; students from all fields would flock to their lectures in what was called *studium generale* only for their own edification, not for credit.

All of these things were facets of a longed-for normality. But the longer the new experience went on, the more it felt like a shock. I found normal life infinitely lacking in excitement and looked for distractions, but did not gain any particular satisfaction from them. Not until one evening toward the end of my studies in Freiburg, on hearing the encoded quotation of the Eroica motif in Richard Strauss's *Metamorphoses* at a concert, did I feel myself understood and could I understand the elderly, disheveled man sitting next to me. His eyes wet, he abruptly turned to me and said that from today he would never attend another concert. Not for the rest of his life! He didn't need to go to the concert hall to weep! He could do that at home. At his age, anyway. And he couldn't hold back the tears any longer. It had started with an adagio, he explained, but now any musical perfection made him lose his composure. He asked me to excuse him. With increasing age, I would become familiar with these tears.

The next day I called on Fritz Werner at his bookstore. He came toward me, beaming behind the thick lenses of his glasses. "At last!" he exclaimed. "Good news for you! Two books at once. First the titles: one is Thomas Wolfe's *Look Homeward, Angel*; the other, Hemingway's early novel *The Sun Also Rises*. Both cloth-bound. And now, put on a happy face!"

I thanked him and went down Salzstrasse to the former Adolf Hitler Strasse, which was now called Kaiser Joseph Strasse once more. When I reached the intersection I was struck by the thought that now things are as they should be. For the first time in your life, you are free. You go to the bookseller and without making an application or getting a special permit simply buy—for about twenty marks, which is all they cost—two works of American literature. But then the next thought is already there: Are you really free? All I did was buy books. Perhaps normality is harder than freedom. It begins now. Would I be able to cope with it? And, if so, how?

ELEVEN

•

Retrospect and a
Brief Look Ahead

Long after my return from the war and captivity, I continued to struggle with normalcy. I even had problems with the idea itself. The whole world was talking about how we had to get back to normal conditions, but as soon as I asked what these were, the old commonplaces were brought up. Yet there had been a dictatorship and an unparalleled collapse that had left behind a people and a land in ruins. No one could really say to what extent the former rules and conditions were still valid or why they should be reestablished. For anyone with eyes to see, the preceding years had swept away almost everything. To what should we cling?

Furthermore, these doubts as to the principles of existence coincided with the long-overdue process of detaching myself from my parents. Of course, my siblings and

I had the greatest respect for what my mother and father had achieved in their lives, and in our occasional discussions we reminded each other not to forget their moral integrity during the Nazi years. This knowledge set certain limits to any conflicts of opinion we might have. But something else (as Winfried also admitted) caused us much greater problems. Unlike the overwhelming majority of Germans, we were not part of some mass conversion. Whenever talk came around to the 1930s and 1940s, many of our contemporaries felt some kind of remorse, but we were excluded from this psychodrama. We had the dubious advantage of remaining exactly who we had always been, and so of once again being the odd ones out.

On top of all this, the chaos of the times had thrown up another problem: I had two fathers. One was the man of the 1930s, a product of the Hitler years, inclined to rage and a black wit; the other was the figure who returned from Russian captivity, physically worn out, his intellect and spirit contracted. His wit, which gave us pleasure in our younger years and, in part, also a kind of apprenticeship, only gradually reemerged, and then only for moments at a time. My father had always loved sayings with the brevity of aphorisms. I remember the phrase with which, during Hitler's Reich, he had often commented on some arbitrary decision by insignificant people who had suddenly acquired power. It was "Endure the clowns!" and it soon became a motto with a proverbial force in our family. At any rate, given his propensity for formulas as signposts, Father recommended the phrase to us as a guiding principle for the coming years, perhaps for the rest of our lives. I once heard him draw to a close a discussion of an episode which had occurred during the Nazi years with the maxim "One sometimes has to keep one's head down, but try not to look shorter as a result!"

It was a life full of privations, which, after a promising beginning, he had chosen in full awareness of the consequences; indeed, it had meant the sacrifice of any kind of future. Of the many heroic speechmakers who take the platform at commemorative ceremonies nowadays, I have often asked myself which of them would have done the same as my father? For compensation, my father had only the knowledge of meeting his own rigorous principles. And if this consideration did not make everything good and sometimes drove my mother, in particular, to despair, it nevertheless provided him with a significant degree of satisfaction.

My mother, on the other hand, though she held the same views as my father in political matters, had a much more difficult time dealing with day-to-day life. For her, family came before principles; only once did this imperceptibly smoldering difference of opinion burst out into the open. She got nothing but the burdens, caring for the pots, the washboards, and the tiled stove. And all the while, she wanted to get each one of us through those times, alive and at the same time "with decency." Long after the war we heard her say, with a touch of bitterness, "He had his circles of friends, Hans Hausdorf, Dr. Gans, Dr. Meyer, and many more besides. I had the burden of five children. Not that I'm complaining. But it was a lop-sided arrangement. I don't think I was made for a life like that. But then who is? We paid a high price."

At the end of the 1940s something else stood in the way of normality. We were young, enterprising, and, especially after the limitations of the Nazi years, suscep-tible to intellectual whims of one kind or another. Yet judgment, discernment, and common sense were also demanded of us. Inevitably there was friction as these two sets of demands came into conflict. Yet no one could give a convincing answer to historical questions in the narrow sense, how Hitler and all the havoc he had caused could have come about. It was certain that only a minor-ity had wanted the war or had wanted to settle in Byelo-russia and beyond that to the Ural Mountains, and no one had been keen to defend the heights of the Caucasus against Muslim mountain tribes. Nor did the simplistic faith in a Nordic race have more than a tiny number of supporters.

Altogether it was not abstruse arguments such as these that had brought Hitler to power; the motives deriving from the personal experiences of individuals were much more determining. These included infla-tion and the world economic crisis, together with the collapse of the middle classes on whom the stability of the state depended. Everyone who had been affected by such troubles feared falling even deeper into the abyss. In addition, there were the ideological conflicts of the body politic and the trend of the time to totalitarian or at least dictatorial systems—especially when a master of

The author in 1946 as a prisoner of war,
drawn by Alfred Sternmann

moods and demagoguery like Hitler was staging his oratory so attractively and powerfully. Consequently, broad but fickle sections of the population, who were essentially well disposed to the republic, believed themselves to be threatened by radicals of the right and left; they increasingly surrendered to the idea that nothing less than the spirit of the age was against them. With Hegel in one's intellectual baggage one was even more susceptible to such thinking.[1]

Nevertheless, the question still being asked is how these ideas were capable of driving such an old and civilized nation out of its mind. How was it possible that the leaders of the National Socialist movement were able to overcome the constitutional safeguards with so little resistance? And, furthermore, how was so much disregard of the law possible in an order-loving country? I once heard my father say that the Germans were no longer German: "They have lost their passion for introspection and discovered their taste for the primitive. Their model is no longer—as it once was—the reflective scholar type of the nineteenth century. He prevailed for a long time. Today, however, it is the tribal warrior, dancing around a stake and showing his chief a painted grimace. So much for the nation of Goethe!"

---

1 Fest here refers not to the Hegel whose reception, especially via France, has dominated so much of postmodern Western thought. He writes of the founder and main representative of German Idealism as he was popularly dispensed in German secondary schools and universities well into the 1960s. One of the seminal modern thinkers, Georg Wilhelm Friedrich Hegel (1770–1831) has profoundly changed speculation in most fields of philosophy from logic to ontology and from philosophy of history to aesthetics.

The most obvious explanation for the success of
National Socialism was that—like all groups ready to
use force and then endowed with funds—it attracted
opportunists. That is attested to by the mass defections
of spring 1933, when hundreds of thousands went over
to the Nazi Party after the seizure of power, as well as
by the almost instantaneous and complete disappearance
of the party in 1945. No one wanted to admit to having
supported a lost cause. For years people had ignored the
atrocities of the regime and fawned on those in power:
senior civil servants, employers, generals, and the rest.
Each person soothed his conscience in his own way. The
conduct of the actress Adele Sandrock will always represent the exception. At "afternoon tea for ladies" at the
Reich Chancellery, when Hitler burst out with invective
against the Jews, she supposedly interrupted him: "My
Führer! In my presence not a word against the Jews,
please! All my life they have been my best lovers!" But
perhaps that was only an anecdote passed on in a whis-
per. Then one put the party badge in one's buttonhole
and went to cheer along with the rest. Then there followed, after 1945, the Great Denial.

The attitude in the early years after the war was later
described as a "communicative silence," which was not
simply a form of repression. Disillusionment, shame,
and defiance combined to form an opaque refusal of
guilt. In addition there was a tendency to belatedly con-
struct heroes. Some invented acts of resistance; others (as
part of the game of contrition) sought out a prominent
place on the bench of the self-accusers. But in all their

lamentation, they were very ready to defame anyone who didn't do as they did and constantly beat their sinful breasts. When Günter Grass or any of the other countless self-accusers pointed to their own feelings of shame, they were not referring to any guilt on their own part—they felt themselves to be beyond reproach—but to the many reasons which everyone else had to be ashamed. However, the mass of the population, so they said, was not prepared to acknowledge their shame.[2]

Seen as a whole, what I had experienced was the collapse of the bourgeois world. Its end was already foreseeable before Hitler came on the scene. Solely individual characters survived the years of his rule with integrity—no classes, groups, or ideologies. Too many forces in society had contributed to the destruction of this world, the political right just as much as the left, art, literature, the youth movement, among others. Basically, Hitler had merely swept away the remaining ruins. He was a revolutionary. But because he was capable of hiding behind a bourgeois mask, he destroyed the hollow facade of the bourgeoisie with the help of the bourgeoisie itself: the desire to put an end to it all was overpowering.

---

2 This was a right-wing hobbyhorse after the war and Fest loves to ride it. While antifascist himself, he cannot abide—echoing the sentiments of most German conservatives—the assumption of national shame and guilt urged upon the nation by most of its left-wing postwar writers. These include Günter Grass (born 1927), whose many novels and essays were the first and most successful attempts to deal meaningfully and critically with the Nazi experience. This was seen as inappropriate for serious art and as demeaning to the German nation. He was accused by CDU politicians of "befouling his own nest," an opinion Fest obviously shares.

Of the twelve families at 13 Hentigstrasse, only one tenant was a member of the Nazi Party. As far as I know, it was not much different in the neighboring buildings. If asked, each person living in our building would have passionately defended middle-class and civil virtues. Yet, inwardly, this stratum of society had decayed long before, so that I was essentially brought up in accordance with the principles of an outmoded order. Its rules and traditions right down to its poetic canon were passed on to me. It kept me at a distance from the times to some extent; simultaneously, it put some solid ground under my feet, which helped to sustain me in the years that followed.

As is evident in retrospect, each member of our family had his or her own distinctive way of coping with the challenges of the age and, taken all together, we were a reflection of the various possibilities of evasion in the face of the regime. My father's stubbornness was coupled with a contempt that never diminished and allowed of no compromise. My mother's opposition derived from her quite different set of values, impregnated by religion, which she was able to bring into play with often surprising skill. Wolfgang was able to checkmate every difficulty with his wit and charm. I drew attention to myself with acts of impudence that my parents observed with some concern, but which also had a political aspect. Winfried had his level-headed introversion. My sisters faced life each in her own way, in part quietly, in part defiantly, and had no problems either with the world or with regarding it ironically. We sometimes defined the behavior of friends in accordance with this family catalogue of types. Everyone in our close circle of friends had their own way of getting through the times halfway undamaged.

Also among those things that survived the Nazi Reich, despite the heavy losses, was for a few years a link between Germans and Jews. In the Berlin of the first years after the war I still encountered brilliant, educated, and charming witnesses to this past, and I regard it as one of the strokes of luck of my life that during the 1950s I experienced a brief revival of this world in the home of the respected doctor Walther Hirsch. He had been born around the turn of the century and in his Grunewald villa he tried to conjure up once more the luster of the 1920s and to revive the memory of the vanished days of his youth. At the soirees which he held at his home every couple of weeks I got to know Fritz Kortner and Joachim Prinz, Wolfgang Lukschy, Hans Scholz, and Sebastian Haffner, as well as Jean-Pierre Ponnelle, Melvin Lasky, and the painter Heinrich Heuser, and many more.

Long after midnight, when most of the sixty or so guests had taken their leave, a circle of about a dozen remained behind, and each time three of them were called on to enter a kind of competition for the best story of the night. Anyone who was present will remember tales that were developed in masterly fashion and brilliantly told, and often the winner was the host himself or the writer Hans Scholz, whose great success was yet to come. I still regret that these tales were never recorded and collected. They are gone and lost forever, like the German-Jewish community.

Many voices—most prominently that of Gershom Scholem—have argued that the much-discussed German–Jewish symbiosis never existed. That is very understandable as a response to injustice stretching over generations, and above all to the horrors of the Hitler years. But as a conclusion it remains inaccurate. The relationship between Germans and Jews was always deeper and more profound than, for example, that between Jews and the French or Jews and the English or the Scandinavians.

The sense of fellowship was based above all on three things. There was first of all a delight in speculation, imaginatively taking an idea as far as it will go, even into entirely new realms of thought. Further, there was an inclination toward complicated structures of ideas, which possibly have a theological aspect and, ultimately, a utopian goal, because world and man are unceasingly searching for salvation. And, finally, there should be mentioned an obsessive love of music to the extent that it becomes almost a metaphysical background, as did German music, notably from Beethoven to Richard Wagner. This common interest can be found in the relationship between Richard Strauss and Hugo von Hofmannsthal or Bertolt Brecht and Kurt Weill, and in many outstanding conductors from Otto Klemperer to Leonard Bernstein. So, perhaps the Germans' hatred of the Jews and the genocide may be interpreted as a kind of fratricide, even if one remains aware of how debatable as such an assertion is.

Such affinities were mostly destroyed by the Holocaust, and Walther Hirsch's moving attempt to resurrect them in his house could not last longer than the lifetimes

of those involved. Today the relationship between Germans and Jews is atrophied and largely trivialized. There
are no great communities of interest anymore, no visible
results. Among my notes I found some record of conversations with Dr. Meyer just before I went to Freiburg.
They sound like an anticipated epitaph. "We have no
future," he once responded to a remark by me about how
things would go on. "With our end the world ends. All
of us here are appearing in a tragedy. But it has no fifth
act. There is no continuation. Our book of life suddenly
breaks off. Someone has simply torn out the last page."

The shattered country to which I returned in 1947
was not so much a world of restriction and lack of freedom of movement, as it is often viewed today. There was,
in fact, plenty of free space to be found. Efforts at restoration by leading figures and various governments—
for which they are criticized even today—were helpless
attempts to find a way back to certain rules without
which life as a society is impossible.

Intellectually, too, these were years without rules. We
took the freedoms that were available for granted. It was,
in fact, this temptation that stopped me from returning
to Berlin immediately and beginning my studies at the
Humboldt University, because I could not imagine that
in the eastern sector of the city there would be the same
freedom as in Freiburg.[3] There, in addition to my stud-

---

3 The Humboldt University building was located in the Soviet sector of Berlin
at the time; it was to become the flagship university of the GDR. In 1948, professors leaving because of the Communist influence on teaching and administration
founded the Free University of Berlin in West Berlin.

ies, I continued to read about the Italian Renaissance and to extend my knowledge of the fall of the Roman Empire. I read everything I could find by Thomas Mann, picked up all the American literature I could get hold of—from John Steinbeck to William Faulkner—as well as the more recent French writers from Raymond Aron to Emmanuel Mounier; and I went to the theater whenever I could. Among the productions that have stood the test of time are Sartre's *Les Mouches*, Christopher Fry's *The Lady's Not for Burning*, and Thornton Wilder's *The Skin of Our Teeth*. Then I came across Hugh Trevor-Roper's *The Last Days of Hitler* and Curzio Malaparte's *Kaputt* and was deeply impressed.

Toward the end of my period of study I got to know Eckart Peterich, who was very amused to discover that he had once influenced my notion of the ideal profession.[4] With him was his daughter, charmingly nicknamed "Coccolo," and both of them invited me to their grand house high above Florence on the "other side" of the Arno. The two weeks that I spent reading and writing in the topmost tower room of the villa once again made the profession of "private scholar" a tempting one, even more so when we drove out to the country seat of the Peterichs in the middle of a pine forest in the then still rural Forte dei Marmi. Here I got to know, for the first time, the daily routine of a scholar living in sophis-

---

4 Eckard Peterich (1900–68), who lived primarily in Florence and wrote about myth, religion, and art in classical antiquity, is the prime exemplar of the "private scholar" young Fest always wanted to be.

ticated and affluent circumstances: in a Mediterranean
landscape, occupied with studies by day and entertaining friends in the evening, sitting at well-spread tables
late into the night.

The country home welcomed guests from all over
the world. I met Ernst Jünger and Aldous Huxley, Hilde
Spiel and Peter de Mendelssohn, Luigi Barzini, Indro
Montanelli, and Elio Vittorini. Arthur Koestler dropped
by one day with an excitingly good-looking woman, and
among the guests for the month was a retired British general who told stories about India and other places full of
adventure, but preferred to spend the evenings by the
fire, saying nothing. It was striking that in these cosmopolitan surroundings no one treated me as a member of
a nation that had fallen into disrepute. All those present
felt themselves to be Europeans or at least saw themselves as part of a European-American cultural context.

The successful French writer André Germain, who
lived in a palazzo in Florence, called several times; his
young, homosexual secretary had just run away; but
what particularly incensed Monsieur Germain was the
fact that he (the secretary) had persuaded the wife of
the British consul general in Florence, of all people, to
take off with him. At that time Monsieur Germain was,
rather bizarrely, working simultaneously on a biography
of Lucrezia Borgia and another on Benito Mussolini.
Years later I found the latter in the library of Gaston Gallimard, when I myself had become a Gallimard author.
I assisted André Germain as a secretary for a while and
during that time wrote about two dozen short stories,

which an agency sold to a number of small newspapers for me, and for which I received about ten marks each. In addition, I took extensive notes on the age of the Borgias.

Italy—at least in the part I got to know—had everything that Germany (for me) lacked: warmth, lightness, naive animality, and theatrical sparkle. And, like my father, I experienced the country as an overwhelming antipode. It did not have the fadedness, the delicate patina of the day before yesterday which I had so often found striking on trips to France. After two months in Forte dei Marmi I felt as if I were at home and at the same time far from the world. For how long, I asked myself, could both be combined? When I couldn't find an answer I felt an ever greater desire to return to Germany.

In early 1950, soon after my return, I began to address more precise topics. The first essay that I offered Northwest German Radio, and which was also in memory of the "Romantic" Reinhold Buck, had the somewhat high-flown title "German Romanticism in the Twilight of Contemporary Experience."[5] I've forgotten the topics and titles of my subsequent reflections, but I remember that despite my considerable reluctance, the Hitler years found their way into almost every manuscript. Gradually, the American broadcasting station RIAS[6] became the focus of my early journalistic efforts. I saw my future

---

5 Writing essays, radio plays, or short narratives for the radio was one of the most readily available and frequently used ways to make a little money for both established and aspiring authors.

6 RIAS: Radio im Amerikanischen Sektor (Radio in the American Sector)—i.e., the American Sector of Berlin.—Trans.

preferably as a publisher or as the author of reflections on the reciprocity between the events of the day and the "spirit of the age."

At the same time I was writing my doctoral thesis at the Free University of Berlin, which was just establishing itself. It investigated within a legal context the influence of advertisers on the daily press. The thesis was almost complete and a date set—some considerable time in the future, due to overcrowding in the new institution—for the oral examination, when I received an offer from the RIAS. After a long conversation with my father, who advised me to finish my thesis first, I turned it down, but shortly afterward I received an even better offer. This time I accepted. Soon after taking up my post, the deputy director, Mr. Bloomfield, whom I had already met privately once or twice, asked me to his office and suggested, among other things, that I edit or, preferably, write a series of broadcasts on German history. The idea was to treat the period from the dismissal of Bismarck in 1890 up to the year 1945 in a number of increasingly detailed individual essays elaborating the reasons for the disaster. To be taken into consideration was that listeners in the Soviet Zone of occupation were getting a completely distorted picture of the German past.

A lengthy discussion ensued, in the course of which I argued against the proposal to the best of my ability. Something like that was better placed in the hands of a professional editor, I objected. At Freiburg University I had attended several lectures by Gerhard Ritter, Hans Herzfeld, Gerd Tellenbach, and other well-known historians, but I had avoided contemporary history as much as possible. I had never been sufficiently interested in it. Consequently, for both professional and personal reasons, I did not feel myself qualified to produce a series of programs on the period proposed.

Mr. Bloomfield remained adamant; I even had the impression that it was my very objections that lent force to his insistence. But for myself, I kept on thinking—on top of everything else—of a conversation I had recently had with my father about a commentary I had written on the 1932 German presidential election. He had praised the piece for its formal aspect, but objected that my "high style" was inappropriate when writing about the "Nazi gang." Then came the words I have never forgotten. Hitler and his rule was no subject for a serious historian, he said. It was nothing more than a "gutter subject." Hitler's supporters came from the gutter and that's where they belonged. Historians like myself were giving them a historical dignity to which they were not entitled.

My father's view, I argued, betrayed an old-fashioned and much too exalted conception of history. Nobody was ennobled by being in a history book. History simply recorded the course of events. Historians wrote about series of events, men of violence, ham actors, and murderers, just as they did about saints. But my father had experienced and suffered the Hitler years, so his objections were understandable. The younger generation, on the other hand, wanted to know how those years had come about.

My father remained unimpressed, and I began to understand just how much he continued to feel the

injustice of those times, when the best years of his life
had been stolen from him. I had wanted to study Col-
leoni, the Gonzagas, and Lorenzo the Magnificent, and
now I had exchanged them for the inferior riffraff of
Ley, Streicher, or Sauckel—they did not deserve any
"literary enhancement," he insisted toward the end of
our conversation.[7] He was quite able to see the tensions
which followed from his position, but it was impossible
to escape from this dilemma. I should therefore return
to my old preference, the Italian Renaissance. I told him
that I had mentioned that preference to Mr. Bloomfield
but he indicated that after the Hitler debacle airtime for
such remote topics might become available at best ten
years from now.

When I called on Mr. Bloomfield again, he turned
out to be as obdurate as my father had been, whom he
wanted to meet after hearing my report. In the end he
asked me to "simply get started" working on the series.
If that did not, in the long run, agree with me it would
not be hard to find some other kind of project in addition to the ones I was responsible for now. To put an end

---

7 Fest senior here lists several notables of the Nazi regime who were tried as war
criminals by the Nürnberg Tribunal and found guilty. Ley committed suicide while
the other two were hanged.

   Robert Ley (1890–1945) headed the Deutsche Arbeitsfront (German Labor
Front), in charge of all aspects of the organization and welfare of German workers.

   Fritz Sauckel (1894–1946) wound up in charge of the massive slave labor recruit-
ment which involved as many as five million people, many of whom were mistreated
and died.

   Julius Streicher (1885–1946) was Nazism's most heinous anti-Semite and Jew
baiter; his hysterical utterances and slanders became too much even for the likes of
Göring and Goebbels and he was forbidden to appear in public by 1940 and dismissed from his party posts. He remained unrepentant all the way to the gallows.

to the pointless quarrel I excused myself and, practically out the door, said to him: "All right, so be it! I should be able to crank out a dozen manuscripts about German history." Mr. Bloomfield stopped with surprise and called me back to his desk. He said: "I am afraid we have misunderstood each other. I did not mean a dozen shows; I was thinking more like eighty. At any rate, I am planning on a program of some length." So we were at loggerheads once again and I replied to him, "You are turning this awful contemporary history into a lifetime occupation for me!" But in the end I agreed to give it a try. It turns out Mr. Bloomfield was more prescient than I was. "It will be more than a try," he said, standing at the door to his office. And that's how I got into contemporary history.

I stayed with contemporary history for many years, but always with a touch of bad conscience, because I could never get the words "gutter subject" out of my head. I still preferred the Renaissance, and read whatever I could in my free time, including Charles de Brosses's *Secret Letters from Italy,* Landucci's *A Florentine Diary from 1450 to 1516,* and the *Memoirs* of Marguerite de Valois. Some of it I eventually forgot, but the Italian Renaissance remains my subject of choice.

In the early 1960s my father died. On the day before his death I spent several hours by his bedside in the hospital, and we talked in broad terms about his times and his life. Some of what was said has found its way into these memoirs, such as his reasons for showing Wolfgang and me the burnt-out Reichstag in 1933. Smiling, he recalled throwing the Hitler Youth leaders out of the house and his letter protesting his being drafted to build antitank fortifications. Reviewing those years, he managed one of his characteristic plays on words which Wolfgang had called "parsing syllables." *"Ich habe,"* he said, *"im Leben viele Fehler gemacht. Aber nichts falsch."* I have, he said, made many mistakes in life. But I have never done wrong.

Part of our time we spent talking about the whereabouts of old friends and those we had lost in the turmoil of war. He quoted an old French popular ballad, *"Que sont devenus mes amis?"* which he had learned from the Straeter family. This led us on to Karlshorst and I told him that with Mother's help and despite all the mishaps, he had made our youthful years happy ones. Then he said, as he was fading away into some state of half-awareness: "Please, tell me a story! Any story!" And some parable about life came to me, a mix constructed of things read and invented. It was probably pointless to base the narrative loosely on the *Odyssey*, but I thought he, being a Prussian *Bildungsbürger*, might find that pleasing.

Much abbreviated, the story went as follows. When man first stepped onto this earth he had to get to know the garden, the animals, and the bushes—just as we did back then in the Hentigstrasse. Once he had become reasonably familiar with all, he might do well to explore the city near and far, as we did when driving to Unter den Linden, to Potsdam, and to the Stechlinsee. At some point he will find himself a wife, start a family, and sally forth into the world where many challenges await, perhaps even a war, albeit not like the one Hitler had started so willfully. On that and other similar occasions he will encounter a lot of useless things and even lose his way. I continued, increasingly leaning on the *Odyssey*: At some point everyone has to deal with a modern version of Polyphemus—the world was still filled with monsters, taking on technological or hierarchical shapes nowadays. Later it would behoove one not to submit to a magical Circe, to pass through Scylla and Charybdis and whatever else one might encounter, not to forget the graceful and barely resistible Nausicaä and her tears. And once one returned to one's home, some stranger or other is occupying it, strutting about, and when they have finally been removed—then what? What was there to add? Then ennui awaits. Nor is there an end to travail—that much, at least, I had grasped. It seemed as if my father, lying below me on his pillow, slightly tilted his head. It even seemed to me as if he smiled one more time.

My professional life continued. First at RIAS, mainly as editor and producer for contemporary history; also a brief, happy time as a kind of impresario of the RIAS Youth Orchestra under Willy Hannuschke at the Brussels Expo of 1958; then from 1961 in charge of TV plays at North German Broadcasting and, a little later, as its editor in chief. That was when my first book, *Das Gesicht des Dritten Reiches* (1963), was published, which collected some twenty portraits from the contemporary history series Mr. Bloomfield had talked me into doing years before. The publication was a success, translated into many languages, and I was asked if I would undertake a biography of Hitler.

Naturally, my father's phrase about "gutter subject" came
to mind yet again; against that, however, there was his
maxim that one should never submit to the opinion of others. As the pressure of the political parties on the broadcasting stations increased and became almost unbearable
for me, I resigned from my broadcasting post to write the
Hitler book. What also persuaded me was that I would at
last fulfill the dream I had had as a fourteen-year-old to
live and work as an independent scholar—as I had written
home in November 1941.

My mother was very worried by my departure from
North German Broadcasting. She saw her own fate
about to be repeated. She said, "I do not like repetitions,"
or, more accurately, she added, she only liked repetition
in music, as well as in lyric poetry and—sometimes—on
the faces of children. Anywhere else they were an indication that things were about to go wrong. "On the subject
of Hitler that is almost inevitable," she said. "You will
always antagonize one side or the other." All my friends,
when asked, advised me not to take the risk and said I
was reckless, but I stuck to my guns, and, as a compensation for the book on the Renaissance which I had now
finally abandoned, I went to Italy, as I would from that
time on almost every year.

Germany was almost suffocating in its limitations,
but whenever I visited Italy it was as if many doors
were opening. Sometimes it seemed to me I was meeting the world and the people of the Renaissance in the
present, albeit reduced in their dimensions. Wherever I
went south of Lake Garda, I had the impression I was

revisiting the "lost paradise" of my childhood years, an overwhelming combination of natural and architectural beauty. It was also a land of sharply etched profiles and entertaining stories. I simply must talk about one of these encounters. One of the first acquaintances I made in Italy was Conte F., from a tiny town near Florence that time had passed by. The tales with which he entertained his friends were a vivid reflection of a multicolored world, despite its distance from the present.

The Conte was a stocky man who turned visibly grayer every time we met, brimming with the solid energy found in many Italian nonurban nobles. He also possessed a defining kind of charm which I likened to that of a condottiere who had been civilized over the course of many generations. But that comparison was met by a short, bellowing laugh and the comment that rheumatism, thick glasses, and an incipient paunch prevented any jumping onto coursers: "Just ask my sons!"

They were called Fabrizio and Camillo. Fabrizio was correct to a fault, pedantic, and had a tendency to be rather stern with himself, while Camillo lived only for *dolce far niente* and would at most act the eccentric Englishman. When I first met the Conte, people talked about the latest of Camillo's scandals. He had invited two of the local worthies to dine with him and a surprise guest in the private room of a local club; when they arrived they found that guest to be a totally naked woman, stretched out on a sofa next to Camillo. As one might expect, he met an unhappy end a few years later, while Fabrizio rose to become a director of a reputable bank. Whenever these names came up I was reminded of Eichendorff's poem about the two "brave lads" or the friends Charles and Sebastian in Evelyn Waugh's *Brideshead Revisited*. I also thought of the two Buddenbrook sons. One of them, Thomas, spends his time abroad acquiring an education and brings home his future bride, while the other, Christian, can only tell stories about Johnny Thunderstorm and sing "That's Maria!"

I was so deeply caught up in my notion of Italy that back then I believed that the Florentine tale of Conte F.'s family was simply a continuation of the Renaissance story, while the English novel or the German tales were mere literature that made visible every calculated thought in every line. It seems to me one could base an entire research project in intellectual history on this observation, and once again I regretted that I had to busy myself with Munich's bohemian circles and Hitler's march to the Feldherrnhalle in 1923. For at the time the Conte told me about his two sons, my intellectual game playing had already ended. The decision had been made some time ago.

Around this time my mother asked me to write down her recollections of the Nazi years. She indicated her willingness to help me record them. When I mentioned that Father did not want anything written down about those years, she replied it was only he who refused to record his experiences. Our conversation lasted all evening. Once or twice it seemed to me that she regarded her life as a failure. I suggested that she had borne a greater burden than my father, but she firmly denied it. "It was his decision," she said, "his responsibility." She had borne nothing but the external burdens, whereas his life had been destroyed. Did one suffer more at the hearth, she asked, or from the utter lack of prospects imposed on one's life? That depends on how one looks at it, I said. Her life, too, had been ruined. She replied that she had never seen it like that and did not want to do so, either. "Ruined" was in any case the wrong word. Only her girlish dreams had been smashed. But where were they ever fulfilled anyway? No matter how much she tried to downplay her own role, I could tell that she was very far from having come to terms with the Hitler period, even if it had been long ago by then.

When Winfried also refused to record his memories, my mother chose to say nothing more about the Hitler period. She remained stubbornly silent, as if she had erased it from her memory as a final sacrifice. However, when she read a draft chapter of my Hitler book, she was moved to observe that, from a distance, world events seem rather grand, whereas if one looks at the fates of individuals, one discovers a great deal of shabbiness, powerlessness, and misery. But once again, she refused to talk about her own feelings.

Some time later she fell ill. When I visited her in the hospital for the last time, a few days before her death, she had begun to lose consciousness with increasing frequency. She talked unceasingly and ever more quickly. With every word that could be understood the misfortune of her life burst out of her. It was the first time I heard her quarrel with fate. She spoke about the

never-ending worry, the constant shortages and making do, the informers everywhere, and, above all, how
much she suffered losing a son in Hitler's war. From time
to time she returned to the world from her confusion,
became aware of me, and managed a sign of acknowledgment by raising her hand from the blanket. After
that she fell into a semiconscious state and damned the
world and her botched life. I had never heard her curse
before, but now it seemed to me she was making up for
it—for all those years of repressed bitterness. I took her
hand, but she hardly noticed and went on cursing. It
lasted for hours. When it had already grown dark, she
managed some coherent words. Once she said, with
lengthy pauses, "The days are no longer lost . . . God
knows they're not! . . . They count again . . . Each one is
another twenty-four hours less! . . . That's what I always
tell myself! . . . That is my comfort."

Two days later nothing was left of the rebelliousness
which had haunted her semiconscious state only hours
earlier, and she passed away in her sleep. After her childhood and the happy early years of marriage, my mother
had increasingly begun to realize that evil exists. It was
easily visible in the simple images which constituted her
world. It was embodied in drunkards, swindlers, murderers, and Nazis. Even long after the end of the Third
Reich she said that one always had to be on one's guard
against evil. Because evil is extremely imaginative. Life
had taught her that. It liked to present itself in a humane
guise, as a lover or benefactor, a flatterer, and even as a
kind of god. Masses of people fell for it.

In a conversation we had a few months before her death, she said that the preferred guise of evil in her time had been the slogans, demonstrations, and festivities of the Nazis and the Communists. When I was young she had always been the one to contradict my father's gloomy view of things, and her plea "Stop being so apocalyptic!" had become almost proverbial in the family. But looking back she had to say that he was right. She still could not understand why so few had seen the naked evil around them: the obscenity of political uniforms, the sheer loathsomeness. Dr. Gans had always said that at the end of time reason would prevail, but she did not believe it. Rather, she was certain that evil would triumph. It required no justification, because people loved it. She had belonged to the wrong generation, she said, and she hoped we would have better luck. That was more or less all that life had taught her. When Winfried and I left her apartment in Zehlendorf, he said that her words were a simple and, in fact, conclusive judgment on the world of political daydreams.

If I remember rightly, it was after this visit and on some other occasions that we discussed the formative influence of our parents and our home. I talked about the many attacks I had come under for not conforming to the left-wing mood of the time, and, laughing, we quoted the nonsense then making the rounds about me. In our youth, Winfried explained, we had been taught a kind of pride in stepping out of line—and that was something none of these "grown-up Hitler Youth kids" realized or understood. Whenever I was asked about my guiding principles, I would always refer to my skepticism and even to a distaste for the spirit of the age and its fellow travelers. I had never doubted my father's *ego non*, to which he had introduced us on that unforgettable day when he instituted our "second supper." The lesson of the Nazi years for me was to resist current opinion. Hence I was never seriously tempted by Communism, unlike many respected contemporaries, who succumbed at least for a while. Several friends from my youth remained in East Germany, and in the years that followed it became evident that the Communist regime there was often more successful at persecuting its citizens and more impenetrable in its bureaucracy than the Nazis, and that it would not have tolerated the survival of such a halfway happy family home as ours had been. At any rate, we never had the feeling as children that we were growing up in a world without a future, unlike some of my schoolmates who lived in the German Democratic Republic. Yet Communism has largely succeeded in not being equated with National Socialism in the long run. That is surely its greatest propaganda victory.

If I look back at the key experiences of my youth, both my background and my education taught me political skepticism. At the time it was mainly directed against the prevailing ideological assumptions. Similarly, I have never understood why the rebels of 1968 and other politically confused and morally self-important young people longed to explain the world from a single point of view. The blindness and horrors of such ideas had only recently been patently manifested in our own country. And as for those older radicals, who suddenly wore jeans and long hair in carefully coiffed disarray—I never found words for them and never wanted to.

For those who could read the signs of the times, the wrongheadedness of all the fashionable nonsense of the age was always evident. Already in the 1930s Communism—and then in its train Nazism—should have caused every unprejudiced observer to take up a position of fundamental opposition toward them. The inhumanity of both ideologies, arising from their formulaic explanations of the world, was all too clear. There were many, however, who could not resist the temptation of making their dreams a reality. Even today, plenty of people remain sentimentally attached to some "ism" or other which has long since failed dismally. Against such nonsense, the much more intelligent words of Henry David Thoreau have always impressed me. "If I knew for a certainty that a man was coming to my house with the conscious design of doing me good," he said, "I should run for my life."

Such observations would later become the topic of some of my works and thus leap ahead of time. I mention them here because they were and are important to me. Another look ahead concerns one of the most important events of our lifetime. Sometimes I am reminded of the pessimistic moods of my father and most of his friends which surfaced again and again. At our garden table one of them once tried to equate the proportion of reason and unreason in the process of world history to a ratio of ten to ten thousand. The gloomy picture of man and history which my father's generation could not get away from reflected the times. I shared in this mood, as when I observed that in all history the liberating trumpet signal of Beethoven's *Fidelio* had hardly ever been heard and was no more than an "opera idea." Yet I feel happy every time I drive down the long road to Glienicke Bridge, where the temperamental Sophie had once flung her arms around my neck and where—after 1961—all roads ended.[8] I am lucky enough to have experienced a historical event in which, exceptionally, reason overcame all blindness and the desire to inflict horror. Then—just once, at least, and in the face of all experience—the sound of the trumpet became audible. It made the wall fall down and forced those in power to surrender it.

On the ninth of November, 1989, I found myself in Palermo, Sicily. I had come home late and had arranged an interview the next morning with a journalist from the Communist newspaper *l'Unità*. It had been agreed that we would discuss recent political developments and the German media and I wanted to tell him about that *"république de lettres"* which was the inspiration and ambitious goal of that part of the *Frankfurter Allgemeine Zeitung* for which I bore responsibility at the time. But when I arrived for the interview, before I had uttered a single word, the journalist jumped up from behind his desk,

---

8 The main road from Berlin to Potsdam crosses Glienicke Bridge, which today marks the boundary between the cities. The building of the Berlin Wall in 1961 cast the boundary in concrete, as it were. From then until 1989 the bridge had a certain notoriety as a place where spies and others were exchanged between East and West.—Trans.

The Freiburg University bookseller Fritz Werner
meeting the author in 1988

spread out his arms and exclaimed, *"Il muro della ver-*
gogna è caduto!" (The wall of shame has fallen!) Assuming he meant the easing of restrictions on travel between
East and West Germany, I said, "Yes, indeed! Things
are getting better." "No, not better!" my interviewer, a
young man with unruly, curly hair, almost shouted. "It

has fallen! Gone! Finished!" Only then did I discover details about what had happened and gave a long interview. I expressed my regret about having to hear about the fall of the wall in faraway Palermo, but he replied that for him my presence on this day was pure reportorial joy. To my annoyance, I could not leave for Berlin immediately, as I had an appointment in Rome that could not be put off. I spent all of the tenth and eleventh of November 1989 in front of the TV, and often thought of Henri IV's words: *"Pends-toi, brave Crillon! nous avons combattu à Arques et tu n'y étais pas!"* (Hang yourself, brave Crillon! We fought at Arques and you were not there!)

Early in the morning of the twelfth of November, 1989, I flew to Berlin.

Postscript

I want to end these memories here. There are many gaps in them. The years they deal with, after all, already lie a generation back and often rely—at least as far as many childhood details are concerned—on stories handed down in the family or questions asked of relatives. I am also aware how some experiences took on a consistency and sometimes a pathos which I would gladly have avoided. "That doesn't quite capture it!" said an inner voice, and received as answer: "But almost every detail has been checked and confirmed by others." Soon afterward the images flowed into each other again and became mixed up in new combinations.

That was not the only difficulty. Other things remained unsaid, because when the necessarily fragmentary memory was dug up it yielded no more than a few disconnected ruins. Or because the peculiar atmosphere of a time—its tone or the color of an experience—could no longer to be captured in words. Because what the memory has preserved is never, strictly speaking, what actually happened. The past is always an imaginary museum. One does not, in retrospect, record what one has experienced, but what time—with increasing shifts in perspective, with one's own will to shape the chaos of half-buried experiences—has made of it. By and large, one records less how it actually was than how one became who one is. And that is not only the weakness, but the justification of memoirs.[1]

The questions arising from these observations recur again and again. I wanted to know "What is truth?," and came up, again and again, against an insight formulated by Sigmund Freud. He wrote to Arnold Zweig that pure biographical truth "cannot be had" no matter how hard we try. There is no better observation, I thought, for the beginning or the end of any memoir. That is why it is included here.

---

1 This is a deliberate echo of Leopold von Ranke's (1795–1886) famous dictum that it is the historian's task to show us *"wie es eigentlich gewesen"* (how things have actually been). Ranke is credited with having founded the modern discipline of academic history, and his requirements for a critical use of primary sources are still valid today, even if his assumptions are no longer universally shared by historians.

Index

Born in Berlin in 1926, Joachim C. Fest was a historian, journalist, critic, and publisher of the renowned newspaper *Frankfurter Allgemeine Zeitung*. Best known for his writings and public commentary on Nazi Germany, he was the much-praised author of biographies of both Adolf Hitler and Albert Speer, and a leading figure in the debate among German historians about the Nazi period. Fest died in 2006.

Martin Chalmers was awarded the Schlegel-Tieck Prize in 2004 for his translation of *The Lesser Evil*, the post-1945 diaries of Victor Klemperer. His recent translations include *December* by Alexander Kluge and Gerhard Richter, *Part of the Solution* by Ulrich Peltzer, and *Summer Resort* by Esther Kinsky.

Born in the then Czechoslovak Republic in 1935, Herbert A. Arnold was educated in Germany and is professor emeritus of German and Letters at Wesleyan University in Middletown, Connecticut.